The Philosophy of Modern Art

by the same author

*

EDUCATION THROUGH ART

ART NOW

ART AND SOCIETY

ART AND INDUSTRY

THE MEANING OF ART

THE GRASS ROOTS OF ART

THE ART OF SCULPTURE

ICON AND IDEA

*

THE CONTRARY EXPERIENCE:
Biographies

SELECTED WRITINGS:
Poetry and Criticism

THE CULT OF SINCERITY

ESSAYS IN LITERARY CRITICISM

COLLECTED ESSAYS IN LITERARY CRITICISM

THE FORMS OF THINGS UNKNOWN:
Essays towards an Aesthetic Philosophy

THE TRUE VOICE OF FEELING

ANARCHY AND ORDER:
Essays in Politics

WORDSWORTH

*

COLLECTED POEMS

MOON'S FARM

THIS WAY DELIGHT:
A book of poetry selected for the young

The Philosophy of Modern Art

collected essays by

HERBERT
READ

faber and faber

LONDON · BOSTON

First published in this edition 1964
by Faber and Faber Limited
3 Queen Square London WC1N 3AU
Reprinted 1969, 1975, 1977, 1982 and 1985

Printed in Great Britain by
Whitstable Litho Ltd., Whitstable, Kent

To my esteemed master
in the philosophy of art
WILHELM WORRINGER

ISBN 0 571 06506 6

Contents

I

I. THE MODERN EPOCH IN ART   *page* 17

II. THE SITUATION OF ART IN EUROPE AT THE
     END OF THE SECOND WORLD WAR   44

III. THE FATE OF MODERN PAINTING   58

II

IV. HUMAN ART AND INHUMAN NATURE   73

V. REALISM AND ABSTRACTION IN MODERN ART   88

VI. SURREALISM AND THE ROMANTIC PRINCIPLE   105

III

VII. PAUL GAUGUIN   145

VIII. PABLO PICASSO   153

IX. PAUL KLEE   164

X. PAUL NASH   174

XI. HENRY MOORE   195

XII. BEN NICHOLSON   216

XIII. CONSTRUCTIVISM: THE ART OF NAUM GABO AND
     ANTOINE PEVSNER   226

IV

XIV. ENGLISH ART   249

INDEX   271

Preface

The Philosophy of Modern Art is perhaps a grandiloquent title for a collection of essays written on various occasions over a period of fifteen years. I cannot claim that I had a coherent plan in mind all this time, and different purposes have required different styles of address. To mention one particular anomaly: the reader is bound to be disconcerted by the way I shift with little or no warning from the position of the spectator *ab extra* to that of the creative artist.

But what, if not philosophic, is this activity I have indulged in, not only in this book, but for the best part of a lifetime? It is not critical, for I have never pretended to assess the value of particular works of art, or to arrange artists in an hierarchy of worth. It is not historical, for though I am conscious of connections, and eager to trace the re-emergence of traditions, I am not systematic enough to give the complete picture of a period, nor confident enough to define a school or classify a generation. The method I adopt may be called philosophic because it is the affirmation of a value-judgment. To be precise: I believe that among the agents or instruments of human evolution, art is supremely important. I believe that the aesthetic faculty has been the means of man first acquiring, and then refining, consciousness. Form, the progressive organization of elements otherwise chaotic, is given in perception. It is present in all skills—skill is the instinct for form revealed in action. Beyond this physiological and instinctive level, any further progress in human evolution has always been dependent on a realization of formal values.

The realization of formal values is the aesthetic activity. Aesthetic activity is biological in its nature and functions; and human evolution in particular, and by exception, is differentiated from animal evolution by the possession of this faculty.

The evidence for this belief is not presented systematically in this book, but the nature of this book is determined by this belief. There is no phase of art, from the palaeolithic cave-paintings to the latest developments of constructivism, that does not seem to

13

Preface

me to be an illustration of the biological and teleological significance of the aesthetic activity in man. Such is the hypothesis that
underlies these essays, and gives them whatever logical coherence
they may possess.*

A note will be found at the end of the volume which gives
particulars of the original publication of the essays. Two of the
number perhaps require a word of explanation to justify their
inclusion. I thought that 'English Art' would serve to show that
my appreciation of the art of the present is not independent of a
deep affection for what I deem to be most genuine in the art of
the past; and that 'Surrealism and the Romantic Principle' would
show that my philosophy of art is not restricted to the arts of
painting and sculpture.

H. R.

Stonegrave: January 1951

* I have given a more direct formulation of this hypothesis in the Conway
Memorial Lecture for 1951, entitled 'Art and the Evolution of Man' (London,
Freedom Press).

I

1

The Modern Epoch in Art

The heart that beat for this world has been almost extinguished in me. It is as though my only bond with 'these' things were memory. . . . One relinquishes this world and builds into a region beyond, a region which can be all affirmation. The cool romanticism of this style without pathos is astounding.
PAUL KLEE. *Diary*, 1915

i

In discussing the origins of naturalism in the Middle Ages, Max Dvořák warned us against the folly of trying to fix a specific 'beginning' to anything so underground as the first growth of an artistic style. The modern movement in art, which in general is a reversal of the movement discussed with such brilliance by Dvořák (in his *Idealismus und Naturalismus in der gotischen Skulptur und Malerei*), offers no exception to this rule. Its origins are extremely obscure, and, like roots, proceed from different levels and contradictory directions. One cannot exclude either the revolutionary romanticism of a Blake or the revolutionary classicism of a David; Constable's scientific naturalism is certainly a factor, but so is the historical idealism of Delacroix (to Cézanne always 'le grand Maître'). The realism of Courbet and Manet; the expressionism of Van Gogh and Munch; the symbolism of Emile Bernard and Gauguin—all these precede and in some degree predetermine the specifically modern movements of fauvism, cubism, constructivism and surrealism. Perhaps we should abandon our biological analogies and think rather of the complex 'movement' of a chronometer; for historical 'time' seems to reduce, on analysis, to such an interlocking of gears and ratchets. It will be said that even the chronometer has a spring at the centre, but this is not necessarily true of the modern chronometer, which may be set and kept in motion by the simple alternation of night and day.

There is, of course, the further explanation offered by the theory of dialectical materialism. For night and day in our metaphor we may substitute rich and poor, bourgeoisie and proletariat,

17

and in the circulation of élites see a sufficient motive power for all the stylistic changes of art. This is not an argument that can be ignored, for art never exists in a vacuum, but is inextricably entangled in the life of society as a whole. If we discover that the modern artist is relatively isolated from society we must not be led to suppose that such isolation is a characteristic of art itself— an island as such is only defined by reference to a neighbouring land-mass.

Nevertheless, economic facts and social movements can only have an indirect relation to the stylistic evolution of art. In the period that concerns us here, there is one broad economic development of the utmost significance—the gradual decline of private patronage due to the severe restrictions imposed on the accumulation of wealth. Private collectors still buy works of art in the open market—to that extent there are still patrons, if only through the medium of the art-dealer. But they no longer *command* the artist like the monastery or the guild, the court or the castle. The position has been so reversed that the contemporary artist must form the taste and recruit the public (through the intermediary of the art critic, in himself a modern phenomenon) on whose patronage he will then depend. The modern artist is miserably dependent on the media of publicity. That is his deepest humiliation.

There is another and a more limited sense in which the course of art is determined by economic factors. Scientific and industrial progress, particularly in the nineteenth century, threw out as by-products certain theories and inventions which had a direct impact on the technique and social significance of art. These have been too often discussed to need more than a passing reference. The formulation of a scientific theory of colour, which at first led to such aberrations as pointillism, has not had any permanent effect on artistic practice—the artist has discovered by now that he must rely on his sensibility and not attempt to particularize from laws of aesthetic effect. But more significant and more permanent in its influence on the development of art has been the invention of photography and of photographic methods of reproduction. The economic consequences of such inventions are serious enough —the public is provided with a cheap substitute for the plastic arts. It may not be aesthetically so satisfying, but it suffices for the low level of sensibility that seems to be a consequence of mass production and mass education. The effect on the artist has been even more profound, for it has relieved him of one of the social

The Modern Epoch in Art

functions of art—that of 'visual aid'. It is true that certain subtleties of imaginative literature will still call for creative illustration; but for instruction and clarification it is better to provide
an *Orbis sensualium pictus* by means of the camera. What has
been effected is a clear distinction between *illustration* and *interpretation*. This may not seem so significant at first, but implied in
it is the distinction between *image* and *symbol*, which, as we shall
see presently, is fundamental to an understanding of the modern
movement in art.

What in general may be admitted in this connection is that
economic and social trends determine and give their fluctuating
shades to broad movements of thought and opinion in every
epoch. The work of art cannot escape the ambience of such intangible effluences (the philosophies and theologies of the period). To
the extent that a work of art is romantic or classical, realistic or
symbolic, it will certainly be beyond the personal control of the
artist. Even the structure of the work of art (the style of composition) may be a matter of taste or fashion determined by social
contacts. But there comes a point in the evolution of art at which
all these imponderable forces are but external pressures which
result, not in a consequential 'line of force', but in a leap into
creative originality of a quite incalculable kind. The dialectical
materialist may still claim that social factors have determined
that anamorphosis, but the quantum in art, as in physics, may be
discontinuous. A brief examination of the concept of *originality*
will perhaps make my meaning clear.

ii

It has often been observed that if we have regard only for
that quality we call 'sensibility', which would throughout history
seem to be the essential element in art, that then no progress
whatsoever is discernible between the cave drawings of the
palaeolithic period and the drawings of Raphael or Picasso. Sensibility is not the only value in art—as successive civilizations
develop their cultures they invariably dilute this basic sensibility
with other values of a magical or logical nature—they *use* sensibility in social contexts, and it is the variations of context that
seem to explain whatever changes occur in the history of art.
There is, of course, a degree beyond which the sensibility cannot
be forced or prostituted—the result is then the *rigor mortis* of

19

academicism, or the moral rot of sentimentalism. The vitality of art would seem to depend on the maintenance of a delicate balance between sensibility and whatever intellectual or emotional accretions it derives from the social element in which it is embedded.

The process is, it will be seen, a dialectical one, and it is certainly one in which tensions and contradictions inevitably develop. One way in which a tension may be relaxed takes the form of a decline of sensibility, and the tension must be restored if art is to survive. What precisely happens in such a crisis is in dispute. The alternative suggestions are: (1) the artist retraces the historical development of his art and resumes contact with the authentic *tradition*; or (2) the artist resolves the crisis by a leap forward into a new and original state of sensibility—he revolts against the existing conventions in order to create a new convention more in accordance with a contemporary consciousness. We may admit that in doing so he merely recovers, in all its actuality, the original basic quality of art—aesthetic sensibility in all its purity and vitality. But the context is new, and it is the synthesis of an untrammelled sensibility and a new set of social conditions which constitutes, in the evolution of art, an act of originality.

We must guard against interpreting 'social conditions' in a sense narrowly economic or political. The artist's awareness of these conditions rarely assumes a politically conscious form, and certainly there is no correlation to be made between such consciousness in the artist and his degree of originality. Courbet, Pissarro, William Morris—these are the politically conscious artists and they have an important place in the history of modern art. But a more important place is taken by artists like Cézanne, Gauguin and Matisse, whose awareness of the social context of their work was never expressed in a political formula. It is only a primitive mind that can interpret the social context as Daumier's third-class railway carriage. The social context is the totality of our way of life, and its impact on the artist may be through a philosophy or a science, or even through a pair of old boots (Van Gogh) or a heap of rubbish (Schwitters).

From this point of view a renewed contact with tradition may have as much revolutionary significance as any originality in style or technique. The validity of a tradition depends on its retention of the element of sensibility. We agree to find this element in the paintings of Poussin; therefore, said Cézanne, let us go back to Poussin and try to recover, in front of nature, the element that made Poussin a great artist. Cézanne implied, not that the modern artist should imitate Poussin's style (which was personal to Poussin), but that a study of Poussin's art might lead to the recovery of sensibility—to the re-animation of his (Cézanne's) ability to 'realize' his sensations in the presence of nature. 'Nature' meanwhile had changed, because nature is but another word for the social context already mentioned. *To renew one's sensibility towards one's environment*—that is the method of both the traditionalist and of the revolutionary. Nevertheless, there is still a degree of originality which is not necessarily covered by the phrase.

The sense of 'reality' is surely one of those conventions that change from age to age and are determined by the total way of life. Not only does the concept of reality differ as between a mediaeval philosopher like St Thomas Aquinas and a modern philosopher like Bergson, but a similar difference also exists on the average level of apprehension (the difference between animism and theism, between supernaturalism and materialism, and so on). The 'reality' of a citizen of the Soviet Union is certainly different from the 'reality' of a citizen of the United States. We have now reached a stage of relativism in philosophy where it is possible to affirm that reality is in fact subjectivity, which means that the individual has no choice but to construct his own reality, however arbitrary and even 'absurd' that may seem. This is the position reached by the Existentialists, and to it corresponds a position in the world of art that requires a similar decision. The interpretation (or even the 'imitation') of reality was a valid function for the artist so long as it was agreed that a general and basic reality existed and was only waiting for revelation. Once this sense of security is removed (that is to say, is destroyed by scientific analysis) then philosophy and art are public auctions in which the most acceptable reality commands the highest price.

This may be a passing phase in philosophy and the world may return to systems of faith and revelation in which art once more resumes its interpretative function. But Existentialism is but the latest phase of a development of thought that reaches back to Kant and Schelling, and it is difficult (from a point of view inside the stream) to see any other direction which philosophy can take (it already carries along with it the contradictions of Christianity and atheism). It is in this mental climate that contemporary art has shown a tendency to usurp the positivist rôle of philosophy and to present its own self-sufficient 'reality'. A certain type of modern artist claims to construct new realities ('réalités nouvelles'), and he will go so far as to assert that his construction is in no way determined even by such vague concepts as universal harmony or the collective unconscious, but is an act of creation in the almost divine sense of the word. Naturally such an artist has to use elements of form and colour which are common to all the arts, and the world has not shown any inclination to recognize his work as art unless it possesses some of the sensuous qualities of the traditional work of art.

The conclusion we are driven to is that originality can only be conceptual, thematic, structural—never sensuous. There are new ways of thinking and doing—we call them inventions; there are new ways of stimulating the senses. But sensation itself can only be modified—coarsened or refined. It has the physical limitations of our animal frame; stretched on that frame the nerve breaks if forced beyond its expressive compass.

At the same time we must recognize, with the Marxists, the historic nature of human consciousness; and, with certain psychologists, the ambiguous nature of this evolutionary acquisition. In terms of art it gave us the symbol where hitherto there had been only the image. Man in his first unreflecting unity with nature needed only the image to project his sensations. Man as a self-conscious individual separated from the rest of creation needed a language of symbols to express his self-ness. The elaboration of that need gave rise not only to conceptual symbols like 'God' but also to a myriad of plastic symbols, some of them constant and archetypal, others temporary and even personal. If we could reconstruct the stages in human evolution which led from the eidetic, vitalistic art of the Palaeolithic period to the symbolic, geometric art of the Neolithic period, we should have a clear conception of the rise of not only human self-consciousness, ethical conscience and the idea of a transcendental God, but also of the origins of that polarity in art which has caused a rhythmic alternation of styles throughout the history of art, and which now exists as an unresolved dialectical contradiction. It is the co-existence of the image and the symbol, as norms of art, which explains the apparent complexity and disunity of the modern movement.

The Modern Epoch in Art

The true understanding of art depends upon an appreciation of the nature and uses of symbolism. Symbolism is one of the two ways in which the human mind functions, the other being the direct experience of the external world (the 'presentational immediacy' of sense perception). Since language itself is already symbolism, and the complicated forms of thought depend on a system of symbols such as we have in the science of algebra, it is natural to assume that there is something primitive and ineffective about the presentational immediacy of sense perceptions. This is far from being the case. It is much more difficult to be faithful to our direct experience of the external world than to 'jump to conclusions' which are in effect symbolic references. The poet, said Gautier, is a man for whom the visible world exists; he wishes, by this definition, to exclude from art those secondary elaborations of perception involved in the use of symbols. As the poet is condemned to use the symbolism of language, the ideal would seem to be quixotic. (Nevertheless poetry continues to reveal a fundamental strife between imagism and symbolism.)

The special position of the visual artist may be illustrated by a quotation from Whitehead's *Symbolism: its Meaning and Effect* (1928). 'We look up and see a coloured shape in front of us and we say—there is a chair. But what we have seen is the mere coloured shape. *Perhaps an artist might not have jumped to the notion of a chair. He might have stopped at the mere contemplation of a beautiful colour and a beautiful shape.* But those of us who are not artists are very prone, especially if we are tired, to pass straight from the perception of the coloured shape to the enjoyment of the chair, in some way of use, or of emotion, or of thought. We can easily explain this passage by reference to a train of difficult logical inference, whereby, having regard to our previous experiences of various shapes and various colours, we draw the probable conclusion that we are in the presence of a chair.'

This clearly illustrates the difference between a perceptive experience (the immediate perception of an image) and the use of a symbol (the image plus its mental associations). Whitehead adds: 'I am very sceptical as to the high-grade character of the mentality required to get from the coloured shape to the chair. One reason for this scepticism is that my friend the artist, who kept himself to the contemplation of colour, shape and position, was a very highly trained man, and had acquired this facility of ignoring the chair at the cost of great labour.'

With this distinction in mind we can perhaps begin to understand what Cézanne meant by 'realizing his sensations'. We can understand what Van Gogh meant when he said that 'a painter as a man is too much absorbed by what his eyes see, and is not sufficiently master of the rest of his life'. (Letter 620.) Van Gogh's letters are full of descriptions of his intense concentration on what a philosopher like Whitehead would call 'presentational immediacy'. For example: 'I myself am quite absorbed by the immeasurable plain with cornfields against the hills, immense as a sea, delicate yellow, delicate soft green, delicate violet of a ploughed and weeded piece of soil, regularly chequered by the green of flowering potato-plants, everything under a sky with delicate blue, white, pink, violet tones. I am in a mood of *nearly too great calmness*, in the mood to paint this.' (Letter 650, written in Dutch.)

This 'mood of nearly too great calmness' is the mood of direct experience, of instinctual awareness in which the eidetic image is, as it were, preserved from the contamination of symbolism—from the need for further reference to other elements in our experience. It has been claimed that the capacity for realizing and retaining the image in a state of perceptive vividness is the quality that distinguishes the artist from other men, but in fact it is the distinguishing quality of one type of artist—the imagist. It was by his insistence on the strict purity of his perceptive experience that Cézanne restored to art some degree of primal rectitude.

At the other extreme of artistic practice the artist abandons himself freely to a symbolic activity. Whitehead has said that 'the human mind is functioning symbolically when some components of its experience elicit consciousness, beliefs, emotions, and usages, respecting other components of its experience. The former set of components are the "symbols", and the latter set constitute the "meaning" of the symbols' (p. 9). An artist of the symbolist type is creating a combination of forms and colours (or of sounds if he is a musician) which will convey a meaning, and in art this meaning always has an aesthetic or emotional tinge. Art of this kind may therefore be defined as 'the symbolic transfer of emotion', and as Whitehead says, this definition is at the base of any theory of the aesthetics of art—'For example, it gives the reason for the importance of a rigid suppression of irrelevant detail. For emotions inhibit each other, or intensify each other. Harmonious emotion means a complex of emotions mutually intensifying; whereas the irrelevant details supply emotions which, because of their irrelevance, inhibit the main effect. Each little emotion directly arising out of some subordinate detail refuses to accept its status as a detached fact in our consciousness. It insists on its symbolic transfer to the unity of the main effect' (p. 101).

This definition of symbolism agrees closely with those definitions of 'synthètisme' which were formulated by Emile Bernard in 1888 and which, through the medium of Gauguin, were to have a revolutionary effect on the whole development of modern art. Bernard wrote:

'Puisque l'idée est la forme des choses recueillies par l'imagination, il fallait peindre non plus devant la chose, mais en la reprenant dans l'imagination, qui l'avait recueillie, qui en conservait l'idée, ainsi l'idée de la chose apportait la forme convenable au sujet du tableau ou plutôt à son idéal (somme des idées) la simplification que l'essentiel des choses percues et par conséquent en rejette le détail. La mémoire ne retient pas tout, mais ce qui frappe l'esprit. Donc formes et couleurs devenaient simples dans une égale unité. En peignant de mémoire, j'avais l'avantage d'abolir l'inutile complication des formes et des tons. Il restait un schéma du spectacle regardé. Toutes les lignes revenaient à leur architecture géométrique, tous les tons aux couleurs types de la palette prismatique. Puisqu'il s'agissait de simplifier, il fallait retrouver l'origine de tout: dans le soleil, les sept couleurs dont se compose la lumiere blanche (chaque couleur pure de la palette y répondant) dans la géométrie, les formes typiques de toutes les formes objectives.'*

This distinction between painting 'devant la chose' and 'en la reprenant dans l'imagination' expresses neatly the two ways open to the artist, and the further insistence on 'simplification' (Bernard) or 'unity of the main effect' (Whitehead) points to that characteristic in symbolic art which can involve a progressive modification of the 'schema' in the direction of abstraction. There is nothing in the paintings of Gauguin which would seem to imply or justify the abstractions of a Kandinsky or a Mondrian;

* Quoted by Maurice Malingue, *Gauguin, le peintre et son oeuvre* (Paris, 1948), p. 35.

nevertheless, there is what Whitehead calls 'a chain of derivations of symbol from symbol' whereby finally the local relations, between the final symbol and the ultimate meaning, are entirely lost. Thus these derivative symbols, obtained as it were by arbitrary association, are really the results of reflex action suppressing the intermediate portions of the chain. By such a chain of derivations we could conceivably establish an association between such apparently disconnected symbols as Gauguin's *Yellow Christ* and Mondrian's *Boogie-Woogie*. Mondrian was fond of describing his art as 'a new realism', but it is clear from his writings that he had invented a new symbolism. Mondrian insists that art is a parallel experience, not to be identified in any way with our experience, of the external world; but in Whitehead's words we would say that such parallelism is an illusion due to the suppression of intermediate links. The creation of a 'new' reality is not within the scope of our human, time-conditioned faculties.

iv

Let us now leave the realm of theory and try to trace what has actually happened in the evolution of art in the modern epoch. We shall not be able to leave ideas entirely out of account, because my main contention is that art has developed in stages that are parallel to the development of thought, and that both developments have intimate connections with social movements. Perhaps a few words will make clear to what extent the formal evolution of modern art has been 'conditioned' by social and economic forces.

I have already drawn attention to the relative isolation of the artist in modern society. The general effect of the industrial revolution on art has been a gradual exclusion of the artist from the basic economic processes of production. This development may be said to begin with the capitalist system itself; that is to say, with the accumulation of individual wealth. The way in which, from the fifteenth century onwards, the 'patron' gradually forces his own personality, even his own person, into the work of art has often been remarked. At first he is the pious donor, humbly kneeling in an obscure corner of the picture; but he gradually grows in size and importance until, in a painting like Holbein's *Virgin and Child with the Burgomaster Mayer and his family* (1526), he is painted on the same scale as the holy figures. Man is as good as God—as a theme for the artist. This humanism gave rise to the development of schools of portrait painting and historical painting which for three centuries constituted the main substance of the plastic arts. But such a development left the artist in a precarious position—dependent, not on the social organism as such (his position during the Middle Ages), but on the patronage of a limited class within that organism. For most of this time he maintained vitalizing contacts with the general processes of production—in our sense of the word he was still an industrial artist who might on occasion turn his hand to the design of metalwork, furniture or tapestries. But by the time the industrial revolution was complete, the artist was cut off from even these subsidiary activities and had become parasitically dependent on his patron.

In such a situation the artist might react in several ways. He might become sycophantic, adopting the point of view of his patron, supporting the existing structure of society, supplying works of art designed to satisfy the tastes and flatter the vanity of his clients. Such, in general, is the bourgeois art of the eighteenth and nineteenth centuries. But such, also, is a situation that implies the progressive degradation of art. No longer drawing any inspiration or force from the organic wholeness of society, the art in such a situation becomes anaemic and sophisticated, and, in any spiritual sense, purposeless. The basis of patronage may spread more widely, as it did throughout the nineteenth century, but the result will only be an art measured to the mean capacities of *l'homme moyen sensuel*. Just as, according to the Marxists, capitalism contains in itself the seeds of its own inevitable destruction, so (more certainly, even) such a relation between the artist and society involves inevitable decadence.

The artist who resists such decadence may react in two distinct ways. If he is socially conscious, he may revolt against the social situation as such and become a revolutionary artist—that is to say, an artist who consciously uses his art to reform the social situation. That type of artist is rare—it implies a use of art in the service of preconceived *ideas* which the true artist cannot accept. Even Courbet, in a political sense probably the most revolutionary artist of the nineteenth century, held that 'the art of painting can consist only in the representation of objects visible and tangible to the painter' and that 'art is completely individual, and that the talent of each artist is but the result of his own inspiration and his own study of past tradition' (open letter to a group of prospective students, 1861). But the same social situation produces in the artist a state of mind in which he turns from what he regards as the false aesthetic values of the past to seek new aesthetic values more consonant with the developing social consciousness of his fellow-citizens. Constable was not politically minded, but when he wrote (Notes for his lectures at the Royal Institution, May 26, 1836) that art 'is *scientific* as well as *poetic*; that imagination never did, and never can, produce works that are to stand by a comparison with *realities*', he was expressing a revolutionary sentiment, a revolt against the art of Boucher which in its turn had been the expression of another and very different social situation. This attitude is still more clearly expressed in a note of June 16, 1836:

'I have endeavoured to draw a line between genuine art and mannerism, but even the greatest painters have never been wholly untainted by manner. . . . Painting is a science, and should be pursued as an enquiry into the laws of nature. Why, then, may not landscape be considered as a branch of natural philosophy, of which pictures are but experiments?'

On that 'experimental' note the modern epoch is announced, and never from that moment until comparatively recently has the artist relented in his experimental attitude. Exactly seventy years later we find Cézanne writing in almost the same terms as Constable (letter of September 21, 1906):

'Shall I ever reach the goal so eagerly sought and so long pursued? I hope so, but as long as it has not been attained a vague feeling of discomfort persists which will not disappear until I shall have gained the harbour—that is, until I shall have accomplished something more promising than what has gone before, thereby verifying my theories, which, in themselves, are easy to put forth. The only thing that is really difficult is to prove what one believes. So I am going on with my researches. . . .'*

Research, experiment—these words describe the efforts of all the great artists that fall within these seventy years—Millet, Courbet, Manet, Degas, Monet, Pissarro, Renoir, Rodin, Whistler, Seurat, Van Gogh—it is all a persistent attempt to correlate art and reality. It is the research, not of the absolute, but of

* Trans. Gerstle Mack, *Paul Cézanne* (London, 1935), p. 390.

the concrete, of the *image*, and behind it all is not only the divorce of the artist from the processes of production, but also the concurrent attempt to establish a philosophy of reality, a phenomenalism that owes nothing to divine revelation or universal truths, but brings to the analysis of human existence the same faculties that the artist brings to the analysis of nature. Constable, Cézanne, Picasso—Hegel, Husserl, Heidegger; these names represent parallel movements in the evolution of human experience.

But this movement, in art, was not to remain unchallenged. To the image as representation is opposed, as we have seen, the symbol as interpretation, and there is no doubt that the 'synthètisme' of Bernard and Gauguin was a conscious reaction against the scientific attitude in art. The theoretical basis of this reaction was given in the definition of 'synthètisme' by Bernard already quoted, but what that theory involved in practice was first shown by Gauguin. We can best appreciate the antithetical nature of the contradiction by considering what form and colour meant respectively for Cézanne and Gauguin.

Both artists went through an impressionist phase, and their divergence developed as they felt dissatisfaction with the results of their practice of the impressionist technique. Both artists, incidentally, found a meeting-place in Pissarro, who is the chief *point de repère* for the whole revolution. What Cézanne learned from Pissarro was of fundamental importance for his subsequent development, but it did not affect the direction taken by that development. Cézanne felt that the analytical methods of the Impressionists had led to a certain dissolution of reality; they had, as it were, realized the vitality of objects, the vibrancy of light, the vividness of colour, at the cost of the essential nature of these objects—their solidity—indeed, their reality. The analysis of light and colour had led to a separation of colour and form, and this Cézanne felt to be a betrayal of the painter's function. Without sacrificing the real advances made by the Impressionists, he set himself the task of realizing and presenting the solid structure of objects. He arrived at a method which he called 'modulation' (as distinct from the Impressionists' 'modelling') in which volume was represented by local colour changes. His own words must be quoted:

'For progress towards realization there is nothing but nature, and the eye becomes educated through contact with her. It becomes concentric through observation and work; I mean that in an orange, an apple, a sphere, a head, there is a focal point, and this point is always nearest to our eye, no matter how it is affected by light, shade, sensations of colour. The edges of objects recede towards a centre located on our horizon.'*

This rather obscure passage is illuminated by a letter of December 23 of the same year:

'This I declare to be indisputable—I am very dogmatic: an optical sensation is produced in our visual organ which causes us to grade the planes represented by sensations of colour into full light, half-tones and quarter-tones (light does not exist for the painter). Necessarily, while we are proceeding from black to white, the first of these abstractions being a sort of point of departure for the eye as well as for the brain, we are floundering, we do not succeed in mastering ourselves, in ruling over ourselves. During this period—we go to the great masterpieces the ages have handed down to us, and we find in them a solace and a support.'†

One further question, for it is essential for an understanding of the origins of modern art to be quite sure that we first understand what Cézanne was after:

'Now the idea to be insisted on is—no matter what our temperament or power in the presence of nature—to produce the image of what we see, forgetting everything that has been done before. Which, I believe, should enable the artist to express his entire personality, great or small.

'Now that I am old, almost seventy, the sensations of colour which produce light are a source of distraction, which do not permit me to cover my canvas or to define the delimitations of objects when the points of contact are so tenuous, fragile; the result is that my image or picture is incomplete. Then again the planes are superimposed on one another, from which springs the Neo-impressionist system of outlining the contours with a black line, an error which should be opposed with all our strength. Now if we consult nature we shall find a way to solve this problem.'‡

'I regret my advanced age, on account of my sensations of colour',—such was the recurrent complaint of Cézanne in his

* Letter of July 25, 1904. Trans. Gerstle Mack, *op. cit.*, p. 380.
† Trans. Gerstle Mack, *op. cit.*, p. 381.
‡ Trans. Gerstle Mack, *op. cit.*, pp. 382-3.

ast years. He felt a certain opposition between the surface sensuousness of objects and their real nature—his eyes were, as it
were, dazzled by the brilliance of light and colour. Light and
colour were not the same thing as *lucidity*. ('I am becoming more
lucid in the presence of nature, but—the realization of my sensations is always painful. I cannot reach the intensity which appears
to my senses . . .')—(September 8, 1906). And then, in his final
letter to Bernard, who significantly enough was the *agent pro-
vocateur* in this struggle for theoretical expression (significantly,
because he played the same rôle for Gauguin), he says: 'I am
progressing towards the logical development of what we see and
feel by studying nature; a consideration of processes comes later,
processes being for us nothing but simple methods for making
the public feel what we ourselves feel, and for making ourselves
intelligible.'

There were, therefore, in Cézanne's final phase, two stages in
the production of a work of art: first, the realization of sensations,
by which he meant a 'logical' analysis of percepts, of what the
eye actually sees; second, processes by means of which this
analysis could be presented to the public.

Cézanne was an extremely intelligent but simple man, and
his efforts to explain his intuitive processes are not very clear.
What in his stumbling way he seems to have grasped is the principle of the 'good *Gestalt*'. Without going farther into the theory
of perception than would be justified in a general essay of this
kind, it is difficult to give a convincing account of this term, but
the underlying idea is that visual perception itself only makes
sense, only becomes coherent, by virtue of an organizing faculty
within the nervous system. We should not be able to cope with
the multiplicity of impressions which the eye receives were we
not, at the same time, capable of organizing these impressions
into a coherent pattern. In the words of a *Gestalt* psychologist:
'Perception tends towards balance and symmetry; or differently
expressed: balance and symmetry are perceptual characteristics
of the visual world which will be realized whenever the external
conditions allow it; when they do not, unbalance, lack of symmetry, will be experienced as a characteristic of objects or the
whole field, together with a felt urge towards better balance—
the stimulations which under ordinary circumstances affect our
eyes are perfectly haphazard from the point of view of the visual
organizations to which they may give rise. The organism—does

the best it can under the prevailing conditions, and these conditions will not, as a rule, allow it to do a very good job (good, from
the point of view of aesthetic harmony). A work of art, on the
other hand, is made with that very idea; once completed it serves as
a source of stimulation specifically selected for its aesthetic effect.' *

Before Cézanne the principle of composition in painting was
architectonic—the picture-space was 'organized' as an architect
organizes his building, and inevitably questions of balance and
symmetry were taken into consideration. Cézanne's paintings are
analysed and criticized as if they conformed to this principle, and
such a method does indeed 'work', though it ignores the essential
virtue in Cézanne's compositions. For architectonic composition is
a priori; it fits the objects of perception into a preconceived pattern, a system of perspective and elevation, which is not necessarily inherent in perception itself. A landscape by Claude or
Turner is as artificial as a garden, and as much the result of
intellectual preconceptions. But a landscape by Cézanne begins
with no preconceptions—nothing but the direct contact of eye
and nature, and the 'composition' is determined by what happens
'in the eye'—the automatic selection of a focal point, limitation
of boundaries, subordination of details and colours to the law of
the whole. The 'whole' is the *Gestalt*, but the psychologists recognize that the process does not end there—that there are 'good'
and less good *Gestalten*. 'It is characteristic of a good *Gestalt* not
only that it produces a hierarchical unity of its parts, but also that
this unity is of a particular kind. A good *Gestalt* cannot be changed
without changing its quality—in a masterpiece of painting no
line, no form, no colour, can anywhere be changed without de-
tracting from the quality of the picture.' (Koffka, *op. cit.*, 247–8.)

I think there is no doubt whatsoever that Cézanne was trying
to realize the good *Gestalt*. By intuitive processes he had hit upon
a scientific truth which psychology subsequently discovered by
experimental research. Cézanne, therefore, still remains within
the characteristic development of nineteenth century art—as
much as Constable he is an artist who regards landscape painting
as a branch of natural philosophy. But Cézanne's natural philosophy was not destined to be understood by many of his followers,
and it was largely on a misinterpretation of his purpose that
cubism came into being (its subsequent development is another

* K. Koffka: 'Problems in the Psychology of Art'. *Art: a Bryn Mawr Sym-
posium*, 1940.

question). But before we discuss the influence of Cézanne let us return to the challenge to the scientific attitude in art made by Gauguin.

v

One's first inclination is to treat Gauguin as an artist altogether inferior to Cézanne. We cannot doubt his integrity or his sincerity, and the sacrifices he made for his art were certainly as great as Cézanne's. The contrast between the two artists lies in the field of sensibility, of technical accomplishment. Certainly some hard things can be said about Gauguin's technique. He despised the whole business of what he called 'counting the hairs on the donkey'. He had been an Impressionist and had sat at the feet of Pissarro; but his reaction was violent. 'The impressionists study colour exclusively, but without freedom, always shackled by the need of probability. For them the ideal landscape, created from many different entities, does not exist. They look and perceive harmoniously, but without aim. Their edifice rests upon no solid base and ignores the nature of the sensation perceived by means of colour. They heed only the eye and neglect the mysterious centres of thought, so falling into merely scientific reasoning.' (*Intimate Journals*, trans. Van Wyck Brooks (New York, 1936), pp. 132–4.) Form was not to be found in nature, but in the imagination. 'It is well for young men to have a model, but let them draw the curtain over it while they are painting. It is better to paint from memory, for thus your work will be your own: your sensation, your intelligence, and your soul will triumph over the eye of the amateur.' (*Ibid.*, p. 71, 1936.) At every point Gauguin contradicts Cézanne, a fact understood better by Cézanne than by Gauguin. 'He never understood me,' said Cézanne. 'I have never desired and I shall never accept the absence of modelling or of gradation; it's nonsense. Gauguin was not a painter, he only made Chinese images.' To which Gauguin would have replied (in words he wrote to Daniel de Monfried): 'The great error is the Greek, however beautiful it may be. . . . Keep the Persians, the Cambodians, and a bit of the Egyptians always in mind.' (October, 1897.) Or: 'It is the eye of ignorance that assigns a fixed and unchangeable colour to every object. . . . Practise painting an object in conjunction with, or shadowed by—that is to say, close to or half behind—other objects of similar or different colours. In this way you will please by your variety and your truthfulness—your own. Go from dark to light, from light to dark. The eye seeks to refresh itself through your work; give it food for enjoyment, not dejection. . . . Let everything about you breathe the calm and peace of the soul. Also avoid motion in a pose. Each of your figures ought to be in a static position. . . . Study the silhouette of every object; distinctness of outline is the attribute of the hand that is not enfeebled by any hesitation of the will. . . . Do not finish your work too much. . . .' One could go on building up the contradictions, but they all amount to this: *the laws of beauty do not reside in the verities of nature.* The work of art is in some sense a suggestive symbol, stirring our emotions rather than stimulating our sensations.

Between these two points of view, these two distinct conceptions of art, there can be no compromise. Most of the contradictions and varieties of modern art spring from their antithetical opposition. No synthesis within the realm of art seems to be possible; it is not obvious why it should be desirable.

vi

The situation as it developed towards the end of the century was not, however, to remain a simple antithesis. If, for the sake of brevity, we describe the aim of Cézanne as the representation of the real, and that of Gauguin as the creation of beauty, there still remained another ideal of which Van Gogh became the leading exponent. Provisionally we might call it the expression of emotion, but the phrase needs a particular definition. The word *express*, however, inevitably recurs in all our attempts at definition, and Expressionism is the name which has been given to this tendency in modern art. 'To *express* the love of two lovers by a marriage of two complementary colours, their mingling and their opposition, the mysterious vibrations of kindred tones. To *express* the thought of a brow by the radiance of a light tone against a sombre background. To *express* hope by some star, the eagerness of a soul by a sunset radiance. Certainly there is nothing in that of stereoscopic realism, but is it not something that actually exists?'—these words of Van Gogh written at Arles in 1888 show the beginnings of a divergence of aim which in the years to follow was to modify profoundly the evolution of modern art.

Such a humanistic ideal in art was, of course, no new thing. It goes back to Rembrandt, if not farther, and in this tradition are such painters as Delacroix, Millet and Israels—all favourites of Van Gogh. Even Courbet and Manet contribute to the tradition, though their main significance lies elsewhere. Another quotation from Van Gogh's letters will serve to define this tradition and separate it from contemporary trends like Impressionism:

'What a mistake Parisians make in not having a palate for crude things, for Monticellis, for clay. But there, one must not lose heart because Utopia is not coming true. It is only that what I learned in Paris is leaving me, and that I am returning to the ideas I had in the country before I knew the impressionists. And I should not be surprised if the impressionists soon find fault with my way of working, for it has been fertilized by the ideas of Delacroix rather than by theirs. Because, *instead of trying to reproduce exactly what I have before my eyes, I use colour more arbitrarily so as to express myself forcibly*. Well, let that be as far as theory goes, but I am going to give you an example of what I mean.

'I should like to paint the portrait of an artist friend, a man who dreams great dreams, who works as the nightingale sings, because it is his nature. He'll be a fair man. I want to put into the picture my appreciation, the love that I have for him. So I paint him as he is, as faithfully as I can, to begin with.

'But the picture is not finished yet. To finish it I am now going to be the arbitrary colourist. I exaggerate the fairness of the hair, I come even to orange tones, chromes and pale lemon yellow.

'Beyond the head, instead of painting the ordinary wall of the mean room, I paint infinity, a plain background of the richest intensest blue that I can contrive, and by this simple combination of the bright head against the rich blue background, I get a mysterious effect, like a star in the depths of an azure sky.

'In the portrait of the peasant again I worked in this way, but without wishing in this case to produce the mysterious brightness of a pale star in the infinite. Instead, I think of the man I have to paint, terrible in the furnace of the full harvest, the full south. Hence the stormy orange shades, vivid as red hot iron, and hence the luminous tones of old gold in the shadows.

'Oh, my dear boy . . . and the nice people will only see the exaggeration as caricature.' *

* Letter 520. From: *Further Letters of Vincent van Gogh to his Brother.* 1886-1889 (London & Boston, 1929).

The Modern Epoch in Art

The whole theory of expressionism, in its strength and weakness, is in this letter. Its strength lies in its humanism—in the fact that art cannot be limited to the search for any absolute, whether of reality or beauty, but must ever return to the essential dignity of our common human qualities, our human nature. Its weakness lies in the imprecision of its terminology—in words like mystery and infinity which, when it comes to the point of translation into practice, into terms of form and colour, have no real meaning. There are no 'infinite' shades of blue, and brightness is no mystery—that, at least, would have been Cézanne's opinion. Gauguin would have been more in sympathy with this language, but he was not really interested in painting a postman, for example, 'as I feel him', but rather in using any suitable model for the creation of an independent aesthetic entity— a work of art that creates and contains its own emotional values and is not dependent on the evaluation of a human context. For Gauguin the work of art, as a symbol, must be detached from any particular occasion, just as a crucifix is detached from the Crucifixion.

Van Gogh had no immediate following in France. It was in the far North, in Scandinavia and later in Germany, that expressionism had its widest expansion. Here the dominant figure is the Norwegian Edvard Munch. Munch was born ten years later than Van Gogh (in 1863), and he may to some extent have been inspired by the Dutchman. There is certainly a close affinity of aim, and even of style, between the two artists. But a countryman of Ibsen's had really no need of external inspiration, and though Munch modified his style after his visits to France, he may be said to have been born with the desire to express himself forcibly. His scope, however, is not quite the same as Van Gogh's: it is more objective. It is true that he could write in his diary in 1889 words which are quite reminiscent of those we have quoted from Van Gogh's letter of the previous year: 'No more painting of interiors with men reading and women knitting! They must be living people who breathe, feel, suffer and love. I will paint a series of such pictures, in which people will have to recognize the holy element and bare their heads before it, as though in church.' (Quoted by J. P. Hodin, *Edvard Munch*, Stockholm—Neuer Verlag—1948, p. 28.) But in Munch's subsequent paintings, as in the work of the expressionist school generally, there is an element of despair, leading to remorseless analysis and maso-

chism, which was not characteristic of Van Gogh. This Kierke-
gaardian morbidity in Expressionism is a sufficient explanation
of its failure to appeal more strongly to the Latin races. There is
plenty of wonder in Expressionism, but little joy.

vii

By 1900 the three forces I have described—Realism, Symbolism and Expressionism—were ready to radiate into the new
century. Their courses, however, were to be intricate and confused; only Expressionism developed with any logical consistency,
though its inner despair was to destroy it. But meanwhile, in
Kokoschka, Beckmann, Nolde, Heckel, Schmidt-Rottluff, Rohlfs,
Soutine, Chagall and Rouault (not all of whom acknowledge the
title of Expressionist) it produced artists of great talent and
achievement.

The development of Realism has not been so uniform. In his
last phase Cézanne, in his desire to emphasize the solidity of objects, had formed a style which is not merely architectonic in
a metaphorical sense, but patently geometrical in a structural
sense. The framework of the structure, perhaps a pyramid or a
diamond, becomes dominant, and a considerable degree of distortion of the natural object is tolerated in order that the subject
may conform to the perception of a 'good *Gestalt*'. Between 1907
and 1909 Picasso and Braque gave a further accentuation to this
geometrical scaffolding and thereby affected what can only be
described as a quantum-like jump into an altogether different type
of art. Both Picasso and Braque were to retreat from their discovery, but it was taken up by Juan Gris, who did not, however,
live long enough to pursue the new inspiration to its logical
limits. This was done first by artists in the immediate vicinity
(Marcel Duchamp, Gleizes, Delaunay, etc.), and almost simultaneously in other centres—Munich (Kandinsky, Klee), Moscow
(Tatlin, Malevich, Gabo), Amsterdam (Mondrian) and London
(Wyndham Lewis). This general tendency to abstraction, as we
may call it, bore fruits of very various kinds, and became confused with such irrelevancies as machine-age romanticism. But at
its best and purest—in, for example, the work of Mondrian, Gabo
and Ben Nicholson—it undoubtedly expresses some profound
need of the age. It may be derided as a flight from reality, but
there are at least two possible defences;—it flies from a dis-

37

credited reality to create a 'new reality', a realm of the absolute, of mystical purity; and in doing so it makes use of laws or elements that are fundamental to the structure of the physical universe. Whatever the explanation, the movement has shown vigour and tenacity for forty years, and the contempt of the critics and the neglect of the public have not sufficed to discourage its exponents.

A much more consistent use of Cézanne's discoveries was made by Henri Matisse. Matisse was not particularly interested in Cézanne's search for solidity, but he did take over Cézanne's insistence on a focal point in perception and consequently in composition—he too is an artist of the good *Gestalt*. But other influences were at work—Gauguin, perhaps, and certainly the discovery of Oriental art (more particularly in Matisse's case, of Persian art). This led Matisse to a complete breakaway from Cézanne's binding of colour to form. Colour is released, as in Gauguin's painting, to play its own dynamic and symbolic rôle. The result is a decorative pattern, but a pattern which still takes its organization from nature and the laws of perception. 'An artist must possess Nature. He must identify himself with her rhythm, by efforts that will prepare the mastery which will later enable him to express himself in his own language.' (Letter to Henry Clifford, February 14, 1948.)

'L'exactitude n'est pas la vérité'—this slogan of Matisse's has been the excuse in our time for much painting that is neither exact nor true. The exhaustion of the scientific impulse in art, which had lasted from Constable to Cézanne, put artists under the necessity of discovering a new principle of organization. Such new principles as have been discovered are either conceptual or instinctual. Cubism, the early 'metaphysical' paintings of Chirico, futurism (with some exceptions), constructivism, neo-plasticism, etc.,—these are all attempts to impose a law of harmony on the visual perception of the artist. (A futurist such as Boccioni could announce the somewhat contradictory intentions of (*a*) 'opposing the liquefaction of objects which is a fatal consequence of impressionistic vision' and (*b*) 'the translating of objects according to the lines of force which characterize them'—thus achieving a new plastic dynamism, a pictorial lyricism. The short life of the futurist movement is probably to be explained by such inner contradictions.) A conceptual art is in effect a classical art, and it is not difficult to find a correspondence between Mondrian and Poussin, Gleizes and Sir Joshua Reynolds.

The Modern Epoch in Art

In general, however, the instinctual principle has prevailed in modern art since about 1910. Picasso has resolutely refused to treat cubism as a canon of art, external to the immediate intuitions of the artist. 'Mathematics, trigonometry, chemistry, psychoanalysis, music, and what not have been related to cubism to give it an easier interpretation. All this has been pure literature, not to say nonsense, which brought bad results, blinding people with theories. Cubism has kept itself within the limits and limitations of painting, never pretending to go beyond it. Drawing, design and colour are understood and practised in cubism in the spirit and manner that they are understood and practised in all other schools. Our subjects might be different, as we have introduced into painting objects and forms that were formerly ignored. We have kept our eyes open to our surroundings, *and also our brains.*' (Statement of 1923; my italics.)

There are one or two further remarks of Picasso's which serve to bring out the essentially instinctual nature of his activity. For example (from the same 'Statement' of 1923): 'Among the several sins that I have been accused of committing, none is more false than the one that I have, as the principle objective in my work, the spirit of research. When I paint, my object is to show what I have found and not what I am looking for.' Again, from his conversation with Christian Zervos, 1935: 'How can you expect an onlooker to live a picture of mine as I have lived it? A picture comes to me from miles away: who is to say from how far away I sensed it, saw it, painted it; and yet the next day I can't see what I've done myself. How can anyone enter into my dreams, my instincts, my thoughts, which have taken a long time to mature and to come out into the daylight, and above all grasp from them what I have been about—perhaps against my own will?' (Quotations from *Picasso* by Alfred Barr. Museum of Modern Art, New York, 1946.) These statements directly contradict everything for which Cézanne stood—his patient research for the form inherent in the object, his laborious efforts to reproduce this form with scientific exactitude. The result of such a new attitude was an explosive liberation of expression, not only in Picasso himself, but throughout the whole civilized world. It is part of my contention that a long process of germination had been taking place in the social consciousness of the same civilized world —Picasso is preceded by Hegel, Marx, Bergson, Freud, by revolutions in science, economics and social organization. But genius

39

is the capacity to focus diversity—the ability to draw into a single burning point of light the discoveries and inventions of a whole generation. Picasso had this gift and his influence accordingly has been universal. It is safe to say that there has never been an artist who in his own lifetime has had so many imitators. Well may Picasso himself exclaim: 'To repeat is to run counter to spiritual laws; essentially escapism.'

viii

The general effect of the revolution in painting established by Matisse, Picasso, Braque and their immediate contemporaries was subjectivist in character, and the same generalization can be made of other arts (Proust, Joyce, D. H. Lawrence). This development in the arts had been supported by the new hypothesis of the unconscious first clearly formulated at the turn of the century by Freud. Again it must be emphasized that the causal connections are not necessarily direct. A writer like D. H. Lawrence may be tempted to justify the nature of his art by a direct appeal to psycho-analysis, but he is the exception rather than the rule. Subjectivism is a mental climate, announced more than a century ago by Kierkegaard and Hegel. It is a climate that has 'prevailed' for the past forty years, and though we may be rather tired of it, there is no sign of an immediate change.

A specific product of this prevailing climate has been the Surrealist movement. The Fauvistes had always imposed limitations on their spontaneity. They disclaimed any plan of campaign, any programme, but they always sought an 'objective correlate' for their sensations. The objectivity of this correlate was always determined by universal qualities which, in their sum, may be called Harmony. 'What I dream of,' Matisse once wrote (*La grande revue*, December 25, 1908), 'is an art of balance, of purity and serenity devoid of troubling or depressing subject-matter, an art which might be for every mental worker, be he business-man or writer, like an appeasing influence, like a mental soother, something like a good armchair in which to rest from physical fatigue'—a naïve confession which nevertheless describes the normal function of art. The Surrealists rejected this 'bourgeois' conception of art in favour of an activity which should be fundamentally disturbing and essentially impure. The first Manifesto of the Surrealists was not published until 1924, but a very necessary preparation had been taking place during the previous ten or fifteen years, years in which the harmonic conception of art was gradually discredited. The chief instigator in this destructive movement was undoubtedly Duchamp, and the surrealists have always honoured him as their forerunner. But the futurists, along with Chirico, Picabia and the sculptor Archipenko also played their parts, and the foundation of the Dada group in 1916 (in Zürich) was the first conscious negation of the aesthetic principle in art. The way was then clear for a new principle, and it was announced by André Breton as *automatism*—'pure psychic automatism, by which it is intended to express, verbally, in writing or by other means, the real process of thought. It is thought's dictation, all exercise of reason and every aesthetic or moral preoccupation being absent.'

Attempts have been made to find precedents for surrealism in the art of the past (Arcimboldo, Bosch, Goya), but they are mistaken, because however fantastic in their conceptions, these artists were always guided by aesthetic preconceptions. Surrealism is a completely revolutionary conception of art, and the only question is whether it is still 'art'. We should deny the term 'science' to an activity that refused to recognize the laws of induction; we have the same right to deny the term 'art' to an activity that rejects the laws of harmony. But the surrealists have not consistently practised what they have preached, and the colour harmonies of Miró, the balanced compositions of Ernst and Dali, the dynamic rhythm of Masson, constitute objective correlates of an aesthetic nature in spite of the artist's intention to rid himself of such categories. In fact, 'pure psychic automatism' only takes place in the unconscious (and we only become aware of it in emerging from a state of unconsciousness, that is to say, in dreams). As soon as we attempt to translate unconscious phenomena into perceptual images, the instinctive laws of perception intervene—we automatically project the good *Gestalt*, the composition that obeys aesthetic laws.

Nevertheless, an immense liberation of aesthetic activity was achieved by this subjectivist revolution. It is not possible to resist the *play* of artists like Miró and Klee—their work simply gives pleasure, and needs no theory to defend it. The work of other surrealists (as of certain expressionists), sometimes intentionally, sometimes unintentionally, is 'troubling or depressing subject-matter' and has its proper place in the case-books of the psychiatrists. One should not necessarily exclude from art the tragic aspects of life—it is perhaps Matisse's limitation that he has— but even in the tragic art of the past the intention was always to 'sublimate' the theme, to resolve the conflict, to create an over- whelming atmosphere of serenity.

ix

Und ich wiederhole: naturferne Kunst ist publikumsfremde Kunst. Muss es sein.

Wilhelm Worringer.

It has not been my aim in this essay to mention every artist of importance, or even to produce one of those charts in which every movement has its appropriate graph. The truth is obscured by such rigid complexities. It is the broad effects that are sig- nificant for my present purpose, and these are complex enough. If I have succeeded, the reader will be conscious of a stream which runs fairly consistently through a tract of time measuring about a century, widening as it approaches our present sea of troubles. But this stream is carrying down with it the sands and pebbles that have ineffectually opposed its progress. This silt accumulates as the river is about to attain its end, blocks the flow and creates a delta—the one stream becomes many separate streams. But here the metaphor breaks down, for the separate streams do not make their way fanwise to the ultimate sea; some turn inland again and are lost in the desert.

This diversion in modern art is due to the failure of the scientific attitude in art. It has not proved possible, or at any rate finally satisfying, to consider art as 'a branch of natural philo- sophy, of which pictures are but experiments'. In art, 'l'exacti- tude n'est pas la vérité.' 'We all know that art is not truth. Art is a lie that makes us realize truth, at least the truth that is given us to understand.' (Picasso.) Art is a closed system, and it is 'true' in the degree that its rhetoric convinces us, pleases us, comforts us. It has no spiritual mission; it is accused of having no social function.

The artists themselves have recognized their isolation. 'Uns trägt kein Volk,' cried Klee—the people are not with us. But it is useless to blame the artist for that isolation—as well blame the weathercock for not turning when there is no wind. (It is true,

42

there is a kind of weathercock that does not turn because its hinges are rusty—the academic artist.) The climate of the age (*Zeitgeist, usw.*) is the creation of a thousand forces, and perhaps the Marxists are right in giving priority, among these forces, to economic trends. But the failure of the Soviet Union, after more than thirty years of strenuous effort, to produce a new art on the basis of a new economy, proves that the inspiration of the artist cannot be forced. We must wait, wait perhaps for a very long time, before any vital connection can be re-established between art and society. The modern work of art, as I have said, is a symbol. The symbol, by its nature, is only intelligible to the initiated (though it may still appeal mysteriously to the uninitiated, so long as they allow it to enter their unconscious). The people can only understand the image, and even this they distrust in its eidetic purity, for even their vision is conventional. It does not seem that the contradiction which exists between the aristocratic function of art and the democratic structure of modern society can ever be resolved. But both may wear the cloak of humanism, the one for shelter, the other for display. The sensitive artist knows that a bitter wind is blowing.

2

The Situation of Art in Europe at the end of the Second World War

We might begin this estimate of the situation that existed in Europe at the end of the Second World War, and that still exists, by contrasting the achievements of two decades. The first of these decades is the one we have recently lived through—the years 1939–48. The other is chosen more arbitrarily, but it too includes a world war—the years 1909–18. The contrast is, as anyone must admit after a moment's reflection, a dramatic one. In the earlier decade art was everywhere in a ferment. In France the post-impressionist movement was developing the more explicit phases known as fauvism and cubism: in Italy there was the futurism of Marinetti and Severini, and the metaphysical school of Chirico and Carrà; dadaism was born in Zürich and presently evolved into surrealism in France and Germany; in Germany and Scandinavia the expressionist school came into existence; in Russia Malevich, Gabo, Pevsner and Tatlin launched the suprematist movement, to develop after the Revolution into constructivism; in Holland Mondrian and Van Doesburg were establishing the movement known as neo-plasticism; even England had a new movement—the vorticism of Wyndham Lewis.

It may be objected that there was nothing very healthy about this ferment—that it was a feverish state of nerves symptomatic of the social unrest which came to a head in the First World War. I have no wish to deny a certain connection between the social and economic condition of Europe in this decade and the art of this same period, but that is an intricate question into which I do not propose to enter at the moment. Any interaction of this kind cannot be isolated within decades, and I do not see any fundamental difference of a *social* kind between the two periods—at least, the differences due to social revolution might be assumed to favour the later decade. Let us ask rather what survives from the earlier agitated decade. We cannot claim finality of judgment, but year by year it becomes clearer that in the art of painting if in no other art, the unquestioned masterpieces of our epoch belong to that decade—the best works of Chirico, of Matisse, of Léger, of Braque and, I would say of Picasso. It may be a prejudice of mine, but I know it is shared by other critics, who also believe that the genius of Picasso was never so clearly and so firmly revealed as in the canvases of his so-called 'classical Cubist' period.

Twenty years pass and we were once more involved in preparations for war and war itself. A decade superficially similar to that of 1909–18 has followed and we can now look back on it as objectively as our despondency allows. What is quite obvious is that there has been no general ferment at all comparable to that of the earlier decade. Not a single new movement in art has been born, and the only new 'ism' of any significance, existentialism, does not touch the plastic arts as yet.* Great art, of course, does not need a theory or a movement to justify it. Indeed, after the ferment of the 'teens and 'twenties, it is conceivable, indeed probable, that the natural phase to follow is one of refinement, distillation, or what in more philosophical terms we might call a synthesis. Many younger artists today seem to be conscious of this necessary step, and in Paris in particular there is an apparent effort to retrace the paths of the past forty years, to plot a general direction, to advance again on an agreed point, profiting by the experiments and discoveries of the older generation. Admirable as much of this painting is—I am referring to the work of artists like Pignon, Lapicque, Manessier, Tal Coat, Gischia, etc.—it seems to me to suffer from the defects of deliberateness: it is decidedly academic in spirit, I find more hope, because there is more enterprise, in the work of some of our young English painters. To them I shall come presently, but first let us consider the French situation, which is the situation of European art in general.

The modern movement in the arts which began to reveal itself in the first decade of the century was fundamentally revolutionary, and it affected all the arts—the prose of Joyce and the music of Stravinsky were as much a part of it as the paintings of Picasso or Klee. When I characterize this movement as *fundamentally revolutionary*, I attach a literal meaning to these well-

---

* There are painters in Paris who claim to be existentialists, but their philosophy has no distinctive plastic expression that I can see.

worn words. There are two senses in which one can be revolutionary. One can set out with a definite aim—to replace a monarchy by a republic, for example—and if one achieves that aim, the revolution is complete, finished. One is no longer a revolutionary. But that is not the kind of revolutionary that Picasso was, or Klee, or Joyce—I am not so sure about Stravinsky. These painters and writers had no new constitution in their pockets: they did not know where they were going or what they might discover. They were quite sure about the sterility and rottenness of the academic standards which then prevailed everywhere, but they had no preconceived ideas about new standards. They were explorers, but they had no compass bearing. 'The important thing in art,' Picasso once said, 'is not to seek, but to find', and that might be given as the motto of the whole movement. These artists projected themselves into the future, into the unknown, not knowing what they would find, relying on the concrete evidence of their senses to find a way to the genuine work of art.

It might be here remarked that this attitude was anything but idealistic—it was, in fact, very much the attitude now defended by Jean-Paul Sartre, on the philosophical and political plane, as existentialist. Sartre's philosophy is said to derive from Heidegger's philosophy, but to a considerable extent I believe it to be a philosophical synthesis based on the practical activity of modern art. It is not without significance that it is precisely in Paris, where the revolutionary attitude in art has prevailed so long, that this new philosophy has arisen. I said a few moments ago that existentialism is not concerned with the plastic arts: I am inclined to suggest now that it is for the very good reason that art has in this respect anticipated philosophy.

A revolutionary philosophy, Sartre has said, must be a philosophy of transcendence. In political philosophy this would seem to mean that we must regard any immediate revolutionary attitude as contingent because the system of values at any time current in a society is a reflection of the structure of that society and tends to preserve it. When a revolution has been carried through, a new situation then exists which demands a new revolutionary attitude, an attitude which was not conceivable in the pre-volutionary situation. The new systems of values will be the expression of a structure of society which does not yet exist, but which must be anticipated in order that what *does* exist may be transcended. Sartre's revolutionary man, therefore, 'must be a contingent being, unjustifiable but free, entirely immersed in the society that oppresses him, but capable of transcending this society by his efforts to change it'.

The revolutionary artist of whom Picasso is the most convenient prototype is precisely such a contingent being, entirely immersed in his visible world, but making every effort to transcend the symbols which are conventionally used to represent this world. The revolutionary artist is born into a world of clichés, of stale images and signs which no longer pierce the consciousness to express reality. He therefore invents new symbols, perhaps a whole new symbolic system. Then the academicians come along and try to generalize his symbols, to conventionalize them, to make them good for all time. Many artists, once revolutionary, fall into the same contented frame of mind. We might not call them reactionaries, but in the ceaseless unfolding of existence, it is reactionary to stand still. Or, as Sartre puts it, the slightest human act must be construed as emanating from the future; therefore even the reactionary is oriented toward the future, since he is concerned with making a future that is identical with the past.

I think it will be obvious that between this conception of perpetual revolution and what is usually meant by a synthesis there exists a contradiction. There is no justification in modern philosophy, however, for regarding a synthesis as a stasis—as a fullstop. A synthesis is merely the meeting-place of two ideas, and from their conjunction arises a new idea. But each new idea is in its turn a thesis which merges into an endless dialectical chain, and the only finality is something we agree to call the Truth, which seems to recede with every step we take towards it.

With these considerations in mind, we should approach the whole conception of a synthesis of styles with a certain degree of caution, perhaps of scepticism. The desire for a synthesis of the arts is part of that general longing for social stability which is the natural reaction to any period of revolution. In effect, this is nothing but a more or less conscious determination to consolidate the power of a new social élite, and 'classicism' is usually the catchword for the cultural aspects of such a consolidation. The reactionary—the man who wants to make a future identical with the past—seeks to establish recognized standards of taste, an official type of art, an academic tradition which is universally taught and automatically accepted. From this point of view, the revolutionary art of the period can be transformed into the academic art of the period of consolidation.

Let us next observe that this work of synthesis in the arts is not attempted by the originators of the revolution. Some of these originators—Picasso, above all—have continued to display a restless revolutionary energy. Even when, as in the case of Paul Klee, for example, the development was restricted to a very personal idiom, it remained consistent—it did not attempt to compromise with a general tradition of contemporary art. No: the search for a synthesis is the work of epigoni, of second generation disciples and followers, and not of the masters of the modern movement. The masters themselves remain revolutionary, or become openly reactionary (Chirico, Derain).

The work of those artists who have remained revolutionary for a period of forty years must now be examined to see if we can detach any progressive elements. I have already admitted that in my own opinion the best work of Picasso, Braque, Léger, Chirico, and, I would add, Rouault, belongs to the past—to the decade of 1908–17. I do not in any way dismiss their later work, which is rich and diverse and makes for a cumulative effect which cannot be ignored. But the high peaks of their extensive achievement lie in the distance.

I believe that in other cases the development has been more gradual and has been rising all the time to heights we cannot yet measure. But before I mention any names, I would like to recall certain historical trends within the period in question.

The modern movement in art has four main phases or divisions, which are most conveniently labelled Realism, Expressionism, Cubism and Superrealism. Realism does not come into question, though artists like Picasso and Matisse use a realistic style for particular purposes, and in a later essay (see pages 100–4) I shall discuss the desirability of maintaining a tension between realism and abstraction. (Incidentally, it is no new suggestion—it is the theme of Shelley's *Alastor*, for example.) But in our present historical circumstances realism has contributed little or nothing to the development of modern consciousness—to the development, that is to say, of our specific vision of the world (*Weltanschauung*). Expressionism has been significant for the Nordic peoples of Europe, especially for Scandinavia and Germany, and later I shall consider its present status. But let us begin with Cubism, which has a certain chronological priority.

The cubism which was discovered and exploited for a few years by Picasso, Braque and Juan Gris, was *analytical*. That is to say, it was directed to the revelation of an aesthetic aspect of the natural world, and it claimed, by reducing the appearance of objects to their significant forms, to tell us something about the essential nature of these objects. Juan Gris was not satisfied with such an analytical attitude. He wished to give priority to the formal values in composition, and he therefore established a theory and practice of *synthetic* cubism. In synthetic cubism the realistic elements are subordinated to the architectural structure of the painting, but nevertheless they remain realistic.

Synthetic cubism, while not dependent on the real object in the same sense as analytical cubism, returns to the object by a process of concretion: the object emerges from the canvas like the image of a lantern-slide in the process of focusing. But the focus, when precise, reveals, not an illusory image of some familiar object (for example, a guitar), but a different order of reality with distinct values, only related to the object by suggestion or association. Poetry emerges from the forms, a species of nostalgia is created, as essence is distilled. But what the process involved, and what Gris could never wholly reconcile himself to, was a certain degree of abstraction (a word which has proved obstinately necessary in all this debate). 'I never seem to be able to find any room in my pictures for that sensitive, sensuous side that I feel ought to be there', he wrote in 1915, and that remained true to the end. It produced in his work that *inquiétude* or *Angst* which gives some justification to the description of Gris as a tragic figure. The truth is that the way to 'purity', in art as in any other spiritual exercise, demands not merely a renunciation of the grosser sensations associated with 'a too brutal and descriptive reality', but also a progressive refinement of sensuousness itself.

Gris died in the middle of his career, and Picasso and Braque found the method of cubism too strict for their revolutionary aims. But cubism had contained within itself the seeds of a far stricter discipline, of which there were two aspects or divisions. Analytical cubism, by reducing the natural appearance of objects to a structure of plane surfaces, easily suggested a further stage in which the plane surfaces were divorced from any dependence on the essence (essential Nature) of the object, and became an end in themselves. That is to say, the forms arrived at by the analysis of the structure, say, of pears on a dish on a table, were *abstracted* and realized or appreciated as geometrical forms with their own proportions and colours. It became more and more difficult to recognize the objects from which the composition had originated, and finally an object was no longer taken as the source or origin of a composition: the composition was non-figurative from its inception, an invention of purely formal relationships. This non-figurative cubism had nothing in common with either analytical or synthetic cubism, and has been strongly repudiated by Picasso, for example, who maintains that all plastic art must necessarily proceed from a sensuous awareness of the natural world.

But non-figurative cubism—no longer calling itself cubism, but rather non-objective, or non-figurative art, more popularly *abstract* art, has had an extraordinary expansion, not only in Europe, but even in the United States, where abstract artists have proliferated in a manner which requires some explanation. This non-figurative offspring of cubism easily degenerates into a very precise and precious academicism. To balance forms, calculate proportions and harmonize colours can be an intellectual exercise rather than an act of creative imagination, and it is certainly, on this calculating intellectual level, no longer an activity which can be called revolutionary. It can be called other names—'escapist', for example, for it can be produced in an ivory tower. A more insidious danger is a tendency towards a merely decorative function, and this type of cubism has, indeed, been exploited by industry, and 'cubist' wall-papers, 'cubist' linoleum, 'cubist' lamp-shades and 'cubist' electric fittings became a bourgeois fashion some twenty years ago, and seem to have taken a permanent hold on certain markets—for the very good reason, perhaps, that geometrical designs are easier to produce by machinery than naturalistic motives.

However, in spite of all this vulgarization and academic fixation of abstract art, there exists a progressive front which cannot be so easily dismissed. It is found in its purest and most revolutionary form in the paintings of Ben Nicholson. In Nicholson's work there has never been any question of academic fixation: he has advanced from experiment to experiment, always maintaining the vitality and naivety of an extremely sensitive artist, and avoiding any temptation to be satisfied with a purely decorative function. I know that this latter statement can be challenged—there are sensitive critics who, charmed by Nicholson's sensitive execution and his invariable good taste, are not only contented with such positive gifts, but declare that there is nothing else to seek behind the decorative façade. But there is. Certain forms have a universal significance—they 'echo', as we might say, the basic structural forms of the physical universe, the 'harmony of the spheres'. Ben Nicholson's intuitions of form go far beyond any decorative arrangement of shapes and colours, and being intuitive they have nothing in common with the academic compositions of even such a considerable artist as Kandinsky. Kandinsky, for whose career and work I have a considerable respect, was not so pure an abstract artist as Ben Nicholson: he used his abstract forms to illustrate subjective themes. Behind his compositions there was always an 'idea'—perhaps a philosophical idea or a musical idea—for which he tried to find the plastic equivalent. In Nicholson's case, as in the case of another pure abstractionist to whom Nicholson has always been allied, to whom, indeed, he would acknowledge a considerable debt, Piet Mondrian, there is no precedent idea. The idea is the form, the form the idea. The composition is conceived, *ab initio*, in plastic terms. It cannot be translated into any other language, and is not itself a translation from any other language.

This front of pure abstraction—of, we might also say, the concrete harmony of universal forms—has historical contacts and intimate relationships with another form of abstract art which we call constructivism. Constructivism is actually of independent origin: it developed from the movement known as Suprematism which was founded in Moscow in the year 1913, and architects and engineers had as much to do with its formulation as studio painters or sculptors. In 1920 as a result of a fierce debate involving the principles of Marxism, dialectical materialism, socialist realism, and I know not what else, a group under the leadership of Gabo and his brother Antoine Pevsner seceded from the suprematist movement and established the constructivist movement. The price of their integrity was political exile, and it was in Germany (in Berlin and later at the Bauhaus in Dessau), in Paris (where Pevsner settled), and in London (where Gabo eventually came), that constructivism was developed as a revolutionary movement in the arts. The theoretical background of the movement is to a large extent identical with that of the abstrac-

51

tionists, but constructivism has always been in revolt against the whole conception of studio art, of the cabinet picture, the petty bourgeois longing for a nice painting to hang over the fireplace. Constructivism, as its name indicates, is closely allied to engineering, and it seems to establish a non-figurative art which makes use of specifically contemporary materials—steel, plastics, aluminium—and which uses technical methods of construction. What we therefore get, in a typical construction of Gabo or Pevsner, is something which breaks away completely from the whole tradition of European academic art, with its canvases and gilt frames: we get a work of art which is more at home in a factory or on an airport than in an art gallery or a gentleman's residence. We get something so completely revolutionary that it requires a considerable readjustment of our faculties of perception to accept it as art at all. But none the less these constructions of Gabo and Pevsner, when we analyse them, are found to be as fundamentally aesthetic as the Parthenon. That is to say, in harmony and proportion they conform to the same fundamental universal laws as the art of the past. Their uniqueness, their revolutionary significance, lies in the extension which they exact in the perception and sensuous apprehension of these concrete physical phenomena.

I am now going to pass, rather abruptly, to a consideration of that other phase of contemporary art which, in the past thirty years, has developed phases of revolution and reaction: superrealism*. Here the ground I tread on is full of pitfalls and booby-traps. I shall proceed cautiously.

Between the First Surréaliste Manifesto of 1924 and the latest manifestation of superrealist activity, which was the Paris Exhibition of July 1947, the personnel of the movement suffered many changes, but one factor has remained permanent—the intellectual inspiration and integrity of André Breton. Breton has an analytical intelligence of the same order as Leonardo's—a curiosity of universal range which seeks the power which knowledge alone can give. His research has been directed in particular to the mystery of the human personality or psyche, and has inevitably led to an association with the revolutionary technique of psychological research which we owe to Freud.

* I have always tried to use the English word *superrealism* to indicate the generic style of this school of painting and sculpture; and the French word *surréalisme* to indicate the movement associated with the name of André Breton, which included literature as well as the plastic arts.

Applying Freudian methods to the problems of artistic creation, Breton evolved a theory and indeed a practice of aesthetic automatism which is the essential feature of surréalisme.

The traditional canons of classical aesthetics are abandoned— harmony, proportion, rhythm are treated as at best incidental features of fundamental psychic manifestations, and as features which are by no means essential to the creation of a work of art. The work of art, it is said, derives its power from the unconscious —more particularly from that deepest layer of the unconscious which the Freudians call the Id. Art, therefore, whether in the form of poetry or painting, even architecture, is potent and aesthetically effective (the surréalistes do not claim to be pleasing) to the extent that it projects significant symbols from the Unconscious. Latterly it has been recognized that the proliferation of discrete or unconnected symbols is not fully effective—it is, indeed, merely confusing. For this reason there has been an increasing emphasis on the organization of symbols into effective patterns or myths. The object of surréalisme (and of superrealism in general) might now be described as the creation of a new mythology.

I believe that from the beginning an exclusive devotion to a theory of aesthetic automatism was a mistake. In the first place it involves a surrender of intellectual freedom—for what, in a personal sense is creative or responsible in a purely automatic projection of the images of the unconscious, which in themselves may be collective in their origin rather than personal? But in the second place, the process of automatism is not essentially artistic at all, but, if you like, scientific. Art, in the fundamentally revolutionary sense which I have defined always involves an original act of creation—the invention of an objective reality which previously had no existence. The projection of a symbol or image from the unconscious is not an act of creation in that sense: it is merely the transfer of an existing object from one sphere to another—from the mental sphere, for example, to the verbal or plastic sphere. The essential function of art is revealed in a coordination of images (whether unconscious or perceptual does not matter) into an effective pattern*. The art is in the pattern, which is a personal intuition of the artist, and not in the imagery.

* Since this was written I have read a paper on 'Perceptual Abstraction and Art', by Dr Rudolf Arnheim (*Psychological Review*, Vol. 54, 1947), which gives a more scientific account of the process, but does not, I think, contradict this general statement.

Imagery can be released by hypnosis, by intoxication, and in dreams: but it does not constitute aesthetic expression, or art, until it has been given expressive form. The myth is not necessarily such a form. Myths have usually been evolved in the collective unconscious of peoples, and only slowly precipitated in the form of narratives. It is only when such narratives are shaped into epic poetry that they become works of art. I do not believe that a myth can be synthetically created out of symbols automatically projected from the unconscious of a few individuals associated in a movement like surrealism: but even if it could be created in this way, it would still have to be conceived in epic form before it could claim to be a work of art.

I will not go so far as to say that this particular phase of superrealism has reached a dead end: artists such as Breton, Max Ernst, Tanguy, Mirò, Matta and Lam are full of resource, and often they are artists in spite of their theories. Mirò, for example, has never been a doctrinaire surréaliste and his paintings risk being accepted for their beauty rather than for their symbolic significance. I would say the same of Matta and Wilfredo Lam, in whose work a free revolutionary energy is always manifest.

The theory of psycho-analysis—in its Jungian rather than its Freudian elaboration—has revealed the presence in the psyche not only of significant symbols of a figurative kind, but also of more abstract archetypal forms. Jung has shown, for example, how throughout history the unconscious has repeatedly expressed itself in a formal pattern which he calls the *mandala*, a more or less complicated design divided into quadripartite sections. Other forms and shapes are biologically significant—the phallus, for example. But the world is, as it were, haunted by significant forms. Our attention is held by the contour of a particular hill, by the shape of a rock or a tree-stump or a pebble we pick up on the beach. These shapes appeal to us, not because of any superficial beauty, any sensuous texture or colour, but because they are archetypal. That is to say, they are the forms which matter assumes under the operation of physical laws. When these forms are mathematically regular, as in the convolutions of a shell or the structure of a quartz crystal, we can easily account for their appeal under the laws of proportion and harmony. But most of these shapes are more complex and irregular, and we are not consciously aware of the processes which have determined their outline or mass. The beauty of a leaf, a flower or a seed is obvious:

the beauty of a bone, a fungus, or even of the solution of a mathematical problem is not so obvious. But the appeal of the unknown is often stronger than the appeal of the known: it is strong because it is mysterious, because it has not been dissected and analysed. We invest such forms with our own feelings, of sympathy or of fear. This possibility of identity with an inanimate object is the basis of primitive animism. We used to accuse the savage of worshipping 'stocks and stones', but now we recognize that these stocks and stones may have significant form.

It is in this direction that one phase of European art has continued to advance during recent years. Two artists in particular have explored this superreal territory, this world of animistic forms—Picasso in painting and Henry Moore in sculpture. But one must mention also the work of Lipchitz, of Laurens, or Arp ... If I now mention Henry Moore's work in more detail, it is not only because it is more familiar to me, but also because I believe that it has a more consistent direction than the work of other artists exploring this territory. Its consistency is perhaps due to certain limitations—an obsession, for example, with female forms, with the symbolic forms of fertility and gestation. But such limitations are often characteristics of the major artist and are certainly no argument against the stature of any particular artist. The life of art lies in the transformation of forms, as a French philosopher of art has said*, and this life can be manifested within the infinite variations which spring from a single central theme. Moore has shown in his war sketches, in his drawings of coal miners, and in his *Madonna and Child*, that he can, if necessary, depart from his central theme. But in doing so he still expresses himself with a formal simplicity which derives its significance from a primitive or animistic quality of the forms themselves. I believe the same is true of many of Picasso's recent paintings, which have a family likeness to the masks used in the magic rites of certain primitive peoples.

Finally, I come to the expressionist movement, which has been the typical art movement during these years in Scandinavia, Germany and Austria, and has hitherto left Western Europe untouched. The original source of the modern expressionist movement is undoubtedly Van Gogh, a Dutchman, but it gained general significance with the work of Edvard Munch, a

* Henri Focillon in *The Life of Forms*. Trans. by C. B. Hogan and G. Kubler, New York (Wittenborn, Schultz, Inc.), 1948.

Norwegian. Its exponents, in the period we are now considering, have been Germans like Max Beckmann, Otto Dix and George Grosz; Belgians like De Smet, Permeke and Fritz van den Berghe, and, lastly but not least, a Czech like Oskar Kokoschka. Rouault, in his independent way, belongs to this movement, and so does an Eastern European Jew like Chagall. But essentially the movement has geographic roots: it is the art of Northern Europe, and the typical work of artists of the past, like Mathias Grüne-wald and Jerome Bosch, is fundamentally expressionist.

Expressionism, briefly, may be defined as a form of art that gives primacy to the artist's emotional reactions to experience. The artist tries to depict, not the objective reality of the world, but the subjective reality of the feelings which objects and events arouse in his psyche, or self. It is an art that cares very little for conventional notions of beauty; it can be impressively tragic, and sometimes excessively neurotic or sentimental. But it is never merely pretty, never intellectually sterile.

During the period we are considering something like an 'iron curtain' has been drawn between the expressionist art of Northern Europe and the movements concentrated in Paris. Now, partly as a result of the dispersion caused by Nazism and the war, expressionist influences have been spreading. Kokoschka has been in England, Beckmann and Chagall in the United States, and almost every country has had its refugee expressionist painters. Independently of these direct influences, I think that northern countries, cut off from the propaganda of Paris, have been discovering the congeniality of expressionism—they suddenly recognize in it their natural mode of expression, their pictorial language. Whatever the reason, there is certainly a strong expressionist element in the work of the younger school of painters in Great Britain—and significantly, the most energetic members of this group come from the north—from Scotland. I am referring to Robert Colquhoun and Robert MacBryde. But an expressionist element will be found in the work of many other young British painters today, and in France we find a similar development represented in the work of Tailleux, Berçot and Dubuffet.

That concludes my survey of the present situation of art in Europe. Perhaps the activity of some of our younger painters goes some way to soften the extreme contrast which I drew at the beginning of this essay between the two decades, 1909–18 and 1939–48. But though I personally find much that is stimulating and fresh, not only in the recent work of artists of the older generation such as Picasso and Léger, but also in the work of new and comparatively unknown artists like Colquhoun and Mac-Bryde, Butler and Paolozzi, nevertheless, in historical perspective, there can be no doubt where revolutionary energy has been most manifest. The work of the younger men is still but the prolonged reverberations of the explosions of thirty or forty years ago. The general effect is a diminuendo.

I shall perhaps be accused of praising my own generation at the expense of an uprising generation. Apart from the fact that I really stand between the two generations, that is not my real intention. My aim has been to represent a consistent revolutionary attitude. If a new generation arises to dethrone the giants of the past, no one will give it a warmer welcome than I. My whole reading of the history of art tells me that change is the condition of art remaining art. Art is never transfixed, never stagnant. It is a fountain rising and falling under the varying pressure of social conditions, blown into an infinite sequence of forms by the winds of destiny.

3

The Fate of Modern Painting

'I write poems for poets and satires or grotesques for wits. . . .
For people in general I write prose and am content that they
should be unaware that I do anything else.' This opinion, expressed by Robert Graves in a foreword to *Poems* 1938–1945, is
one which most poets will be found to share; and even if they
have not dared to express themselves so frankly, their activities
suit Mr Graves's words. Their work has no appeal to people in
general, and never could have had such appeal.

Painters, for reasons which can perhaps be explained historically,
but which are not logical, still maintain a different belief, and a
vast organization of exhibitionism, salesmanship and propaganda
has been built up to support their belief. But I see no *civic* difference between the poet and the painter: each is an individual
giving expression to a personal vision which may or may not be
of great social importance, but in one case society can ignore the
creative gift with impunity, in the other case it is now to be
bullied into accepting it and paying for it out of public revenue.

If we go back four hundred years, there is no difference in the
treatment meted out to any type of artist. The painter, the poet,
the musician or the architect, may have had a patron—another
individual blessed with wealth and power—or he may not have
had a patron; but all were treated alike, according to the patron's
estimate of their merits.

The economic structure of society has changed, and during the
past three centuries, and latterly at a devastating speed, the basis
of patronage, which in its final form was the private fortune, has
been undermined. As a consequence of two world wars, and of
the gradual conversion of most societies to some form of socialism,
incomes have been equalized; and wealth, of an order which
permits largess, has been whittled away.

The poet has long since accommodated himself to this new
situation. He usually takes a job in a bank or a publisher's office,
and writes his poetry in the bus, or at week-ends. Or he may give

The Fate of Modern Painting

up poetry for some more popular form of literary entertainment —that is to say, he commercializes his talent, becomes a copywriter for the advertising agent, or a script writer for Hollywood. But then he is no longer a poet in any serious meaning of the word.

The painter has never accepted the new situation. He has made various attempts to adapt his craft. Hogarth, for example, hit upon the idea of making prints of his paintings and selling them at a popular price to a large public. But photography and other techniques of reproduction took the profits out of that practice, and today the engraver or etcher is just as clamorous as the painter for some form of patronage.

Now that the private patron is threatened with final liquidation, painters demand that the State should become their patron. It is not only the painters who make this demand, but a whole host of interested critics, art historians, sociologists, politicians and priests. Their claims have been formulated without any qualms of modesty in the report on *The Visual Arts* sponsored by the Dartington Hall Trustees. * 'It is essential', we are told, 'for the well-being of painting and sculpture in this country that Government patronage of living art in all its forms should be continued and extended. It is necessary that private patronage should be encouraged, and that in local galleries and by travelling exhibitions the public should be able to enjoy and buy contemporary art. The Government should also support painters and sculptors by buying their work for the national collections and by commissioning them for specific purposes. The Government should either commission artists to decorate public buildings, or introduce legislation on the lines of that in Sweden and some other countries, where a percentage of the total building cost of all public buildings is required to be spent on their decoration by artists. Assistance should be especially directed to tide promising young painters and sculptors over the difficult years between leaving college and establishing themselves. It is useless to consider a larger place for art in the life of the nation without first securing the livelihood of the artist.'

There are many other such arguments in the Report of this Arts Inquiry. It is true that there is an underlying intention to keep private patronage alive, but the economic facts presented in this same report merely serve to make clear the futility of such an

* Published by the Oxford University Press. 1946. 10s. 6d.

intention. Works of art can only be bought with painful sacrifice on the part of individuals, and even these few willing buyers are not sufficient in number to support the thousands of people who choose to become painters and sculptors. The writers of the report realize this clearly enough, and they have no hesitation in suggesting that the State should become the universal patron.

There are several aspects of the question which are not considered in this report, nor in general by advocates of State patronage. In this paper I would like to examine three of them:

I. The actual process of State patronage—who in effect is the the patron and by what machinery is choice exercised?

II. The material consequences of State patronage—what becomes of the works of art purchased by the State and what is their actual effect on the public?

III. What is the effect of State patronage on the artist, and eventually on the quality of the art produced?

A critical examination of State patronage under these heads mgiht lead us towards some general principles which imply quite a different solution of the problem.

In the first place, let us ask who actually is the patron in State patronage. The State is often rightly described as a machine: its total effect is inhuman. But the cogs in the machine are nevertheless human beings—perhaps not *ordinary* human beings, for in the first place they were selected as possessing special qualifications, and a few years' service as a cog may have had some effect on their characters: a well-worn cog has polished teeth. But ministries of education, museums and art galleries, advisory councils and selection committees, are composed of administrative officers, executive officers and clerks. Patronage, that is to say, the selection of artists to work for the State and of works of art to be bought by the State, would presumably be exercised by officers of the administrative grade, with perhaps the assistance of advisory committees. The administrators—even if museum or gallery officials—will not necessarily be men of sensibility or taste: they have been appointed for their presumed efficiency in administration. But even supposing that they are men of taste, and are advised by men of taste, whose taste shall they represent when it comes, say, to the purchase of a painting or the giving of a commission? Let us remember that we are not concerned with the art of the past, where a certain consensus of opinion can guide the administrator. A decision has to be made which is, or should

60

The Fate of Modern Painting

be, the direct exercise of a native sensibility.

But will it be? Will it not rather depend on the prejudices and casual knowledge of the individual in question—whom he has met, what he has read, what he thinks will please the Press? If it is a committee which is to exercise the choice, the situation can only be worse. I have served on many such committees, and in my experience only one of three things can happen:

1. something is chosen which offends nobody, because its virtues are negative;
2. a little bit of everything is chosen to please everybody;
3. the committee agrees to be realistic and to allow one member to make the choice for all of them: the committee, that is to say, resigns its functions in despair.

The first two possibilities merely lead to compromises: they do not imply intelligent patronage and can hardly be said to encourage the best in art. The third possibility is equivalent to the administrator's own choice, and the State is really paying for the indulgence of one man's taste, to which it then proceeds to give the sanction of its anonymous authority.

But administrators change, committees change. A patron of old was at least consistent, even dictatorial. The State as a patron is fickle, and in a very short time a collection of modern works of art accumulated by a government or a municipality is distinguished by its incoherence and dimness.*

Proposals have been made for improving the administration of art services—for consolidating the national and provincial museums, for recruiting staff on a more intelligent plan, for establishing art centres which will act as agents of education and propaganda, bringing the public into contact with the State's purchases, inducing them to appreciate the administrator's taste. Such measures would introduce order where there is at present almost complete chaos, but they would only intensify the indecisiveness of the patronage to be exercised by such an efficient machine.

Now let us consider the physical aspect of the problem. The products of State patronage can be disposed of in two ways. If they are *objets d'art*, easel paintings and pieces of sculpture, they can be accumulated and housed in galleries and museums. No limit

* 'Les fruits les plus accomplis du pompiérisme académique'—the Paris newspaper *Combat* on an exhibition of modern British paintings from the Tate Gallery (June 19, 1946).

is set to such official collecting. The national collections in London already comprise hundreds of thousands of objects, but most of these are antiques. We are, presumably, to collect and house hundreds of thousands of novelties. What we don't house in the capital we shall distribute to provincial cities and towns, even to village colleges and women's institutes. A hundred years ago a humble workman could buy a Staffordshire pottery figure and put it on his mantelpiece. He can no longer buy Staffordshire figures, or anything like them; but the State will buy a picture for him and hang it in the local art centre.

The second way in which the State can patronize art is to use it in its own buildings. It can have painters to paint murals in the post offices; it can put mosaics in railway stations and stained glass in town halls. I see no objection to such a policy, except the one already mentioned: the choice has to be made by an official or a committee. Such results as we see around us already merely reflect the indecisiveness which is bound to be the result of official selection. They are eclectic, inconsistent, incoherent: they cannot be otherwise because there is no common tradition, no prevailing sense of style. Without a tradition to guide them and the infallibility of a sense of style, the guardians of public taste can only express their own separateness, their individual tastes and whimsies. If they wish to be popular, their choice will be vulgar; if they have any inclination of their own to follow, it will inevitably be esoteric, 'highbrow'.

Now let us assume that the State has had a run for its money— a run of a century, shall we say, which is not a long period in the history of art. What, at the end of such a period, will be the position? Museums and art galleries will have proliferated—every city will have several, and no town but will have its art centre. We may restrict the size of the units, but that will only increase their number. Facilities of travel will meanwhile have developed enormously, and there will be no reason why every citizen should not see every museum in his own country, and as many as he likes abroad.

But will he want to? There are museums enough already to satisfy a normal need, and these museums are full enough, many of them too full. But a museum of *modern* art, it will be said, may exhibit some new thrill, touch some hitherto unexercised chord of sensation. One painting in a thousand may do this, but the search will be arduous and long. There are a thousand easier and better ways of attending the muses. Clough's revised commandment applies with devastating effect to works of art:

> Thou shalt not kill; but need'st not strive
> Officiously to keep alive.

If it is objected that I am applying the sentiments of a roué of the arts to material intended for the common man, the ordinary citizen of a paternal State, then I must ask for a consideration of the psychological facts. Suppose by propaganda and other inducements we have persuaded this common man to pursue the pilgrimage of art, to expose himself to the impact of a civil patronage exercised on his behalf by his anonymous mentors—what then? When we visit some national or municipal art gallery and observe the people about us—those dim, bored figures gingerly skating over waxed floors, drifting like chilled bees from one fading flower to another—can we believe that anything important is happening to them? 'How the diabolic Whistler,' wrote Timothy Shy at the time, 'would have enjoyed the reopening of the Tate, photographs of which showed three citizens indomitably tackling the pictures and six more reclining hopelessly on a settee, already dazed, sewn up, exhausted, and knocked out by British Art. We never forget a Voice from the Middle West heard in the Uffizi at Florence. "All this darned Art," it wailed, "it just makes your feet hot." ' In a rare case, one in ten thousand, a dormant sensibility may be awakened. But unless that common man is by present standards very uncommon, the mere fact that he is a man, and has therefore undergone the normal processes of education and social integration, means that he is already deaf to any appeal that the work of art might have for him. His aesthetic sensibility has been killed at school, probably before the age of twelve. It cannot now be revivified, except by some treatment equivalent to psycho-analysis. Do not let us deceive ourselves: the common man, such as we produce in our civilization, is aesthetically a dead man. He may cultivate art as a 'culture', as a passport to more exclusive circles of society. He may acquire the patter of appreciation, the accent of understanding. But he is not moved: he does not love: he is not *changed* by his experience. He will not alter his way of life—he will not go out from the art gallery and cast away his ugly possessions, pull down his ugly house, storm the Bastille where beauty lies imprisoned. He has more *sense*, as we say.

The Fate of Modern Painting

Finally, let us consider the effects of State patronage on the artists. Again, a complicated psychological problem of which only the outlines can be indicated.

First, there is the question of what one might call the scope of art—the aim or intention which is present, perhaps only half-consciously, in the mind of the artist. For a private patron, the artist used to paint with a definite notion of what was expected of him—he knew that the painting would be hung in a living-room, that it would be lived with, that it would have to please a specific 'taste'. But the painter who aims at State patronage—with what preconceptions shall he paint? The picture will be hung in some bleak or pompous gallery—he cannot be sure where it will be hung: it must please the taste of some obscure or unknown official before it is offered to the appreciation of a wandering, indifferent public. Not exactly an inspiring prospect for the painter. In some cases, it will mean the abuse of the artist's talent: for example, if he is essentially a miniaturist, he will force himself to paint on a monumental scale. But assuming he can accommodate himself to the scale and environment of a public gallery, the painter must then consider his anonymous patron. The State with us is not yet a political instrument; where it is the painter must consider the ideology and prejudices of the party in power. But even where the State is still politically neutral in its administration, the painter has still to consider the aims and ideals of the bureaucracy. Again, it is the indefiniteness, the imprecision of the process that is baffling, that fails to inspire. When a painter painted for the Catholic Church, or for the Court of a king, he had a fairly exact idea of what was expected of him: he was faced by a definite task—to paint an altarpiece for a particular position in a particular church. But how shall a contemporary painter set about painting a picture to be bought by the Arts Council and circulated round a thousand art centres?

Let me now suggest another way of looking at the whole problem. Let me return to my starting point, and paraphrase Robert Graves's statement. *Pictures should be painted for painters. For people in general artists should design useful things and be content if the public is unaware that they do anything else.*

Mr Graves would probably admit that within the term 'poets' should be included putative poets—mute inglorious Miltons who have a mental poetic activity. In the same way my paraphrase would include putative painters—people who have retained their aesthetic sensibility, are consciously aware of a desire to exercise it, but have never had the chance. With that qualification, the statement will stand as an indication of my way of looking at the problem.

The whole business of what is called 'cabinet' painting—painting little rectangles of canvas or board to be hung in private living-rooms—is a relatively recent development in the history of art. It corresponds very closely with the rise of capitalism and was called into being by the acquisitive society, by the bourgeoisie which wanted to invest some of its wealth in *objets d'art*, in relatively small works of art which could be moved from one house to another, and which in case of financial need could easily be disposed of piecemeal.

Before the sixteenth century painters were craftsmen. Generally speaking, they were not exclusively painters. They had workshops which would turn out any job of interior decoration, and the jobs were usually handed out to them by the Church, sometimes by the city council, sometimes by a prince. But it was always commissioned work, and it was always work with a specific function. The orders which the Church gave to the glass-painter—an obscure corner of the history of art of which I used to have some expert knowledge—were as detailed as a modern contract for building a factory. All the great medieval painters, and Renaissance painters right down to the time of Michelangelo, were craftsmen carrying out formal contracts.

Then, as time went on, the painter and the sculptor were left to their own devices, to express, as we say, their own personalities. There were still specific jobs to be done—portraits to be painted, for example—but in general the artist began to invent free subjects—still lifes, landscapes, *genre* subjects, finally what we call abstractions. A medieval patron would have been quite incapable of understanding why he should pay good gold for a functionless construction of circles and squares. If such a proposal had come within his comprehension, he would have been outraged: he would probably have ordered the insolent painter to be executed.

I am not suggesting that no great works of art were produced in the epoch of cabinet painting. From Giorgione to Picasso a host of exquisite creations, the expression of a great artist's subtle vision and fauntless technique, were produced for the capitalist market, for the private delectation of merchant princes and rampageous tyrants, for men of taste who also happened to be men of wealth. But the whole basis of that kind of production has gone. The merchant prince is now the controller in some Government department, with a fat salary but so heavily taxed that he has no money left to indulge in any but the most modest patronage: the tyrants have been tamed and the man of taste has been impoverished. Admittedly, here and there a private fortune is still large enough to leave a margin for indulgence—but it is a shrinking margin. Only in America does private patronage survive on a considerable scale. We must also, at this point, take into consideration the influence of modern developments in architecture, which leave little room for the hanging of pictures in a house or flat. Contemporary sensibility prefers unencumbered surfaces, unbroken lines, and a maximum of light. I know modern painters who live in modern houses where they do not exhibit even their own paintings. The studio is a place apart, a workshop where objects are made for people who still live in bourgeois houses, or (hopefully) for the State's art galleries.

In short, the cabinet picture has lost, or is quickly losing, all economic and social justification, and to try and keep it alive by State patronage is like trying to keep the dodo alive in a zoo. Indeed, there is more than a fanciful parallel between the museum and the zoo; they are both places where we keep rare and eccentric specimens at public expense. And why not, to be logical, put the artist himself in the zoo: let him have a comfortable cage with a northern light, and there let him produce obsolete art objects to be hung in an aquarium-like building next door.

Cabinet painting is a defunct art, perpetuated by defunct institutions. I do not know what proportion of the sixty thousand students attending art schools in Great Britain any one year are taught easel painting: it is certainly a large proportion, and even if it is a small proportion, easel painting has nevertheless a prestige and a status in art education which is part of the defunct tradition of capitalistic art. The Royal Academy exists to perpetuate this tradition, and a whole system of academic education is geared up to its obsolete standards. No harm would be done to art, in any vital sense of the word, if all this vast machinery of life-classes and antique classes were abolished. The Royal Academy Schools, the Royal College of Art, the Slade School, and many local art schools, are not only perpetuating a defunct tradition: they are luring thousands of young men and women into an obsolete vocation where they can only experience poverty, dis-illusion, and despair.

What, then, shall we put in the place of our futile art schools? There is no simple answer to that question, because what is really involved is a complete social reorientation towards art. I advocate a reform of education which puts art where it should always have been—right in the heart of things. Let us begin with the primary schools. If we can reform our methods of teaching and our attitude towards the objectives of education so that some native aesthetic sensibility is preserved in children, and children are no longer brutalized and anaesthetized by the bludgeoning process of 'learning'—that is to say, hammering conceptual knowledge into their innocent minds—then there would be some human material to work with. You can't make the silk purses of art out of the sow's ears of school certificates. You can't expect the flowering of the creative instinct in an epoch which condemns its children to a *via dolorosa* of examinations.

If we get the foundation right, if we produce children who are healthy, sensitive and wise, rather than children who are brawny, 'clever'* and efficient, we can then train them in the techniques of production. Then we can safely teach them how to use tools and machines, because with sensitive fingers and vivid minds they will be incapable of producing or consuming the hideous things they are content with now. Some of them we can teach to be specialists in design—to be industrial designers and architects. To others we can give commissions to work, commissions as specific and detailed as those the medieval artist received. And then, in good time, an art as great as medieval art will take shape.

As for painting easel pictures—well, why not if you, a useful citizen, feel so inclined? You will have your own time in which to paint, just as the poet has his own time for writing verses. You can give your pictures as tokens of regard to your friends, or you can make a little pocket-money by this private hobby. You might paint a great picture in your spare time, just as T. S. Eliot wrote a great poem in his spare time. But you will not any longer, if you are a reasonable person, expect your fellow-taxpayers to support you while you indulge in an activity which no longer has any economic sanction.

---

* *Clever* etymologically means something with sharp claws (hence, 'clever as a cat') and that, of course, is the predatory concept of education which we have evolved under the influence of a competitive economy.

The Fate of Modern Painting

If these facts, and my deductions, are admitted, we should then consider whether any useful purpose can be served by the various institutions and organizations which have already been brought into existence. In other words, can we redirect the policy and practices of our museums and schools of art, our ministries of art and education, our art councils and international committees, even UNESCO itself—can we so reorientate the activities of these bodies that they serve art in a creative and not merely conservative fashion?

There is, admittedly, no direct solution of cultural problems. Let me reaffirm once again the *radical* nature of cultural growths. Art is an organic phenomenon, a biological process. Like flowers and fruit, plumage and song, it is a product of the life-force itself. I am not trying to reduce art to materialistic factors. I am prepared to admit that human life has a qualitative distinction, a certain spirituality or higher consciousness, which transcends but does not separate it from the rest of animal creation; and by reason of this evolutionary variation, man's art has perhaps a deeper, at any rate a different, biological significance, compared with the song of the nightingale or the plumage of the peacock. But, nevertheless, all these phenomena are within the same scale of creative evolution. Art is human, not divine: profane, not sacred. It does not descend in pentecostal flames: it arises, like a green sap; like a seminal fluid, it issues from the body, and from the body in an unusual state of excitement. This is true whether we are literal, and think of the body of the individual artist; or metaphorical, and think of the body of society. Now, though we are quite clear about the psychology of artistic creation in the individual, and even our classicists admit that art is a physical afflatus of some kind, we have never given much consideration to the psychology of artistic creation in a society. We sometimes speak of 'an inspired age', or 'a creative epoch', but then we are only speaking metaphorically. But the facts correspond to the figure of speech: eras, no less than artists, have their afflatus, and a society can be inspired. And that is the problem we should study—the relations between the forms of society and the forms of art, the interflow of vitality from organizations to individuals, the generation of creative activity in the group, between persons and associations. When we have considered those problems in all their aspects—climatic, ethnic, economic, social—then, perhaps, we shall be in a position to give direct support and encouragement to the arts.

The Fate of Modern Painting

Our present activities are futile. We take what exists—the detritus of a defunct civilization—and we assume that by sifting it, cementing it, mixing it with bureaucratic gold or circulating it in unusual channels, we can re-create a past glory, build the foundations of a new civilization. All we can create in that way is an *ersatz* culture, the synthetic product of those factories we call variously universities, colleges or museums. The universities never have produced an art, and never will. All our technical colleges and public schools, even our primary schools and infant schools, are all so many slaughter-houses, institutions for anaesthetizing the artist, for eradicating sensibility, for repeating endlessly and without variation the stamp of a civilization without art.

We must begin again, modestly, patiently. From our historians we must expect a more exact analysis of the social conditions which have produced art in the past. From our psychologists we must expect a more exact analysis of the creative process in man, not merely in the individual artist, but as a process occurring between man and man, for art is not only creation, but also communication. And from our educationists we must expect a remodelling of the educational system which will preserve and refine man's innate sensibility, to the end that the practical activities of life are no longer clumsy and inept, abortive or destructive; but by securing a perfect equilibrium of the sensuous and intellectual faculties, ensure the first requisite of a creative age.

II

4

Human Art and Inhuman Nature

Most of the controversies about art, from ancient times to the present day, have been concerned with the relation of man, in the shape of the artist, to nature, in the shape of the artist's subject matter. The activity we call art is a technical process by means of which we depict, or represent,—what? The simple assumption is that the artist depicts the external world, the things he sees with his eyes. If that is the sole aim of the artist, then he has, at different historical periods, seen nature very differently. Take the commonest object, say a tree, and then compare the representation of a tree in Chinese painting of the Sung dynasty, in Byzantine mosaics, in Gothic glass painting, in a painting by Gainsborough or Corot, and in a painting by Cézanne. These five trees, if set side by side, would have little in common except roots in the ground and branches in the air. We can give all kinds of explanation for these distinct visual images depicted by artists at different periods of history, but we end inevitably with an overall theory of relativism. The artist paints what he wants to see, a human or individual version of that inhuman abstraction called Nature.

What do we mean by Nature. We spell the word with a capital N and it then means something very near to God—the totality of creation, the living or evolving world, with man at the apex. In the jungle Nature, still wearing a capital, becomes red in tooth and claw and distinctly unattractive. When we spell the word with a small 'n' nature shrinks to matter for immediate observation, even for minute observation under a microscope. Obviously nature is a very flexible term—so flexible that Oscar Wilde found it possible to suggest that nature is the creation of art.

Wilde's jest, as was usually the case, expressed a profound truth, but a truth not easy to grasp. Between *nature*, as universal indiscriminate growth, and *man*, as a being endowed with self-consciousness, there is a contradiction. Man has become aware of what is going on in the universe, of the how and the why of

73

things, and instead of just passively submitting to the instinctual drives which he possesses in common with other animals, he takes control, as best he can, and attempts either to adapt himself to his condition, or to change his condition. He becomes a nomadic animal, seeking his food in favourable places. He then takes a still bolder step—he stops wandering and adapts his surroundings to his needs. He creates an artificial environment which most people have in mind when they talk about nature, and which Wilde had in mind when he talked about art.

The Greeks and Romans probably had the same idea as Oscar Wilde—at least, their words for what we call art were equivalent to our words for skill and technique. That is to say, the arts, like agriculture and building, were methods of imposing the human will on matter—organic or inorganic as might be. As such the arts continued to be thought of in most civilizations at most periods, until, in the course of time, an ideal Nature was evolved in the imagination of certain poets and philosophers, and Art was ordered to imitate this ideal. In fact, art became the approved method of realizing this ideal, of giving it visible shape.

The next step needs careful attention. By the middle of the eighteenth century it had been agreed that Art is the imitation of an ideal Nature. Then, between about 1780 and 1830, the general conception of nature changes completely (idealism is discredited, science takes over); it is no longer ideal, but fascinating in its irregularities, particularities, variations and visual actuality. But, at first, the idea of art does not change. It must still imitate, and now it must imitate, not the ideal but the actual—the visible, palpitating reality of things. The imitative function of the artist remained the same, but the new reflection in the mirror he dutifully held up to nature at first gave people a shock. When Constable's *Haywain* was exhibited in the Paris salon of 1824 it created a sensation—it was a revolutionary painting in the eyes of the public of that time. To that same public artists such as Géricault, Delacroix and Courbet seemed to be introducing disturbing innovations, and the limit of indignation seemed to be reached when Manet's *Olympia* was first exhibited in 1865.

After Manet came Degas, Monet, and Pissarro and the whole of what at the time was regarded as a complete break with the past—the Impressionist movement. I need not mention minor phases of that movement such as the pointillism of Signac and Seurat, except that they do serve to indicate the source of all this restlessness in art. It was essentially, from Constable onwards, the impact of science on art—science in a broad sense which would include meteorology, which Constable studied,* the science of colour, which most of the Impressionists studied, and later, ethnology, which spread a knowledge of the art of primitive people. The whole period is characterized by a general diffusion of knowledge, and the changes in art are due to the absorption, by the artists, of some aspect of this knowledge. It was not always an intelligent application of science—it is generally admitted now that the 'divisionist' and 'pointillist' techniques were based on a misunderstanding of the physiology of perception.

No artist, in the whole of this development, was so significant as Cézanne. Cézanne can hardly be called scientifically minded, in the sense that Seurat was; he never betrayed any particular interest in science as such, and the strength of his character comes from a certain peasant-like naïvety. But nevertheless Cézanne had been influenced by the temper of the age, and his whole attitude to nature, which is analytical, and to the technique of art, which is experimental, is essentially scientific. Analysis is the key-word for his whole procedure, and analysis is a scientific word.

Round about the turn of the century another science was lying in wait for the artist—the science of psychology, and it is the impact of this science which has been decisive in our own time. Again, the artist may not have had any direct knowledge of the science, but a general state of awareness was created which decisively influenced the artist. The artist was made aware of the science of human nature. Psychology established the validity of individual variations of type, and even the desirability of freely expressing the characteristics of one's own type. As a consequence the artist felt entitled to a new freedom, a freedom from convention and tradition. His art became the expression of his unique personality.

We can measure the distance travelled in this century of evolution by retracing our steps and contrasting such personalism in art with the eighteenth century formula for art. Reynolds, who is the typical representative of the former tradition, said in one of his *Discourses* that 'the whole beauty and grandeur of Art consists . . . in being able to get above all singular forms, local customs, particularities of every kind. . . . The painter corrects

* See *Constable's Clouds*, by Kurt Badt. (London, Routledge & Kegan Paul, 1950.)

Human Art and Inhuman Nature

Nature by herself, her imperfect state by her more perfect. His eye being enabled to distinguish the accidental deficiencies, excrescences, and deformities of things, from their general figures, he makes out an abstract idea of their forms more perfect than any one original.' This is putting the artist firmly in control of Nature in order to create an ideal of Beauty. The criterion of the modern artist is Truth rather than Beauty, and to this extent modern art is still keeping pace with natural science.

Though modern art in general is a continuation of the scientific trend of the nineteenth century, nevertheless a break in this relationship took place about forty years ago and has been gathering pace ever since. About 1909 Picasso painted his first cubist picture and a new movement was born. This soon split into two, as movements mostly do, and cubism became either analytical or synthetic. Analytical cubism was still a continuation of the scientific attitude—what was 'analysed' was the structure of nature. But Juan Gris, who was responsible for the breakaway known as synthetic cubism, proposed that the work of art should begin with an aesthetic reality—that is to say, with an abstract pattern designed within the two-dimensional space of the picture frame. Representational elements *might* afterwards be introduced to fill in the abstract design—to give it sensuous substance. But the basis of the work of art was no longer Nature, but Idea— something conceptual, geometric, architectural.

Finally, along came artists who said: Why bother to introduce representational elements at all? Why not let your geometric or architectural structure speak for itself, in terms of pure form and colour? And they proceeded to paint pictures and carve materials in conformity with such principles. Thus a new type of art was born which has been called abstract, constructivist, neo-plastic and several other names, but all these varieties of abstract art agree in rejecting the notion that Art is in any way dependent on Nature. They neither 'screen' Nature, in the manner of Reynolds, nor respect Nature, in the manner of the Impressionists; they will have nothing whatsoever to do with Nature. Some of them may attempt to represent what is fundamental to Nature —namely, the laws of harmony inherent in the physical structure of the Universe itself; but others claim to be independent even of this given quantity, and to invent an entirely new reality.

It will be noticed that the theories of art at both extremes of this development agree in stressing the freedom of the artist—the artist is not a slave to Nature, or to the science of nature. His mind is emancipated—free to express, not himself (for that would still be a kind of slavery) but a new vision, a new order of reality, an ideal beauty. Art is harmony—I believe that no other definition can include such a wide range of objects which mankind in all ages and countries has agreed to call beautiful. It may be that Nature contains all the elements, in colour and form, which go to the composition of a work of art, just as the keyboard contains all the notes necessary for the art of music. But Whistler, who used this analogy, went on to say that 'the artis is born to pick and choose, and group with science, these elements, that the result may be beautiful—as the musician gathers his notes, and forms his chords, until he brings forth from chaos glorious harmony'.

The faculty which enables the artist to accomplish this magical result is generally known as the imagination. I am not going to attempt to definite this faculty—it has been done before by critics such as Coleridge—but I would like to quote a description from Ruskin's *Modern Painters* of the way it works:

'Such is always the mode in which the highest imaginative faculty seizes its materials. It never stops at crusts or ashes, or outward images of any kind; it ploughs them all aside, and plunges into the very central fiery heart; nothing else will content its spirituality; whatever semblances and various outward shows and phases its subject may possess go for nothing; it gets within all fence, cuts down to the root, and drinks the very vital sap of that it deals with: once therein, it is at liberty to throw up what new shoots it will, and to prune and twist them at its pleasure, and bring them to fairer fruit than grew on the old tree; but all this pruning and twisting is work that it likes not, and often does ill; its function and gift are the getting at the root, its nature and dignity depend on its holding things always by the heart. Take its hand from off the beating of that, and it will prophesy no longer; it looks not in the eyes, it judges not by the voice, it describes not by outward features; all that it affirms, judges, or describes, it affirms from within.'

This, it will be seen, is a very subjective version of the imaginative faculty—there is no idea of building up an ideal Nature from visual images. All that kind of sensuous experiences, so to speak, ploughed into the ground of the mind, and in due course there emerges, from this ground, a new growth, with original sap, vital and fruitful.

All of which, it may be said, is fanciful theory. Let us get down to the facts, more particularly the commonsense facts of English art. Ruskin was writing about Turner, an artist with his eccentric moments. Let us bring into the discussion artists of a more solid kind, such as Hogarth and Constable. If we review the development of English art between Hogarth and Turner, perhaps a theory of the imagination more reasonable than one based on Turner alone will emerge.

The effort of a hundred years is in question—beginning, say, with Hogarth's *Marriage à la Mode* (1744) and ending with Turner's *Rain, Steam and Speed* (1844). The inclusion of Hogarth prevents any easy generalizations about the romantic nature of the English genius—or, indeed, similar generalizations about the nature of romanticism, for if we are going to claim the painter of *Marriage à la Mode* as a realist, as an artist 'engagé', according to the fashionable doctrine, by social realities, then what are we to call the painter whose 'sketches' of clouds and trees were not only based on an observation scientific in its exactitude, but reinforced by a determined study of the scientific literature of the period? Nothing is more trivial and perverse than a theory which assumes that because an artist directs his attention towards human beings or social actions, he thereby becomes in some sense more 'realistic', or even more 'classical', and is therefore in some undefined sense 'greater', than the artist who prefers to paint landscapes or still-life. One might as well say that the science of anthropology is more realistic or more important than the science of geology. Just as in this case it is the scientific method which matters—and which should be the sole object of our judgment—so in the other case it is or should be the aesthetic method which matters. From this point of view, differences of some importance are observable.

Ruskin, in the passage I have quoted, was writing a hundred years ago and at the end of the period covered by the three artists I have taken as representative. He was trying to distinguish a difference in the quality of the imagination present in certain works of art. It would be simplifying too much to say that Constable, Turner and Bonington had one quality in common, not shared by Hogarth. As a matter of fact, Ruskin himself distinguished sharply between the imaginative powers of Constable and Turner. 'There are some truths', he wrote, 'early obtained, which give a *deceptive resemblance* to Nature; others only to be obtained with difficulty, which cause no deception, but give *inner and deep resemblance*. These two classes of truths cannot be obtained together; choice must be made between them. The bad painter gives the cheap *deceptive* resemblance. The good painter gives the precious non-deceptive resemblance. Constable perceives in a landscape that grass is wet, the meadows flat, and the boughs shady; that is to say, about as much as, I suppose, might in general be apprehended, between them, by an intelligent fawn and a skylark. Turner perceives at a glance *the whole sum of visible truth open to human intelligence.*'

A logical fallacy will be obvious in this argument; for if a fawn is 'intelligent' it is presumably just as capable as Turner of perceiving '*the whole sum of visible truth*'. Later on in his work, Ruskin was forced to distinguish between two kinds of imagination, and to qualify the kind possessed by Turner as 'noble'—an ethical qualification as blatant as any put forward by our modern protagonists of 'engagement' in art, of socialist realism, of nationalism, etc.

Let us be quite frank about this issue. When Constable says, 'There is nothing ugly; I never saw an ugly thing in my life: for let the form of an object be what it may, light, shade, and perspective will always make it beautiful'—he too is making an ethical judgment. It is not light, shade, and perspective which in themselves transform ordinary or even ugly objects into works of art; they are rather transformed by the artist's feeling and associational values . . . 'old rotten planks, slimy posts and brickwork, I love such things', Constable confessed. 'Painting is with me but another word for feeling.'

On that note we can reconcile Turner and Constable, and Ruskin with them both. Indeed, the primacy of feeling is the bracket in which we can include the whole romantic movement —not only the painters but the poets, philosophers and architects. In Hogarth, generally speaking, the primary act is one of judgment, of criticism, of rational selection. Feeling is worked up to cope with the selected facts. Not that Hogarth is the perfect contrast to Turner or Constable: Reynolds, with his conscious idealism, his canon of perfection, his declared aim of 'correcting Nature', is the true English representative of classicism. Compare with Constable's 'There is nothing ugly', Reynolds's 'All the objects which are exhibited to our view by Nature, upon close examination will be found to have their blemishes and defects'. Hogarth played with the classical Ideal, but he had not the intellectual power to achieve it. His predominant aim was social criticism, or social honesty when it was a question of a direct portrait.

What distinguishes all the Romantic painters, from both the Realists and the Classicists, is their preoccupation with landscape. Constable could on occasion paint a very competent portrait; Bonington (who died at the age of 27) promised to be a master of portraiture. Across the Channel romantic painters like Delacroix and Courbet and even Corot excelled in portraiture. There is nothing inconsistent, therefore, between romanticism as such and the art of portrait painting. Why, then, the almost exclusive devotion of the English romanticists to landscape?

Here we touch upon something fundamental in English art, which is only to be understood as the contest between two philosophies of life—on native, indigenous, instinctive, the other imported, imitated, acquired. The native tradition is a Northern tradition, allied to the tradition which stretched right across Scandinavia, Russia, Northern China. The imported tradition is the Mediterranean tradition. The contrast between these two traditions has often been described—and this is not the place to discuss the subject generally. But the fundamental distinction is the one which finds expression precisely in this attitude to Nature. In the North the concept of nature may differ from time to time and from place to place; it may be negative, as in Celtic art, transforming natural objects into decorative pattern, or it may be affirmative, as in the art of the period we are studying, striving to reproduce the 'dewy freshness' of the scene. But affirmative or negative, the concept is there all the time, breaking out in the margins of a manuscript, in the tracery of a stained-glass window, in stone capitals and chased silver, above all in poetry.

In Latin countries, however, nature has no existence, except as the unessential background to human activities, as *décor*. There are exceptional artists, like Leonardo, who are inspired by a scientific curiosity which includes natural facts in its scope. But Man, in godlike isolation, is the singular subject of Greek sculpture, of Italian painting, of Latin literature. Even in the Romantic period which concerns us now, it is Byron, a 'humanist', who can be assimilated by the Continent. Wordsworth, a much greater poet, is ignored.

The predominance of landscape in English painting is to be explained, therefore, as indigenous—as the expression of an innate Northern necessity, and not as a romantic category. To call Constable romantic is misleading; he is not in any sense an introvert, but rather a modest craftsman, interested in the efficiency of his tools, the chemistry of his materials, the technique of his craft. His preparatory 'sketches' are no more romantic than a weather report. But they are accurate, they are vividly expressed, they are truthful. By contrast, a painting like the *Calais Gate* is theatrical, exaggerated, unreal; in the popular usage of the word, it is infinitely more 'romantic' than anything Constable ever painted.

Turner is another question. His sketches are precise, even more precise than Constable's. Constable admired them greatly. An early painting like *A Frosty Morning* (1813) does not differ greatly in conception from Constable's *Hampstead Heath*. But what shall we say of the *Interior at Petworth* (? 1830) or *Rain, Steam and Speed* (1844)? Natural truth, in any sense conceived by Constable, is no longer in question.* Ruskin had to defend his hero on the grounds that truth of another kind was being presented, and it needed nothing less than a new theory of art. This theory was the theory of Expressionism, a modern word; but though Ruskin did not use the word, no one has more precisely or more eloquently formulated this theory. What he wrote in defence of Turner can be used in explanation of any great expressionist artist since his time—Oskar Kokoschka, for example. The passage I have quoted is the most succinct statement of the theory that I can find in *Modern Painters*. Ruskin called the faculty involved 'Imagination', but he agreed that 'the name is of little consequence'. Whatever it is to be called, 'this penetrating, possession-taking faculty' is 'the highest intellectual power of man'. 'There is no reasoning in it; it works not by algebra, nor by integral calculus; it is a piercing pholas-like mind's tongue, that works and tastes into the very rock heart; no matter what be the subject submitted to it, substance or spirit.'

There is perhaps a further refinement in Ruskin's theory which should be noted, for it serves to distinguish Turner from some

---

* Constable himself found (May 17, 1803) that 'Turner becomes more and more extravagant, and less attentive to nature'.

modern expressionists. A work of art, said Ruskin, is often called imaginative when it merely leaves room for the action of the imagination: when it is merely suggestive, as a few shapeless scratches may be, or accidental stains on a wall. But this is not the real test. 'The vacancy of a truly imaginative work' (and here presumably Ruskin was thinking of works such as the *Interior at Petworth*) 'results not from absence of ideas, or incapability of grasping or disdaining to tell more; and the sign of this being the case is, that the mind of the beholder is forced to act in a certain mode, and feels itself overpowered, and borne away by that of the painter, and not able to defend itself, nor go which way it will: and the value of the work depends on the truth, authority and inevitability of this suggestiveness.'

This distinction might be illustrated by that painting which Ruskin said he would choose were he reduced to rest Turner's immortality upon any single work—*The Slave Ship* from the Boston Museum. Ruskin wrote one of his wonderful purple patches in description of this picture (*Modern Painters*, Vol. I, Pt. II, Sect. v, Ch. iii), a parallel work of art rather than an analysis, a synthetic vision in which every detail focuses to wonderful clarity. Once the spectator has seized the subject (a slaver riding a storm, and throwing her slaves overboard), and then looks into the picture, it will be seen how what appears at first sight to be a confused torment of water and spray, transfused by the rays of the setting sun, is actually packed with realistic incident—agitated fishes, pieces of wreckage, disappearing limbs, despairing hands, hovering gulls, and, in the offing, two ominous sea-monsters with gaping jaws. 'Its daring conception, ideal in the highest sense of the word, is based on the purest truth, and wrought out with the concentrated knowledge of a life . . . the whole picture dedicated to the most sublime of subjects and impressions—the power, majesty, and deathfulness of the open, deep, illimitable sea.'

I may seem to be concentrating too much on Turner, and quoting too much Ruskin, but I have done so deliberately. It would have been more cautious to concentrate on Constable, but he may be safely left to the academic critics. The truth is that

* Less respectfully, Thackeray described them as 'such a race of fishes as never was seen since the saeculum Pyrrhae; gaping dolphins redder than the reddest herrings, horrid spreading polypi, like huge slimy poached eggs, in which hapless niggers plunge and disappear'—thus anticipating the reaction of any modern philistine to an expressionist exhibition.

for many years now the issue of Turner's art has been avoided by art critics, English and American. 'Avoided' is perhaps not the right word, since some of these critics, such as Roger Fry, have expressed themselves in no uncertain terms. But to express dislike or revulsion or disdain is not a scientific attitude. It is the real issue that has been avoided, and this is the clash I have already spoken of, between the Northern and Mediterranean traditions, between Expressionism and Idealism. I do not think any of the exponents of Expressionism, least of all Ruskin, have wished to deny the values represented by the classical ideal. But they do insist that it is not the only way of representing the world we experience, and much as they respect the vision which 'sees things steadily and sees them whole', they would point out that for some purposes the attitude is too detached; that, indeed, the nature and dignity of a truly imaginative faculty 'depend on its always holding things by the heart'.

This is, of course, a rhetorical phrase, but the physical image used by Ruskin brings us back to the personal factor. The human heart is not a machine, guaranteed to mould the feelings to a uniform shape. There is no single way, even no normal way, of representing the world we experience. We experience the world through the subtle medium of a temperament, and if we faithfully represent that experience, we produce something unique, or at any rate, something typical of our temperament. In the end, all differences of style in art reduce to differences of temperament.

If we now assume that the artist is at liberty to express his temperament in his painting, then there ought to be as many types of painting as there are types of persons, and this is indeed what we find. The science of typology—or type-psychology as it is more often called—is comparatively modern. It is true that men have been divided according to their temperaments from early times, and usually into four categories: the sanguine, the choleric, the phlegmatic and the melancholic. A man's mode of expression —his voice, gestures, gait, and actions—corresponds to his constitutional type. Now modern physiologists and psychologists have resumed and at the same time enormously elaborated the study of types, but curiously enough they do not depart essentially from the traditional categories. Jung, for example, still distinguishes four basic types of temperament, though by indicating the dynamic direction of these basic types (inward or outward) he increases the number to eight. The physiological school, basing itself mainly on endocrinology, distinguishes between 'cycloid' and 'schizoid' temperaments, but the cycloid is divided into the hypomanic and the depressive, and the schizoid into the hyper-aesthetic and the anaesthetic. We therefore again have four categories and they correspond fairly closely to the choleric, melancholic, sanguine and phlegmatic types. Without going into all the detailed characteristics of the various types it may be said that most artists fall naturally into one of the four categories. It needs a good deal of careful analysis to decide which category a particular artist belongs to, and if in the end we describe Franz Hals as a typical 'pyknic cyclothyme' or Michelangelo as a typical 'schizothyme', the common reader is not much the wiser. But certainly artists can be classified in this way, and it follows that there is more essential similarity between the same psychological types in different periods than there is between the different psychological types in the same period. In other words, psychological characteristics are stronger than period characteristics.

A painter is not a 'realist' because he happens to be born in a realistic period, or because his government tells him he must be a realist; nor is a painter 'romantic' because he is born in a romantic period, 'religious' because he is born in a religious age, etc. Social and economic conditions may favour one type of artist or suppress another type: the types are nevertheless born and propagated: they come into existence in spite of the ideological prejudices of the particular period and they can only be eradicated by tyrannical force.

Assuming the existence of various types of artist, more or less constant in their appearance throughout history, let us next consider for a moment the complications which are introduced by the purpose for which particular works of art are designed. Such purposes are, of course, of endless variety, but already in the early days of Greek art we can distinguish three distinct types of art differentiated according to their purpose or destination. There was the votive image, dedicated to the gods: the symbol of some feeling of awe or propitiation. There was the poetic myth embodying an ideal, divine or human. And finally there was the representation of the actual, what we call realistic art—the Greeks, with more reason, regarded the ideal as the real, and representational art as merely an imitation of an imitation of the real.

Human Art and Inhuman Nature

These three ends of art persist throughout history, but some-times one and sometimes another is predominant. We might call the three purposes Symbolical, Poetic and Imitative. Naturally, if a painter has a choice in the matter, he will paint for the end most congenial to his temperament: if he is an introverted type he will not normally paint imitative (objective) pictures; if he is an extrovert, he will not paint poetic pictures. But actually it is not so simple as that. Every man, as Paracelsus said, is the son of two fathers: one of Heaven, the other of Earth. He is compounded of mind and matter, body and soul, sensation and sensibility. If he is an artist, he can serve his god or his patron with either side of his nature. It thus comes about that whether art is symbolical, poetic or imitative, it can still be materialistic or transcendental. A Byzantine icon is symbolical: the very prototype of the painting conceived as a votive offering to the divine god. It is entirely transcendental and the emotion it expresses cannot be character-ized as other than religious. We might take for comparison a modern painting by Otto Dix. At first sight it is aggressively realistic, and seems to have nothing in common with the icon. It is an imitation or likeness of the painter and his infant son. But if we look closer we see various symbolical details: the brush in the painter's hand, the honest 'set' of his features, his simplified clothing, the benedictional attitude of the child. We may then remember that Otto Dix began his career as an expressionist painter: that he was converted to the political doctrine known as 'socialist realism': and we then realize that the painting, in its realistic manner, is every bit as symbolical as the Russian icon. But instead of symbolizing the transcendental values of a super-natural religion, it symbolizes the materialistic values of racialism: instead of the Mother, the father; instead of the Christ Child, the Nordic child. I am not criticizing the relative values of these two symbolical paintings: I am merely pointing out that ancient and modern, if we look to intentions rather than appearance, are not so different as they seem.

If the intention of the artist is poetic—that is to say, if his pur-pose in painting a picture is to create a mood, a state of dis-interested pleasure or pleasurable contemplation, then he may still use earthly or heavenly, real or super-real means. Nothing could be more idealistic or 'literary' than the theme of a painting by Poussin, yet the figures he employs, the landscape he sets them in, every detail of plant and flower, is drawn from nature.

85

Human Art and Inhuman Nature

The theme of Chirico's picture, *The Disquieting Muses*, might almost be a satire on the theme of Poussin's *Inspiration of the Poet*. The natural landscape is replaced by an entirely artificial one: instead of trees a prison-like building and factory chimneys: instead of idealized human figures, stuffed dummies and a plaster cast. Yet out of these artificial elements Chirico builds up a poetic atmosphere—not, indeed, the poetry of the *Cid*, but definitely that of *The Waste Land*.

That an imitative art giving a superficially realistic representation of objects existed in ancient times, we know from certain references in Greek literature, but this type of art has never been valued very highly by philosophers or connoisseurs, and extraordinarily little of it has survived from any past age. It was rightly regarded as a clever trick rather than as creative art, and the invention of photography removed the last justification for it. But there is a naturalistic type of art, which while in no sense 'photographic', does try to convey the quality and direct experience of the objective world. It is represented at its best by a landscape painter like Constable or a figure painter like Degas. Its method is selective: it is realized by the painter that perception itself is selective, and that the vividness of our sensations does not depend on the inclusion of every detail, but on the exclusion of everything unessential. It becomes the painter's task to pick out the significant details and combine them in a significant design. It is a question of economy rather than exactitude, of impression rather than imitation. The Impressionist school which concentrated on this purpose is perhaps the only kind of modern art which has no exact parallels in the past: it is true that one can pick out impressionist details in Tintoretto or Tiepolo or El Greco: but these details are incidental in a composition which has quite another purpose.

Naturalistic art, even impressionist art, is still of the earth: is there an art that is an imitation of transcendental values, that is to say, of ideas themselves? I think there is, and that it is the basis of modern 'abstract' art. An art which is concerned in an entirely non-representational manner with the harmonic relationships of lines and shapes and colours is an art which imitates, and imitates very closely, certain very definite and concrete elements. Here is no impressionism, no poetry, no symbolism; but something as exact and representational as a mathematical diagram. Mathematicians claim that some at any rate of their formulas are beautiful:

86

what then is the difference between the plastic representation of such a beautiful formula and an abstract painting? Essentially, there is no difference at all: the mathematician is an abstract artist except that he does not possess, or has not cultivated, the ability to express his conceptions in a plastic material.

Abstract art, which strikes some people as the most strange and uniquely modern of all forms of art, is therefore essentially as old as that art which studies the elements of form and number embodied in the structure of the universe. It is perhaps more consistently intuitive than mathematics, though I doubt whether a mathematician would think so: but otherwise it is mathematics translated into a plastic material.

Here, at the extreme limit of the evolution of art, we must repeat: *Plus ça change, plus c'est la même chose.* Art changes its clothes: clothes change their fashion. The body beneath has sex and temperament, which differ but do not change. Art in all its variety of purpose, in all its fidelity to the multiplex moods of our human nature, is essentially the same today as it was yesterday, and will be the same in the twilight of civilization as it was at the dawn and in the blaze of noon. I know of no test of the genuineness of art other than that suggested by Ruskin—the sense of 'getting at the root' and of 'holding this by the heart'. Art is human, and there is no substitute whatever for the vitality which it should reflect and in itself exhibit.

5

Realism and Abstraction in Modern Art

Modern art offers a confusing variety of movements and mannerisms, and it would be a bold critic who attempted a comprehensive definition of them all. But if we were to arrange all the prevailing styles in an orderly sequence, we should find at one extreme a style which without hesitation we should call 'realistic', and at the other extreme another style which, perhaps not quite so confidently, we should call 'abstract'. We might use other terms to describe these same extremes—terms like 'naturalistic' and 'geometric', 'organic' and 'conventional', 'vitalistic' and 'formalistic', but all these words indicate the same opposed tendencies. If in this essay I adopt 'realistic' and 'abstract', it is because they are in most general use. In addition, they seem to me to be based on common sense, and to have a descriptive aptness which explains their persistence. By *realism* we mean fidelity of representation, truth to nature. By *abstraction* we mean what is derived or disengaged from nature, the pure or essential form abstracted from the concrete details.

From this general point of view, realism will include, not only the attempt to reproduce with fidelity the images given in normal perception, but also those distorted or selected images due to exceptional states of awareness which we call idealism, expressionism, superrealism, etc. In the same way, abstraction will include any form of expression which dispenses with the phenomenal image, and relies on elements of expression that are conceptual, metaphysical, abstruse, and absolute. The fact that such images are expressed as concrete signs or symbols (compositions of lines, volumes, colours, etc.) does not vitiate the use of the word 'abstract'. Our terms refer, not only to the final product of expression, but also to its origins and the process of its creation: stages which, as Croce rightly maintains, can never be separated in a work of art.

Realism and Abstraction in Modern Art

This is perhaps a sufficient excuse for the adoption of the popular usage of such terms; that usage seems to me to have both practical convenience and sufficient scientific validity.

Let us now consider why these two modes of expression, realism and abstraction, should exist side by side, and what justification for them is to be found in the social conditions of our time.

The simplest explanation, and it is one I have myself accepted in the past, is that the two modes of expression correspond to opposite dispositions in the human personality; that one is extravert, the other introvert; one ectomorphic, the other endomorphic. But such correspondences do not work. A realistic painter may be an extravert type or an introvert type; an abstract painter may also belong to either type. In one of my early books, I ventured to apply William James's terminology to the Cubists, and to divide them into the tough-minded and tender-minded types. The types differ, but the style is the same. I am not going to suggest that no correspondence exists between temperament and expression, but I am quite sure that the correspondence which undoubtedly does exist is not along the axis of realism and abstraction.

We get a little nearer to the true correspondences if we consider, not style, but manner. By style I mean the formal mode of expression—realism, superrealism, or abstraction. By manner I mean the actual handwriting, the workmanship, of the individual artist. At its simplest, it is the difference between form and texture—forms may correspond and constitute a style, but within this style there may be infinite varieties of texture. And texture is an infinitely safer index of temperament than is style.

But that is not the end of the matter, as I think will soon be evident if we compare an Attic earthenware drinking-cup (about 530 B.C.) with a Chinese porcelain vase (A.D. 960–1279). Both are very fine pots—the lower one an example of the perfection of texture achieved by a Chinese potter of the Sung dynasty; the other an example of the perfection of form achieved by the Greek potter of the fifth century B.C. But can this contrast be explained as a simple difference of sensibility and temperament in the potters? I very much doubt it. To begin with, the form of the Chinese vase is by no means unworthy of its texture: it might quite reasonably be argued that its form is every bit as good as that of the Greek vase. I doubt, however, if anyone could maintain that the texture of the Greek vase was as attractive as that of the Chinese vase. Both in colour and in tactile values, it is devoid of subtlety and of charm. But is that deficiency due to the temperament of the potter? Or to the method of manufacture? There can be no doubt on this point: in order to obtain precision of form, the Greek potter used measuring-rods and callipers, and the actual surface texture of his pot is due, not, as in the case of the Chinese vase, to the sensitive touch of human fingers, but to the intervention of an instrument. What I wish to demonstrate by this example is that the *intention* of the artist determines the presence or absence of sensuous quality in the work of art, and that this intention, though always aesthetic, may have a prescribed pattern—it may proceed by rule rather than by intuition.

It will be seen that this simple confrontation of two pots has led us into very deep waters—the deep waters of Kant's *Critique of Judgment*, as a matter of fact. If beauty is a mental category in Kant's sense, then it is possible that the formal values in a work of art are the supreme values, and that qualities like texture—which are merely sensuous—are incidental. From this point of view there can be no doubt that the Greek vase excels the Chinese vase as a work of art; and I am pretty sure that such would have been the opinion of Immanuel Kant. Perhaps there are modern philosophers who would agree with him, but no critic of art would dare to be so dogmatic. Indeed, if we were to take the contemporary taste of connoisseurs as a standard of judgment, there is equally no doubt that they would consider the Chinese vase as the greater work of art.

It would be possible, and tempting, to devote a whole essay to this object lesson—most of the psychology of art is involved in it. I must confine myself to one further point which it illustrates. We may agree that there is only a difference of degree between the sensibility of the naked fingers in contact with the clay, and the sensibility of those same fingers grasping an instrument like a pair of callipers. After all, a painter uses a brush, and a sculptor uses a mallet and chisel, and *they* manage to transmit their sensibility to the work of art. There is a distinction, which I will not stop to elaborate, between the artist who works with a static material, like the painter's canvas or the sculptor's stone, and the artist working with a plastic material in movement—as does the potter. But the fundamental distinction suggested by this illustration is that which exists between a conceptual control of form and the sensuous handling of material. The questions we are to discuss are now isolated: (1) what are the comparative values of these two modes of aesthetic expression, and (2) what particular significance have they for our present historical situation?

We may begin by dismissing, as due either to ignorance or prejudice, the view that abstraction, or formalism as it is usually called, is merely an expression of bourgeois decadence. The tendency to abstraction is a permanent feature in the history of art, and at certain periods—the neolithic age, for example—and in certain phases of primitive art, of Celtic art, of Arabic art—it has been the predominant style. It should be quite obvious, even to a dialectical materialist, that if form can be conceived in abstraction, and simultaneously realized or expressed in plastic symbols, such a psycho-somatic process might take place in very different types of society, and can in no *a priori* sense be characterized as 'decadent'. In Hegel's philosophy of art precisely such a realization of idea represents a higher stage in the development of human culture. Even from the dialectical materialist's point of view, the neolithic age must be regarded as an evolutionary advance on the palaeolithic age; and both Celtic and Arabic art are arts of vigorous and vital civilizations. There is, of course, decadent Celtic and decadent Arabic art; but there is no correspondence between the degree of formalism and the stage of decadence —on the contrary, decadence is usually associated with the growth of naturalism. Admittedly there is the contrary process, in which formal ornament is developed from the 'slurring', or hasty execution, of naturalistic ornament, but no correlation exists, so far as I know, between such formal ornament and periods of decadence. In general, the correlation that does exist is between vigorous emergent cultures and geometric ornament; between decadent cultures and languid, over-ripe naturalism.

We must discuss this question, however, at a deeper level than any represented by ornamental art. There is no need to despise ornament as such, but it is usually the work of simple craftsmen and only indirectly, and then unconsciously, expresses any subtlety of apprehension, of comprehension, of reaction to experience. Ornament can be explained in terms of visual comfort, of perceptual stimulation; art goes beyond, and is itself a medium of explanation of emotional, intellectual and metaphysical attitudes.

The origins of the abstract movement in contemporary art have often been traced, and I shall not go over the ground again. But it would be useful at this stage in our argument to refer very briefly to the influence of Juan Gris, for in his brief career he gave the art of painting a new orientation which was to be decisive. It is due to his theory and practice that we owe the important distinction between analytical and synthetic cubism. Analytical cubism is an offspring of realism: it is an attempt to reduce the images given in visual perception to a schematic or structural order. The fact that such a cubistic analysis tended to dissolve the visual image—in such works as Picasso's *Portrait of Kahnweiler* or *Woman with a Guitar*—led Picasso to abandon the analysis at a point where the organic or vitalistic nature of the object was compromised. Though he has continued to make experiments which might be described as 'cubistic', Picasso has never adopted a style of pure abstraction. Nor did Juan Gris carry abstraction to its logical conclusion; though his theory of synthetic cubism involves abstraction as a basis for painting, but only as a basis. Impressed by the fact that a work of art owed its aesthetic power to abstract elements of form and colour—to what he liked to call its architecture—Gris began with a formal arrangement of the picture-space, into which he then worked appropriate representational elements. He elaborated what he called 'a painter's mathematics', and 'only these mathematics are capable of establishing the composition of the picture. It is only the architecture, which can give birth to the subject, that is to say, an arrangement of certain elements of reality called forth by the composition.'*

It will be seen that Gris's theory and practice became an attempt to combine realism and abstraction in counterpoint. He himself used the analogy of weaving. 'Painting for me is like a fabric, all of a piece and uniform, with one set of threads as the representational, aesthetic element, and the cross-threads as the technical, architectural, or abstract element. These threads are interdependent and complementary, and if one set is lacking the fabric does not exist.'

But inspired by the experiments of Picasso, Braque and Gris, certain painters were to attempt to create works of art with only one set of threads—the abstract element. There thus arose several varieties of abstract art which agree only in rejecting the realistic or figurative element. I do not intend to classify them, but they include purely academic exercises in formal arrangement, whose function can only be decorative, as well as attempts to abstract the

* 'On the Possibilities of Painting', *Transatlantic Review*, 1924. Reprinted in *Juan Gris*, by D. H. Kahnweiler. London (Lund Humphries, 1947, pp. 139-44).

essential harmonies of the physical universe—what Mondrian called 'the direct expression of universal beauty'. And finally there is constructivism as expounded and manifested by Naum Gabo.

This whole development occupies a period of about twenty-five years, and disengages the two elements, realism and abstraction, either to recombine them (as does Juan Gris and his followers) or to pursue them in isolation. To many artists the choice presents an agonizing dilemma; others do not understand what is involved in the choice, and fade away into academicism. The possibility that the choice as presented is a false one has occurred to very few artists, but it is precisely these two or three who offer some escape from the dilemma, and a leap forward in the evolution of art. That the dilemma is not a purely personal one is indicated by the political significance which has been given to the problem, particularly in Russia, and by the fact that these developments in modern art have a clear connection with the major philosophical discussions of our time.

We might begin by asking what wider philosophical significance can be claimed for the contrasted styles of realism and abstraction. The explanation which has hitherto prevailed, and which I myself have accepted, sees in realism an expression of confidence in, and sympathy for, the organic processes of life. In other words, realism is an affirmative mode of expression, by which we do not necessarily mean the expression of an optimistic mood—there is such a thing as affirmation of the tragic element in life. But abstraction is the reaction of man confronted with the abyss of nothingness, the expression of an *Angst* which distrusts or renounces the organic principle, and affirms the creative freedom of the human mind in such a situation. An interesting correlation could thus be made between the development of existential philosophy and of abstract art, and certain abstract artists with a philosophical insight have not hesitated to express themselves in phraseology that recalls Heidegger or Sartre. This is particularly true of a constructivist like Gabo, who demands for the artist the right to construct a visible image of that reality which is being created by the contemporary human spirit. 'It is evident', writes Gabo *, 'that no such demand could be warranted

* In a letter to the author; but the same point of view is developed in his lecture, 'A Retrospective View of Constructive Art', published in *Three Lectures on Modern Art*. (New York, Philosophical Library, 1949.)

if I should accept the view prevalent in our philosophies that human thought is striving to discover an eternal truth which is embodied in some stable and universal reality outside us; or that in our striving for knowledge we are pursuing the discovery of that reality which is constant and pure. . . . I maintain that knowledge is nothing else but a construction of ours and that what we discover with our knowledge is not something outside us or a part of a constant and higher reality, in the absolute sense of the word; but that we discover exactly that which we put into the place where we make the discoveries . . .' After making some further remarks—posing questions very much in the existentialist vein—Gabo continues: 'We know only what we do, what we make, what we construct; and all that we make, all that we construct, are realities. I call them *images*, not in Plato's sense (namely, that they are only reflections of reality), but I hold that these images are the reality itself and that there is no reality beyond this reality except when in our creative process we change the images: then we have created new realities.'

It will be seen that we have come full circle in our terminology. By subjecting the phenomenal world to logical criticism, we are left with a clean existential slate; we then create a new and logically consistent reality, and the images which the artist projects to make this reality concrete, the constructions of his imagination and his hands, are the only forms of art which can properly be called realistic.

This philosophy of Constructive Realism, as Gabo calls it, clearly defines the place of the artist in this society of ours. 'If I were an academician', Gabo explains, 'or a believer in a higher reality outside me, as most people are (lucky creatures!), I would have no need for any justification for painting landscapes, or portraits, or social realism. I would rely on my so-called common-sense, on what I see and feel, and I would enjoy it. Or I would fix one point in the distant haze of that unknown reality, would try to approach it as nearly as I could, and would find solace in the fanatical belief that I am the only one who is portraying that reality which is the only truth. I would give myself to intolerance, obscurantism and prejudice, and would be one of those who decry and deride the fellow artist who is seeing things otherwise. But I am an artist who is doing so-called abstract work, and as you so rightly put it, few people know that you have to be another man to penetrate into this world of so-called abstractions which we are painting. I never forget that constructive art is a medium of expression still in its very tender age—it cannot live and grow exposed to all winds and weather. It has to strengthen its roots in the more solid soil of the whole human mind—it has to fit in with all that is troubling and exalting the creative spirit of our age. It also has to have its place not only sociologically but also mentally and spiritually. It has also to have an aim, a direction. . . . If this art is to survive for any length of time at all, or if it is to grow into something at least equivalent in importance to the coming ages as the old arts were for theirs, it can achieve this only if the artist of the future is capable of manifesting in this medium . . . a new image, pictorial or sculptural, which will, in its whole organization, express the very spirit of what the contemporary mind is trying to create and which will become the accepted image of life in the Universe.'

I have quoted so extensively from this private correspondence with Gabo because the ideas he is expressing have been expressed nowhere else; just as the type of art he is advocating has never been so uncompromisingly carried to plastic realization. He is virtually creating a new language, a symbolic language of concrete visual images. This language is necessary because our philosophical enquiries have brought us to a point where the old symbols no longer suffice. Philosophy itself has reached an impasse—an impasse of verbal expression—at which it hands over its task to the poets and painters, the sculptors and other creators of concrete images. It is for this reason that Heidegger turns to the poetry of Hölderlin, and that Sartre the philosopher becomes Sartre the novelist. It is not, I think, thereby implied that the only images of reality we can create are the artist's images; rather, no distinction is made between the images of the artist and the images of the scientist. 'In such a philosophy', says Gabo, 'there is no difference between art and science—they are both art; between technique and knowledge—they are both skill; and in such a philosophy the image of the world of the primitive is just as true and real as the image of the world of Thomas Aquinas and Einstein. It is up to us to choose one or the other according to which of those images appear to me or to you more coherent, more harmonious and more cogent, above all, more acceptable as a means for our orientation in this life of ours.'

By now the position we have reached in our argument is this: that which we call reality is a chain of images invented by man, whose personal existence must be affirmed before he proceeds with his invention. Reality is man-made, and the maker is the image-maker, the poet. Reality accords with the images the artist makes, and derives its validity from such values as integrity, self-consistency, viability, pragmatic satisfaction, aesthetic satisfaction, etc.

An age, a civilization, may accept a particular series of images as concordant, as expressive of its needs. In that way—for images, which are personal images, beget reflections and imitations in other minds—in that way a style is created; in that way a religion is created; in that way a science is created. A style, a religion, a science—each is a self-consistent, coherent image-series. The mistake—a mistake which mankind makes with tragic frequency —is to assume that a particular series of images is eternally real. The reality changes with our circumstances.

We can therefore now express our questions in another way, and as only one question: in the circumstances of our time is there any particular reason why the artist should adopt one or the other of the types of imagery or symbolism represented by the terms realism and abstraction?

In the Soviet Union there is, of course, the very good reason that realism is enforced, with extinction as an artist as the alternative. I do not think that this prejudice in favour of socialist realism is quite so stupid as the Russians themselves make it seem. There must be a vague realization of the existential dilemma of modern man, and a fear that the solutions which seek the creation of a reality in Art or God, offer an escape from the reality which should be Stalin, or the State. It is not a style of art that the communist dictatorship fears: it is art itself, in any form forceful enough to compel the allegiance of man's minds; and they have succeeded in reducing art to insignificance.

I believe that the same iconoclastic tendency is present in certain phases of modern thought not confined to the Soviet Union. There is always the recurrent fear among theologians that Art might in some sense replace God, and ever since Kierkegaard formuled his Either/Or, these religious philosophers have been busy telling us that a reliance on the reality created by the artist leads ultimately to despair. That, as I see it, is the attitude of an age that has lost all contact with the actuality of art—an age that can only conceive art as idea, and is utterly divorced from the creative experience, even in the humble form of handicraft.

Realism and Abstraction in Modern Art

Personally I find it hard to accept any ontology or theory of life which insists on a single and exclusive reaction to experience. There are various modes of understanding and various constructions to express this understanding. Why must we assume that life, which has evolved into such a diversity of creatures, should be expressed in a single category of understanding? The way of art and the way of religion, and equally the way of science or dialectical materialism, are equally valid alternatives, and the only question, in any comparative evaluation, is whether a particular construction furthers the continuance and intensification of the life-process itself. It follows that the imposition of any particular system of reality on any particular society, or the mere prejudice in favour of any particular system, is due to a kind of stupidity, to a lack of tolerance in the presence of life itself. Any construction which has positive meaning for the individual, or for the community, or for life as a whole, has value, has meaning, has relevance. It is what Woltereck* calls a 'mode of resonance' in face of the incomprehensibility of existence, and there is certainly more than one such mode of resonance—not only 'dread' (as Heidegger supposes), but also amazement, joy, curiosity, affirmation, what Nietzsche called a yea-saying.

Various as the forms of these resonances are, they may perhaps be arranged along a polar axis, with transcendental metaphysics at one end and an intense self-awareness of physical vitality at the other end. It is along the same axis that we can place abstraction and realism in art. But again the choice is not imposed on the individual artist. The axis exists *within* the individual artist, if only he can become conscious of it.

This fact I shall attempt to demonstrate by reference to the work of two or three English artists with whom I happen to have been intimately associated. All are artists who have developed alternate phases of realism and abstraction—not, in general, attempting to combine them, as Juan Gris did, and never seeking a dogmatic fixity in one or the other extreme.

The first example is Henry Moore. The greater part of his work could, I think, be described as an 'inward intensification' of subjective feeling, a discovery and an affirmation of the organic life-process. But at the extremes we have, on the one hand, direct transcripts of the human figure such as we find in his *Madonna and Child*; and, at the other extreme, a composition of the kind

* See p. 102 below.

97

illustrated in Plate XI, which has only an indirect reference to the phenomenal world. At the one extreme, therefore, realism; at the other, abstraction.

The contrast in the work of Ben Nicholson is not so clear because, like Juan Gris, when he introduces a realistic motive, it is generally within an abstract architectural design. But both early and late in his career he has expressed himself in a purely realistic style; and at other times, with equal decisiveness, he has created pure abstractions of this uncompromising type (see Plates V-VI).

A still more striking contrast is provided by Barbara Hepworth, for the contrast is embodied in the different media of sculpture and painting. Sometimes the drive to abstraction is carried to its farthest extreme in a construction of greatest purity and harmony. But the same artist, moved by a chance contact with life at a moment of crisis—for example, life hanging in the balance on a surgical operation table—has produced paintings in the style of the realistic art of the early Renaissance. (Plates XIII-XIV.)

The point to notice about these cases is the perfect ambivalence of the process. The change-over from one style to the other, from realism to abstraction or from abstraction to realism, is not accompanied by any deep psychological revolution. It is merely a change of direction, of destination. What is constant is the desire to create a reality, the will to form. At one extreme that will is expressed in the creation of new forms, of what might be called *free* form, so long as we do not assume that freedom implies any lack of aesthetic discipline; and at the other extreme, the will to form is expressed in a selective affirmation of some aspect of the organic world—notably a heightened awareness of the vitality or grace of the human form. In one of her letters to me (6.3.48) Barbara Hepworth describes this ambivalent process with perfect clarity: 'I don't feel any difference of intention or of mood when I paint (or carve) realistically and when I make abstract carvings. It all feels the same—the same happiness and pain, the same joy in a line, a form, a colour—the same feeling of being lost in pursuit of something. The same feeling at the end. The two ways of working flow into each other without effort . . . [The two methods of working] enhance each other by giving an absolute freedom— a freedom to complete the circle. . . . Working realistically replenishes one's *love* for life, humanity and the earth. Working abstractly seems to release one's personality and sharpen the perceptions, so that in the observation of life it is the wholeness or inner intention which moves one so profoundly: the components fall into place, the detail is significant of unity.'

That, it seems to me, is a very revealing explanation of the creative process within the artist, and it suggests a theory of reciprocal tensions, which, whether we call them realism-abstraction, conscious-unconscious, life-death, are expressive of the total world-process. The consciousness of the artist alternates between the two poles of this tension. One pole may be left un-expressed, and then the artist is wholly realistic, or wholly ab-stract. But it seems reasonable to suppose that a better balance, if only in the mental personality of the artist, will be achieved by the open expression of both polar extremes of tension.

Somewhere in this psychic shuttle, this alternation of the positive and negative forces of life, freedom intervenes—the free-dom to create a new reality. Only on that assumption can we ex-plain any form of evolutionary development in human con-sciousness, any kind of spiritual growth. A novelty-creating free-dom exists by virtue of the intensity generated by aesthetic awareness; an evolutionary advance emerges from the act of expression.

What wider philosophical implications these facts of aesthetic experience may have is a question for open discussion. But if I may conclude with a personal point of view, I would confess that it has always seemed to me that the opposition which we make in critical theory between reason and romanticism, and in wider philosophic terms between pragmatism and idealism, cannot be resolved and should not be resolved. It is merely the difference of the particular resonance expressed in that moment when, naked and comfortless on the abyss of nothingness, we question the meaning and the nature of existence. We answer as answer we can—that is to say, according to our particular psycho-physical constitution. We answer with wonder or we answer with dread; and for each answer there is a separate language. But the poetry is in the freedom with which we answer; the art is the affirma-tion, the acceptance and the intensification of the life.

REALISM AND ABSTRACTION:

A FOOTNOTE TO THE PRECEDING ESSAY

The specifically 'modern' movement in art, which began with the first cubistic experiments of Picasso and Braque, is now forty years old. Its vagaries, its violence, its sudden transitions and frequent schisms, suggest that it has developed haphazardly, without premeditation, justifying itself from day to day, pragmatically. But the briefest consideration of the historical facts shows that the philosophical foundations of the modern movement were already established in logical completeness before the creation of any parallel manifestations in plastic form. A spiritual situation existed, and had already been described by the philosophers, before the artists became conscious of the style, or of the choice of styles, implicit in that situation.

The psychological analysis of Lipps, the historical generalizations of Riegl and Wölfflin, and many other works in the wider field of general philosophy, had contributed to the intellectual clarification in question. For the purposes of my present argument there is no need to review such a vast field because, at the critical moment, a brilliant synthesis was made by Wilhelm Worringer, and the dates are not in question. Worringer's dissertation on *Abstraction and Empathy* was completed in 1906 and published in 1908. I doubt if any work of art which deserves the name of *abstraction* was created before 1910. Picasso's *Demoiselles D'Avignon*, which was painted in 1907, is sometimes cited as the first work in the cubist style, but its cubistic elements are very slight, and are taken over from negro sculpture without any fundamental feeling for abstraction as such. Picasso may have been conscious of the stylistic integrity represented by the African sculpture which at the moment influenced him, but he was equally inspired in this composition by Cézanne's late bathing groups, and the attempt to combine two such antagonistic styles in one picture cannot be described as aesthetically satisfying, however important as an historical document. The landscapes painted at Horta de Ebro in the summer of 1909 are the first compositions thoroughly penetrated by a geometrical principle, and it is only in 1910 with such paintings as the *Portrait of*

Realism and Abstraction in Modern Art

Kahnweiler that the will to abstraction has succeeded in completely dominating the organic elements of the subject-matter.

The position in Germany does not seem to have been any different. Kandinsky settled in Munich in 1908, the year in which Worringer's book was published in that city. His paintings began to show a tendency towards abstraction, but it was not until 1910 that he painted anything of a completely abstract character. Was Kandinsky prompted by the philosophical discussions which Worringer's book had provoked in Munich? It is significant that when he himself, two years later, wrote his book *On the Spiritual In Art*, it was published by the same house (the Piper Verlag) that had published Worringer's dissertation. All the members of the *Blaue Reiter* group, which was founded in Munich by Kandinsky and Franz Marc in 1912, were philosophically minded. The extent to which they were philosophically instructed is not known to me, but I am persuaded that a conscious integration of art and philosophy took place at this time. * I would even like to suggest that the comparatively consistent development of the art of Kandinsky and Klee is due to their early acquisition of a philosophical background.

The philosophical situation at the beginning of the twentieth century was the result of a long development of which artists, during the preceding century, had remained serenely unconscious. It is not to be denied, of course, that a close correspondence of feeling and of development exists between transcendentalism and romanticism, but when philosophy began to question the very basis of existence, it was leading in a direction in which art, for the moment, was not willing to follow. The philosophical development which leads from Schelling through Kierkegaard, Nietzsche, and Husserl to Heidegger and Jaspers has no parallel in the plastic arts until we reach Picasso, Kandinsky, Klee, Mondrian and Gabo. Art, even in the extremes of Fauvism, remains positively naturalistic, sympathetically realistic. There is, no doubt, a certain degree of metaphysical *fear (Angst)* in a painter like Van Gogh, but one has only to read his letters to discover how strongly he was resisting this feeling of doom, plunging into a state of apprehension which was crudely vitalistic. The particular kind of 'nullity' which becomes the starting-point of modern philosophy can only be represented in art by an attitude which leaves the artist for the

* This question is resumed in the essay on Ben Nicholson (see pages 216 to 225 below).

moment independent of nature. The possibility of creating a reality through the means of art becomes, indeed, an important aspect of philosophy, for here at any rate is one positive method of vindicating the individuality of the person. Art in this sense becomes the most precious evidence of *freedom*.

The abstract movement in art awaits, therefore, a justification which is already present in the philosophy of existentialism. But existentialism itself is not a coherent body of doctrine, and apart from the distinct varieties represented by such names as Heidegger, Jaspers, Marcel and Sartre, all of which are erected on a basic mood of fear, there is a dialectically opposed reaction to the existential situation which is affirmative, eudemonistic, optimistic. In its historical development this philosophical attitude is closely intertwined with the other, and a philosopher like Nietzsche, for example, embraces both attitudes in tragic dualism. At this point science intervenes, and the biological metaphysics of Bergson constitutes a challenge to the excessive intellectualism of Husserl and Heidegger. Finally it becomes possible (for example, in Woltereck's *Ontology of the Vital**), to oppose a 'natural' ontology to the existential ontology, both acknowledging the same ground, but reacting with opposite feelings. To the dread (*Angst*) of the existentialists Woltereck opposes cheerfulness (*Freudigkeit*), and he claims that this other resonance, which was already known to Artistotle, has no less importance, humanly and ontically speaking, than the Kierkegaard-Heidegger-Jaspers dread born of the consciousness of nothing and the feeling of shipwreck. He goes further and claims that this amazement in face of the world's wonders lacks the narrow self-preoccupation of world 'dread': instead, something positive, lacking in dread, attaches to it, the joyfulness and inner impulse to assimilate, examine, understand, create. And according to Woltereck the sciences as well as the arts are born of this impulse:

'Out of this, even for the single life, genuine and lofty values may arise, for amazement may be heightened until it becomes that which moves and overpowers the whole being. In the experiencing of pure expression in the form of great art, great scenes in Nature, of great—or beloved—individuals, transcendent summits of existence may be attained, as certainly as in the immediate appeal of the transcendent. It depends on the profundity of the experience that falls to a person's lot. The Parthenon, the

* *Ontologie des Lebendigen*, Stuttgart, 1940.

Realism and Abstraction in Modern Art

Eroica, the Moses of Michelangelo may constitute such experiences, but they may also be given to us by a single tree, a single hawk, a single human individual, or by the recognition of a single truth.'

The tendency of *Kunstwissenschaft* has been to recognize contrasted attitudes to nature as period phenomena—abstraction and empathy alternating with, and being determined by, environmental and historical circumstances. We now seem to have reached a stage of intellectual development where an individual choice is possible. That is to say, once we have completed our analysis of the existential problem, then the particular resonance we adopt (fear or joyfulness) is determined by a free exercise of the will. It cannot, I think, be argued that only the positive resonance has any significance for the future of humanity—even Woltereck admits that existential dread undoubtedly possesses, for many of us, a deep ontic significance. He even describes it as 'an especially human mode of resonance', but it is not the only resonance, nor the fundamental mood of man.

We can now turn to modern art which illustrates in its development and scope the philosophical problems which confront the contemporary artist. It would be a too-simple interpretation of the complexity of the situation to make a direct correlation between fear and abstraction and between cheerfulness and empathy. That would be a purely logical *schema*. We must remember that the artist is a human being and not an automaton. He has moods and feelings, and these are not fixed or constant: It is quite possible for the individual artist to alternate between fear and cheerfulness, and to express himself in forms appropriate to each attitude. This has happened, as in the case of Hans Erni, * as a change of total-attitude: in the case of other artists, Henry Moore or Picasso, a frequent alternation of style takes place, much to the surprise and confusion of the naïve public, who expect an artist to be 'consistent'. Such ambivalence in the artist proves that the human will can intervene as a process in the existential dialectic. The freedom to create is thus to be interpreted as a freedom to affirm and intensify the life-process itself (which would imply a naturalistic art) or as a freedom to create a new order of reality, distinct from the life-process, but enhancing the independent spiritual powers of man's isolated consciousness

* This essay was contributed to a volume in honour of the Swiss artist, Hans Erni: *Elements of Future Painting*, ed. Frank C. Thiessing. (Zürich, 1948.)

(which would imply an abstract and transcendental art). The choice will be made according to the disposition of any particular artist, and the choice might be for an inclusive ambivalent attitude, a taking-into-oneself of the complete dialectical process. Some words of Schelling's seem to anticipate such a poetic monism: 'To be drunk and sober not in different moments but at one and the same moment—this is the secret of true poetry. Thus is the Apollonian different from the merely Dionysian ecstasy. To represent an infinite content, therefore, a content which really resists form, which seems to destroy any form—to represent such an infinite content in the most perfect, that is, in the most finite form, that is the highest task of art.'* The definition of 'the most finite form' can only be accomplished by endless research and experiment, and therein lies the best justification of the vagaries of modern art.

Sämtliche Werke, Pt. II, Vol. IV, p. 25.

6

Surrealism and the Romantic Principle*

June, 1936. After a winter long drawn out into bitterness and petulance, a month of torrid heat, of sudden efflorescence, of clarifying storms. In this same month the International Surrealist Exhibition broke over London, electrifying the dry intellectual atmosphere, stirring our sluggish minds to wonder, enchantment and derision. The press, unable to appreciate the significance of a movement of such unfamiliar features, prepared an armoury of mockery, sneers and insults. The duller desiccated weeklies, no less impelled to anticipate the event, commissioned their polyglot gossips, their blasé globe-trotters, their old-boy-scouts, to adopt their usual pose of I know all, don't be taken in, there's nothing new under the sun—a pose which merely reflected the general lack of intellectual curiosity in this country. But in the event they were all deceived; their taunts fell on deaf ears, and though for a time there was no lack of the laughing jackass—an animal extinct in most parts of the world and even in this country generally emerging only from beyond the pale of the ineffectual Cheviots— in the outcome people, and mostly young people, came in their hundreds and their thousands not to sneer, but to learn, to find enlightenment, to live. When the foam and froth of society and the press had subsided, we were left with a serious public of scientists, artists, philosophers and socialists. Fifteen years have now passed by, bringing with them death, destruction, and the diaspora of another world war; but that serious public still remains.

* I am fully conscious of the inadvisability of republishing this polemical essay in a volume which otherwise has some pretension to scientific objectivity. I do so because I feel it would be dishonest to disguise the fact that I am sometimes led away (I do not say led astray) by my sympathies. Those sympathies proceed from my 'cult of sincerity' as a poet; and no doubt this is not the only occasion (even in this volume) when the critic abdicates and the poet takes over.

Surrealism and the Romantic Principle

From the moment of its birth surrealism was an international phenomenon—the spontaneous generation of an international and fraternal *organism* in total contrast to the artificial manufacture of a collective *organization* such as the League of Nations. It would therefore be contrary to the nature of the movement to disengage, as some have suggested, a specifically English version of 'surréalisme'. We who in England supported this movement had no other desire than to pool our resources in the general effort. Nevertheless, an English contribution has been made to this effort, and its strength and validity can only be shown by tracing its sources in the native tradition of our art and literature. The evidences on which the claims of Surrealism are based are scattered through the centuries, the partial and incoherent revelations of permanent human characteristics; and nowhere are these evidences so plentiful as in England. My main purpose in this essay will be to present this English evidence, to unite it with the general theory of surrealism, and to reaffirm on this wider basis the truths which other writers, above all André Breton, have already declared.

In an Introduction which I contributed to the catalogue of the exhibition I asserted, in the cryptic and exiguous manner demanded by the occasion, that 'superrealism in general is the romantic principle in art'. It will be noted that I used a variation of the word 'surrealism'. When it first became essential to find an English equivalent for the original French word, I made an attempt to establish 'superrealism'. Pedantically, euphonically and logically I think I was right; 'superrealism' is not only simple to say, but self-explanatory to the meanest intelligence ('super' is slang, 'sur' is a purely grammatical affix). But I was defeated by that obscure instinct which determines word-formation in the life of a language, and for which I have the greatest respect. The very clarity of the term 'superrealism' was against it; the public wanted a strange and not too intelligible word for a strange and not too intelligible thing; and I bow to that decree. But I do not propose to abandon the word 'superrealism' altogether; I propose rather to make a distinction between superrealism in general and surrealism in particular, employing the first word for the tentative and historical manifestations of what has now become a conscious and deliberate artistic principle. And those tentative and historical manifestations of superrealism I shall identify with some of the essential character-

Surrealism and the Romantic Principle

istics of romanticism—but of romanticism understood in a certain strict and not too comprehensive sense.

No critic of experience will return to a discussion of the terms 'romanticism' and 'classicism' with anything but extreme reluctance; no subject has provoked so much weary logomachy since the scholastics argued themselves out on the question of nominalism. I only take up the discussion again (eating my own words in the process) because I think that surrealism has settled it. So long as romanticism and classicism were considered as alternative attitudes, rival camps, professions of *faith*, an interminable struggle was in prospect, with the critics as profiteers. But what in effect surrealism claims to do is to resolve the conflict—not, as I formerly hoped, by establishing a synthesis which I was prepared to call 'reason' or 'humanism'—but by liquidating classicism, by showing its complete irrelevance, its *anaesthetic* effect, its contradiction of the creative impulse. Classicism, let it be stated without further preface, represents for us now, and has always represented, the forces of oppression. Classicism is the intellectual counterpart of political tyranny. It was so in the ancient world and in the medieval empires; it was renewed to express the dictatorships of the Renaissance and has ever since been the official creed of capitalism. Wherever the blood of martyrs stains the ground, there you will find a doric column or perhaps a statue of Minerva.

Academic critics have not been unaware of this alignment, but have united, of course, to give living colours to the corpse they have embalmed. I have often praised Sir Herbert Grierson's clean handling of this problem; like Brunetière, whose main line of demarcation he follows, he is not altogether unsympathetic towards romanticism, but there is a question of values involved which must be challenged. A classical literature, he writes, 'is the product of a nation and a generation which has consciously achieved a definite advance, moral, political, intellectual; and is filled with the belief that its view of life is more natural, human, universal and wise than that from which it has escaped. It has effected a synthesis which enables it to look round on life with a sense of its wholeness, its unity in variety; and the work of the artist is to give expression to that consciousness; hence the solidity of his work and hence too its definiteness, and in the hands of great artists its beauty . . . The work of the classical artist is to give individual expression, the beauty of form, to a body of common sentiments and thoughts which he shares with his audience, thoughts and views which have for his generation the validity of universal truths.

'Classical and romantic—these are the systole and diastole of the human heart in history. They represent on the one hand our need of order, of synthesis, of a comprehensive yet definite, therefore *exclusive* as well as inclusive, ordering of thought and feeling and action; and on the other hand the inevitable finiteness of every human synthesis, the discovery that, in Carlyle's metaphor, our clothes no longer fit us, that the classical has become the conventional, that our spiritual aspirations are being starved, or that our secular impulses are "cribb'd, cabin'd, and confined" . . . .'*

The particular danger of this argument is due to its false dialecticism. A certain type of society is regarded as a 'synthesis', a natural order or balance of forces, a state of equilibrium; and any deviation from that standard is regarded as abnormal, degenerate or revolutionary. Actually such types of society merely represent the dominance of one particular class—the economic dominance and therefore the cultural dominance of that class. For the stability of such a society a certain uniformity of ideas and modes of expression is a fundamental necessity; and the less novelty these ideas and modes of expression show the better. This explains the constant return to the norms of classical art; for these norms (in architecture we call them the 'orders') are the typical patterns of order, proportion, symmetry, equilibrium, harmony and of all static and inorganic qualities. They are intellectual concepts which control or repress the vital instincts on which growth and therefore change depend, and in no sense represent a freely determined preference, but merely an imposed ideal.

The fallacy we are discussing is logical in its origin. It is a sophism by means of which two terms are conceived as dialectical opposites whereas actually they represent types of action and reaction. This is a very important distinction, and its neglect is the cause of much confusion. In dialectics the thesis and the antithesis are both objective facts, and the necessity for a resolution or synthesis is due to the real existence of a contradiction. But 'classic' and 'romantic' do not represent such a contradiction. They correspond rather to the husk and the seed, the shell and the kernel. There is a principle of life, of creation, of liberation,

* *The Background of English Literature.* London, 1925. Pp. 266, 287–8.

and that is the romantic spirit; there is a principle of order, of control and of repression, and that is the classical spirit. Naturally there is some purpose in the latter principle—the instincts are curbed in the interest of some particular ideal or set of values; but on analysis it always resolves into the defence of some particular structure of society, the perpetuation of the rule of some particular class. To identify romanticism with revolt as Grierson does is true enough as an historical generalization; but it merely distorts the values involved if such revolt is conceived in purely literary or academic terms. It would be much nearer the truth to identify romanticism with the artist and classicism with society; classicism being the political concept of art to which the artist is expected to conform.

It may be as well to forestall at once the criticism that on this showing the artist is merely the individualist in conflict with society. To a certain extent, as I have shown elsewhere*, this is true; the mental personality of the artist may be determined by a failure in social adaptation. But his whole effort is directed towards a reconciliation with society, and what he offers to society is not a bagful of his own tricks, his idiosyncracies, but rather some knowledge of the secrets to which he has had access, the secrets of the self which are buried in every man alike, but which only the sensibility of the artist can reveal to us in all their actuality. This 'self' is not the personal possession we imagine it to be; it is largely made up of elements from the unconscious, and the more we learn about the unconscious, the more collective it appears to be—in fact, 'a body of common sentiments and thoughts . . . universal truths', such as Grierson assumes to be the exclusive concern of the classical artist. But whereas the universal truths of classicism may be merely the temporal prejudices of an epoch, the universal truths of romanticism are coeval with the evolving consciousness of mankind.

It is in this sense, then, that surrealism is a reaffirmation of the romantic principle; and though poets and painters in all ages have clung to a belief in the inspirational and even the obsessional nature of their gifts, repudiating in deeds if not in words the rigid bonds of classical theory, it is only now, with the aid of modern dialectics and modern psychology, in the name of Marx and Freud, that they have found themselves in a position to put their beliefs and practices on a scientific basis, thereby initiating

* *Art and Society*, chap. VI.

a continuous and deliberate creative activity whose only laws are the laws of its own dynamics.

Before passing on to a more precise examination of the romantic principle as actually manifested in English art and literature, there is one further interpretation of the classic-romantic antithesis which is worth referring to, especially as it finds its justification in modern psychology—I mean the theory that the two terms correspond to the general distinction between 'extravert' and 'introvert' types of personality. The comparison is valid enough if it has reference to the personalities involved; what is questionable is the very existence of such a type as an extravert *artist*. To the degree in which he becomes extravert the artist, we would say, ceases to be, in any essential sense of the word, an artist. Now admittedly there is much in the process of producing a work of art which involves, or may involve, an objective attitude towards the materials the artist is using; only the automatic text or drawing is strictly speaking subjective, and though the surrealist insists on the significance of such automatic expression and makes it the basis of his own practice, he is far from asserting that all art must of necessity be produced under such conditions. What he does assert, however, is the absolute impossibility of producing a work of art by the conscious exercise of talents. The notion that a work of art can be created by observing a set of rules is only to be compared with the notion that a human being can be produced in a test-tube.

'Verbal and graphic automatism,' Breton has said, 'only represents a *limit* towards which the poet or artist should tend.' The opposed limit is represented by all those 'arts of poetry', those academic discourses on painting, in which various ages have sought to codify for all time the laws of art. Between these limits we find the whole range of aesthetic expression, but it is towards the limit of automatism, and away from the limit of rational control, that we find the most enduring vitality, the words which live when the poet is dead, when even his name is forgotten—

A rose-red city half as old as time

—a single line surviving from the complete works of a poet, and surviving precisely by virtue of its irrationality.

It is very difficult to determine the factors which lead to the survival of any particular work of art. There is a considerable element of chance, even under modern conditions of publishing and propaganda. We know that contemporary judgment is very uncertain, very arbitrary; every age has its Ossians and there may still be Donnes to be redeemed from a neglected past. We ascribe this fickleness of public estimation to changes in sensibility, but sensibility itself does not change, only the control of it. The sensibility which appreciated the poems of Donne at the time of their first appearance was lively and direct; it needed the colossal irrelevance of a Johnsonian intellect and the general diffusion of a rational spirit to throw them into obscurity. The sensibility which we have now recovered and by virtue of which we once more appreciate the poetry of Donne is the identical sensibility for which his poems were written; and it is no gust of fashion which has re-established his fame, but a revival of poetic sensibility itself—the same revival which has once more placed Shakespeare at the utmost pinnacle of fame, which has given Blake his due eminence and has secured immediate recognition for Hopkins and Eliot. No doubt we are age-bound like the rest and our standards are relative to our circumstances; but it is difficult to imagine, in any form of society congenial to our elementary demands of economic security and intellectual liberty, any return to the standards which tended to exalt a Dryden or a Pope above Shakespeare.

Some recognition of the truth which I am affirming—the identity of art and romanticism—has been given by the philosophers of art; not by all philosophers, but particularly by those who have shown the greatest appreciation of art, or who have been, like Plato, great artists themselves. Plato's description of the poet in *Ion* is well known; I have quoted it before, but I think it should be read again in the present context. Socrates is the speaker:

'For all good poets, epic as well as lyric, compose their beautiful poems not by art, but because they are inspired and possessed. And as the Corybantian revellers when they dance are not in their right mind, so the lyric poets are not in their right mind when they are composing their beautiful strains; but when falling under the power of music and metre they are inspired and possessed; like Bacchic maidens who draw milk and honey from the rivers when they are under the influence of Dionysus but not when they are in their right mind. And the soul of the lyric poet does the same, as they themselves say; for they tell us that they bring songs from honeyed fountains, culling them out of the gardens and dells of the Muses; they, like the bees, winging their way from flower to flower. And this is true. For the poet is a light and winged and holy thing, and there is no invention in him until he has been inspired and is out of his senses, and the mind is no longer in him: when he has not attained to this state, he is powerless and is unable to utter his oracles.'*

It is pointless to observe that because of their irrational character Plato excluded poets from his ideal republic. Within the logic of his rational philosophy, this was inevitable; just as later it was inevitable that Hegel, for quite similar reasons, should come to the conclusion that 'the fair days of Greek art, as also the golden time of the later middle ages, are over'. Both philosophers held the view that a reflective, idealistic and ratiocinative culture was not merely desirable, but actually represented a higher stage in human evolution. They were both right in considering that the sensuous phenomena of art—the completely irrational basis of the imaginative faculty—are inconsistent with such a reflective culture. But what we now assert with the strongest conviction is our disbelief in either the inevitability or desirability of such a culture. The whole evidence of history, as well as of modern psychology, causes us to reject without hesitation such a fool's paradise of idealism. For good or for evil the instinctive and impulsive components of our being are irreducible and irreplaceable, and we ignore them or repress them at our peril. Not merely the neuroses of individuals result from such repression, but there is more and more reason to believe that the mass hysteria manifested, for example, in such a nation as Germany, is the collective aspect of general repressions. The only absolutely pacifist races (if any such still exist) are those which live in a golden age of hedonism such as, apparently, the Minoan civilization enjoyed for many centuries. Unfortunately we do not know enough about the Minoan civilization to relate its freedom from war, for example, its freedom from morality; but we are beginning to know sufficient about our own civilization to be sure that war has no simple explanation in economic forces, but is most probably not unrelated to the frustration of certain primitive impulses during childhood, a frustration which is prolonged and reinforced by adult codes of morality. War is, in theory as in fact, the correlative of religion. The Christian religion in its Calvinistic rigour induced the bloodiest epoch in the world's history. Piety

* Jowett's translation.

and asceticism are inevitably accompanied by masochism and sadism, and the more religion has been deprived of a ritualistic and occult indulgence of the senses, rationalizing itself in the form of moral precepts and social conventions, the deeper the world has plunged into compensatory orgies of hatred and bloodshed. *

Those who have not experienced war at first hand may perhaps entertain illusions about its comparative evil; they may entertain the idea, that is to say, that even its modern intensity of horror is sanctioned by some nobler effects of heroism, of national awakening, of personal regeneration. Such a belief is a pestilential idiocy. There is in modern war neither grace nor dignity. It is mad and inconsequential in its inception; beyond the scope of human control in its conduct—a dreary shattering of human flesh in conditions of physical and mental disgust, a long agony which can only be ended in exhaustion. In spite of this truth, which must be evident to millions of people, we today contemplate a political situation (it would be more exact to say a psychological situation) whose inevitable outcome seems to be another world war even more stupid, more purposeless and more horrible than the last. Everywhere in all countries we meet apparently friendly and peaceful human beings; we exchange visits, books, ideas—not to insist too much on manufactures; we slowly build up an international understanding in which there is no thought of anything but mutual help and general well-being—an indivisible peace. Yet in a few days the face of the world may change. Bugles blow, klaxons screech, an immense machine begins to move and we find ourselves segregated, regimented, drafted into armies and navies and workshops. Bull-necked demagogues inject a poisonous propaganda into our minds and then the storm of steel breaks above us; our bodies become so much manure for an acid soil, and our ideas, our aspirations, the whole structure of our civilization, becomes a history which the future may not even record.†

The astonishing fact is that men can contemplate such a fate and remain passive. Nothing in the world is so disturbing as

---

* It is impossible to ignore the evidence on this question presented by Dr Edward Glover in *War, Sadism and Pacifism* (London, 1933, new edn. 1947). *Cf.* also C. G. Jung, *Aufsaetze zur Zeitgeschichte* (Zürich, 1946), trans. *Essays on Contemporary Events* (London, 1947).

† This paragraph was written in 1936, before the Second World War. There is, alas, no reason to alter it in 1951.

human docility. Man is indeed a wild animal tamed; broken in and made to trot obediently in a ring, to respond to every crack of the whip. He accepts the tips and the kicks, the doles and the charity of his indifferent and cynical masters. Only the fact that history shows that the goad may be driven too deep, that out of extreme suffering will come general revolt—only this melancholy thought saves us from complete despair.

Underlying this condition of humanity are motives no less irrational than those which promote war-mindedness; the capitalist and the socialist no less than the militarist and the pacifist are moved by obscure instincts. Admittedly it is not a very obscure instinct that makes a man desire to triumph over his fellows, to enjoy a position of comparative wealth and ease, to command the admiration of the loveliest women—such desires are elementary and we are only ashamed of them in the degree of our sensibility and altruism. But the individuals who possess this altruism, this sensibility, are certainly not the priests and preceptors whose position and authority is assured by the social system of which they are an integral part. Nothing is simpler to demonstrate than the dependency, in every age, of the official codes of morality on the class interests of those who possess the economic power. The only individuals who protest against injustices—or who make their protest vocal—are in effect the poets and artists of each age, who to the extent that they rely on their imaginative capacities and powers, despise and reject the acquisitive materialism of men of action. *

I am not leaving it open for anyone to suggest that in this respect—in its adoption of a revolutionary political attitude, its protest against injustice and inhumanity—surrealism merely represents a sentimental movement of the heart. Surrealism is anti-rational, but it is equally anti-emotional. If you wish to reduce surrealism to its foundations you will find the only basic elements on which any useful structure can be built—the basic elements of natural science and psychology. The surrealist builds on that materialistic basis. But he builds. He creates. And he has his method of building, his craft of logic, his dialectic.

The philosophical justification of surrealism is to be found, if anywhere in the past, in Hegel. But it is a Hegel deprived for the

---

* It is obvious that the few revolutionary priests who may be included (St Francis of Assisi, Wycliffe, Huss) were in our sense of the word no less poets than priests.

114

most part of those elements which he would have considered of the greatest importance. Just as Marx, for his purposes, turned Hegel upside down, 'sloughed off' the mystical form of Hegel's dialectic, so the surrealist, for his purposes, subjects the philosopher to the same indignity. If I am asked why, in this matter, we should return to Hegel rather than start our philosophy of art afresh, there are various answers to give—answers similar to those which have to be given in the field of political philosophy. One is that Hegel represents a convenient *crux* in philosophy: all previous philosophies seem to meet in him, to be sorted and smelted and reduced to the purest and least contradictory elements of human thought. Hegel is the great scavenger of philosophical systems; he cleans them up and leaves a tidy piece of ground on which we can build. More than that, he provides a scaffolding within which we can build—the scaffold of his dialectic.

This dreaded word *dialectic*—a word which the English-speaking public finds difficult to digest and which even our so-called socialists, with a few exceptions, would willingly forget—this word is actually the name of a very simple and very necessary process of thought. If we consider the natural world, we soon become aware that its most striking characteristic is not permanency, solidity or stability, but *continuous change* or development. Physicists now affirm that not merely the organic world, not merely this earth we live on, but the whole universe is undergoing a process of change. Dialectics is nothing more than a logical explanation of how such a change takes place. It does not suffice to say that 'it grows', or 'it decays', 'it runs down', 'it expands'; these phrases are vague abstractions. The change must take place in a definite way. Between one phase and another of that development there must intervene an active principle, and Hegel suggested that this principle was actually one of opposition and interaction. That is to say, to produce any new situation (i.e., any departure from an existing condition of equilibrium) there must previously exist two elements so opposed to each other and yet so related to each other that a solution or resolution is demanded; such a solution being in effect a new phase of development (temporary state of equilibrium) which preserves some of the elements of the interacting phases, eliminates others, but is qualitatively different from the previously existing state of opposition.

Such is the dialectical logic, elaborated by Hegel for idealistic purposes and brilliantly adapted by Marx for materialistic purposes. As an instrument of thought it enabled Marx to explain the evolution of human society from primitive communism to feudalism and through the various stages of capitalism; it enabled him, moreover, to predict the self-extinction of capitalism and the coming of the socialist state. But that is by the way. What I wish to stress now is that surrealism is an application of the same logical method to the realm of art. By the dialectical method we can explain the development of art in the past and justify a revolutionary art at the present time.

In dialectical terms we claim that there is a continual state of opposition and interaction between the world of objective fact— the sensational and social world of active and economic existence —and the world of subjective fantasy. This opposition creates a state of disquietude, a lack of spiritual equilibrium, which it is the business of the artist to resolve. He resolves the contradiction by creating a synthesis, a work of art which combines elements from both these worlds, eliminates others, but which for the moment gives us a qualitatively new experience—an experience on which we can dwell with equanimity. Superficial critics may pretend to be unable to distinguish such a qualitatively new state from an ordinary compromise, and it is to be feared that in practice most dialectical solutions are of this kind. But a true synthesis is never a reversion; it is always a progression.

That is the central core of the surrealist claim, and any attempt to discredit or criticize surrealism must present an adequate philosophical alternative; just as any criticism of dialectical materialism as embodied in the socialism of Marx must present an adequate philosophical alternative. At present any alternative in art worthy of our consideration is lacking.

To return for a moment to Hegel. He dealt with the subject of art at such length (in his *Aesthetik*) that one would expect to find there some approach to the dialectical interpretation of art which the surrealist now advances. Actually we no more find that than, in his other works, we find an anticipation of Marx. Everything, in his philosophy, is sacrificed to the necessity of making 'ideas', or states of self-consciousness, the supreme forces in creative development. As Marx observed in his Preface to the first edition of *Kapital*:

'My dialectic method is not only different from the Hegelian, but its direct opposite. To Hegel, the life-process of the human brain, i.e. the process of thinking, which, under the name of "the Idea", he even transforms into an independent subject, is the demiurgos of the real world, and the real world is only the external, phenomenal form of "the Idea". With me, on the contrary, the ideal is nothing else than the material world reflected by the human mind, and translated into forms of thought.'

With the surrealists, we might also say, the ideal is nothing else than the material world reflected by the human mind, and translated into images. But 'reflection' and 'translation' are not, for us today, such simple mechanical processes as perhaps Marx implies. For us the process is infinitely complicated: a passage through a series of distorting mirrors and underground labyrinths.

When Hegel generalizes his logic in relation to art, the result is not far from our present point of view. In one place he says:

'This universal need for artistic expression (Bedürfniss zur Kunst) is based on the rational impulse in man's nature to exalt both the world of his inner experience and that of nature into the conscious embrace of mind, as an object in which he rediscovers himself. He satisfies the demand of this spiritual freedom by making explicit to his *inner* life all that exists, no less than by giving correspondingly a realized *external* embodiment to the self made thus explicit. And by this reduplication of what is his own he places before the vision and within the cognition of himself and others what is within him. This is the free rationality of man, in which art as also all action and knowledge originates.' (*Aesthetik*, Introduction, III, i, d.)

But Hegel was not able to continue to treat art as an integral activity. In the name of the Idea he must differentiate between three types of beauty—the symbolic, the classical and the romantic. If in high hope that at least within his romantic category we shall find some anticipation of our theory we turn to that part of his work which deals with romantic art, we find that the terms do not apply to qualities of art in general, but denote specific arts; symbolic art being identified with architecture, classical art with sculpture, and romantic art with painting, music and poetry. In short, Hegel is only concerned to denote the degree of sensuousness in art—which is the negation of the degree in which the Idea, in all its immateriality, is adequately realized. And the Idea is, of course, precisely that mystical emanation of German idealism which the surrealists, no less than the Marxians, repudiate and reject.

Surrealism and the Romantic Principle

It is my ambition some day to submit Hegel's *Aesthetik* to a detailed examination—to do for the realm of art on the basis of Hegel's dialectic something analogous to what Marx on the same basis did for the realm of economics. With such a philosophy of art one could then proceed to a complete revaluation of aesthetic values. I am convinced that the general body of existing aesthetic judgments are *conventional*. For the most part they consist of dogmas handed down by tradition or inculcated by education. They rarely have any real basis in personal experience. We pay lip-service, perhaps to Homer and Sophocles, perhaps to Virgil and Lucretius, Ariosto and Dante, Racine and Boileau, Shakespeare and Milton, and many other names in poetry and the other arts; but very few of these names represent for us *active influences*. I am not suggesting that the whole façade of our culture is false; but it has an architectonic completeness which is historical rather than actual. We look up at this façade and see a magnificent array of saints, all ordered in their appropriate niches; we recognize Homer, Dante, Shakespeare and several others; but for the most part we are ignorant of the identity of the figures and have to consult the guide-book. Our culture is altogether on the guide-book model; Shakespeare has four stars, Milton three, Donne and Blake one. We do not stop to ask on what system, and by whom, the stars were awarded. If we did, we should discover some dusty college of pedants, their noses buried in a profit and loss account of bibliographical data, critical overdrafts and vested interests. If we dared to travel without a guide, to trust our eyes and ears and our contemporary sensibility, the result would be catastrophic. Schoolmasters and professors would wander about helplessly like myopic men deprived of their glasses; textbooks would be irrelevant and teaching an impudent imposition.

Surrealism demands nothing less than such a revaluation of all aesthetic values. It has no respect for any academic tradition, least of all for the classical-capitalist tradition of the last four hundred years. It believes that as a general rule even men of genius during this period—and it has no difficulty in conceding genius where it is due—have been hampered and repressed by the conventions of their education and by their social environment. For poets like Dryden and Pope, for painters like Michelangelo and Poussin, and for many lesser artists, we can only have an angry and in no sense patronizing pity. The spectacle of the immense genius of Michelangelo, for example, caught in the toils of the moral and aesthetic conventions of his day, is a titanic tragedy. On the other hand the exaltation of conforming mediocrities in every age into a position of authority is a melancholy farce.* It is true that only a small proportion of them survive the inevitable ridicule of posterity, but there still remain on every classical Parnassus stuffed corpses that should be thrown on the dunghill.

That such a revaluation would be in effect merely a rehabilitation of romanticism is true enough, if the definition of romanticism I have already given is borne in mind. I would suggest, merely as examples of the tasks awaiting us, and merely in the restricted field of English literature, the following:

(1) *A fuller acknowledgment of the supreme poetic quality of our ballads and anonymous literature.* I do not refer to the actual work of recovering and editing the material; to that ghoulish activity it is time to cry halt. The ballads have become the happy hunting ground of academic competence; they must be rescued from such dead hands and be fully recognized as the most fundamental and authentic type of all poetry. Ballads are partly collective (if not in origin, at least in development) and to some degree automatic, and illustrate the intrinsic nature of surrealist poetry. I include in this category, not merely the familiar Border Ballads, but the popular ballads of more recent times (even Woolworth's Song Sheets) and the vast store of primitive poetry mostly still hidden in anthropological works.

(2) *Driving home the inescapable significance of Shakespeare.* To claim Shakespeare as an ally will be treated as an act of impudence by academic critics, but to justify our claim it is only necessary to point to the history of Shakespearean criticism. The rehabilitation of Shakespeare's genius, after the class and classical denigration of the seventeenth and eighteenth centuries, has been the work of specifically romantic critics, beginning with Coleridge and ending, for the moment, with Middleton Murry. Other critics have tinkered with his text—usually to little purpose —or have elaborated the historical background. But the poetic status of Shakespeare—his relative position among the poets of England and of the world—that depends on the romantic theory of poetry. It is impossible—the very attempt is absurd—to establish the genius of Shakespeare on any classical basis. He breaks all the academic rules.

* For the perfect expression of the resentment of the mediocre talent in the presence of genius, see Aretino's letter to Michelangelo of November, 1545.

Surrealism and the Romantic Principle

A critic who would not be described as romantic—Professor Dover Wilson—published a few years ago a long book on a vexed question: the problem of Hamlet.* Most critics have been puzzled by the incoherency of this, the most famous of Shakespeare's plays—an incoherency which affects not only the action of the play, but also the character of the hero. Various solutions have been proposed, and Professor Wilson reviews them all and finds them wanting. He has great fun demolishing the clumsy or ingenious attempts which have been made to explain the inexplicable; and ends where they might all have begun—by accepting the inexplicable at its face-value, its value as inexplicableness, as irrationality. The heart of the mystery proves to be the mystery itself:

'In fine, we were never intended to reach the heart of the mystery. That it has a heart is an illusion; the mystery itself is an illusion; Hamlet is an illusion. The secret that lies behind it all is not Hamlet's, but Shakespeare's; the technical devices he employed to create this supreme illusion of a great and mysterious character, who is at once mad and the sanest of geniuses, at once a procrastinator and a vigorous man of action, at once a miserable failure and the most adorable of heroes. The character of Hamlet, like the appearance of his successive impersonators on the stage, is a matter of make-up.'

Not since Warton defended the irrational imagery of Milton has such light streamed into the dark cloisters of the academic mind! It is really a very significant event in the history of scholarship. Professor Wilson is not a stray wolf in academic robes—such do occasionally find their way into the fold. He is the authentic type, the adept of a modern apparatus of the most efficient kind. He moves his apparatus into position; sets it in motion to do its carding and sorting and tidy ordering and then discovers that it will not work. Abandoning his apparatus he approaches the work of genius with his naked eye, and is dazzled. Rest, rest, perturbed spirit.†

* *What Happens in Hamlet*. By J. Dover Wilson. (Cambridge, 1935.)

† This critic's acknowledgment of the irrationality of Shakespeare's genius is not confined to this one instance. For example, what can he mean in saying that in *King Lear* Shakespeare 'has fashioned a mirror of art in which, more successfully than any man before or since, he has caught the whole of life and focused it to one intense and burning point of terror and beauty'? (*The Essential Shakespeare*. Cambridge, 1932. Page 127.) It is not in such terms that the academic critic is wont to award his marks.

Surrealism and the Romantic Principle

(3) *The exact relations between metaphysics and poetry.* 'e il pensamento in sogno transmutai'—Dante's line is the perfect description of a process which has yet to be given a full psychological explanation. We think we know how one kind of poetry originates—in inspiration, directly from the sensational awareness of the objective world, or no less directly from the promptings of the unconscious. But we have to admit—it is the only justification of the poetic elements in classical verse— that poetry may be generated by discursive reasoning or metaphysical speculation. In an early essay I described metaphysical poetry as 'felt thought', and I still think that no thought can become poetic unless it is apprehended in its mental configuration—we lack the equivalent of the more exact German word *Gestalt*. But what is still necessary is some explanation of why thoughts or ideas should evoke, not merely a metaphorical imagery, but a sensuous identification with visual images: thought transmuted into dream. Obviously it is some extension of the 'association of ideas' upon which psycho-analysis relies; the poet passes from the idea to the image unconsciously, and for reasons which might be revealed in analysis. But from our present point of view it is only necessary to affirm and prove that even in its most intellectual forms poetry acquires its poetic quality by a process which brings it into line with the irrational sources of lyrical and romantic poetry.

This fact has not been generally acknowledged by critics in the past, but one who enjoys great respect in quarters where the surrealists expect none had some inkling of the truth. 'Although poets often have unusual powers of reflective thought', wrote A. C. Bradley, 'the specific genius of a poet does not lie there, but in the imagination. Therefore his deepest and most original interpretation is likely to come by way of the imagination. And the specific way of imagination is not to clothe in imagery consciously held ideas; *it is to produce half-consciously a matter* from which, when produced, the reader may, if he chooses, extract ideas.'

Some further tasks of revaluation must be referred to more generally and quite briefly:

(4) *Lifting the moral ban.* Though something has been accomplished during the last twenty or thirty years, it is still true to say that poets like Shelley, Byron and Swinburne are judged by standards which must be repudiated. If we can agree that a poet's

work is to be judged by purely aesthetic standards, as in general we judge a painter's work, then we can proceed to the task unimpeded by the irrelevant standards of morality. But if we prove incapable of such detachment—and I admit it is almost inhuman to expect it—if, like Mr Eliot, we believe that 'literary criticism should be completed by criticism from a definite ethical and theological standpoint', then a revaluation becomes all the more necessary. For the ethical and theological standpoint from which we should then judge Shelley would be much nearer to Shelley's ethics and theology than to the ethics and theology of the Church. And the moral shudder that the very name of Byron sends through our bourgeois homes would be intensified by our acclamation. Byron is not, in any obvious degree, a superrealist poet; but he is a superrealist personality. He is the only English poet who might conceivably occupy, in our hierarchy, the position held in France by the Marquis de Sade. The function of such figures is to be so positive in their immorality, that morality becomes negative by comparison. They show, by the more-than-human energy of their evil, that evil too, as Milton was compelled to admit, has its divinity. In short, they reveal the conventionality of all systems of morality. They prove that the most deeply rooted taboos, such as incest, can be thwarted by the individual will; and the courage they manifest in such defiance is so absolute that a figure like Byron becomes the unconfessed hero of humanity. How else explain the enduring fascination of Byron's personality? By all the rules which condemn such lives as worthless and without honour, he should long ago have sunk into an oblivion from which his poetry would not have rescued him. But it is safe to say that no statue in the temple of fame is so securely lodged as Byron's; irrational in his life, he is now the object of irrational devotion.

The case of Swinburne is no less interesting. Though the public is still kept in ignorance of the true nature of Swinburne's character—or wilfully or unwittingly keeps itself in such ignorance —it is no longer to be disguised that the best of Swinburne's poetry is precisely that part of it which most openly celebrates what most people regard as unnatural aspects of human passion —poems like 'Anactoria', 'Faustine' and 'Dolores'. Swinburne during his life was bullied into conformity and bad verse, and his fate is one more unforgivable crime committed in the name of the bourgeois God. It was a crime against beauty, against honesty, against life itself. It should be clearly understood that, in taking up such an attitude towards the case of Swinburne or Byron, there is no question of encouraging vice as such; unnatural behaviour is not in itself interesting or admirable, and is only made anything but dull and distressing by the active aggression of moralists. But Swinburne himself expressed the truth of the matter in a self-defence he was compelled to publish in 1866*:

'The question at issue is wider than any between a single writer and his critics, or it might well be allowed to drop. It is this: whether or not the first and last requisite of art is to give no offence; whether or not all that cannot be lisped in the nursery or fingered in the schoolroom is therefore to be cast out of the library; whether or not the domestic circle is to be for all men and writers the outer limit and extreme horizon of their world of work. For to this we have come; and all students of art must face the matter as it stands. Who has not heard it asked, in a final and triumphant tone, whether this book or that can be read aloud by her mother to a young girl? whether such or such a picture can properly be exposed to the eyes of young persons? If you reply that this is nothing to the point, you fall at once into the ranks of the immoral. Never till now, and nowhere but in England, could so monstrous an absurdity rear for one moment its deformed and eyeless head. In no past century were artists ever bidden to work on these terms; nor are they now, except among us. The disease, of course, afflicts the meanest members of the body with most virulence. Nowhere is cant at once so foul-mouthed and so tight-laced as in the penny, twopenny, threepenny or sixpenny press. Nothing is so favourable to the undergrowth of real indecency as this overshadowing foliage of fictions, this artificial network of proprieties. *L'Arioste rit au soleil, l'Aretin ricane à l'ombre.* The whiter the sepulchre without, the ranker the rottenness within. Every touch of plaster is a sign of advancing decay.'

Swinburne speaks the language of his age, but the case would be no different if we were to translate it into the more technical terms of modern psychology. The dilemma which faces all moralists is that the repression of instincts is apt to breed a worse disease than their free expression; incidentally it entails a feebler art.

(5) That last sentence may, however, need a certain qualification in this sense: that what is repressed may nevertheless find a

Notes on Poems and Reviews. (London, 1866.)

disguised outlet. Without subscribing to the view that art is in every respect a sublimation of repressed instincts (for sublimation usually involves a conformity to collective ideals which completely submerges the individuality of the artist), one must nevertheless recognize—it is indeed one of our main theses—that art is closely linked with these same instincts. Actually it is a question of consciousness. If we are conscious of our instincts and repress them, then we act under duress and produce nothing but intellectual reactions. We try to be good and only succeed in being dull. But if we are not conscious of our instincts, and at the same time allow them to be expressed in a disguised form, then the result may well be interesting. I will return to the psychological aspect of the question presently; for the moment I only want to suggest that certain kinds of literature which are tolerated because they are described as mad or nonsensical—the Prophetic Books of Blake, the nonsense verse and tales of Lear and Lewis Carroll—are actually charged with this unconscious significance. Nothing would be so angrily resented as a revelation of the psychoanalytical significance of *Alice in Wonderland*—the work of a strongly repressed individual; but such significance is obvious and the resistance which its exposure would evoke is only a confirmation of its reality. In our opinion such significance only adds to the value of such literature, and in revealing it we have no other desire than to affirm its importance; that is to say, among the tasks of revaluation we include a reconsideration of all such literature. From our point of view, Lear is a better poet than Tennyson; Lewis Carroll has affinities with Shakespeare.

Many other tasks of revaluation will suggest themselves to the reader who has seized our point of view. I am sure, for example, that the whole field of English fiction must be reviewed, though I do not feel competent to make any proposals myself. It is possible that 'Monk' Lewis, Maturin and Mrs Radcliffe should, relatively to Scott, Dickens and Hardy, occupy a much higher rank. For myself I find them all equally difficult to read. I prefer the *Arabian Nights*, or Franz Kafka. It seems to me that fiction, that is to say, the prose narrative, awaits a complete transformation. In so far as it is to justify itself as art, it must be transformed into poesy. For fundamentally there is no distinction between prose art and verse art; there is only the one verbal art which is poesy.

As for English Painting, there too we must insist on a complete revision of values. The pen is more irresponsible than the brush; we print things which we dare not depict. That is a crude aspect of the general truth that poetry is an art of wider scope and deeper significance than painting, and this will remain the truth even when the art of painting is completely emancipated from the prejudice of naturalism. But during the many centuries in which painting has been hampered by this prejudice, it is obvious that its close adherence to a standard of objective verisimilitude would give only a minor and exceptional scope to any superrealist elements. I would, of course, claim that the art of the Middle Ages, except in so far as occupied with the mass-production of ecclesiastical symbols, was wholly of a super-realist character; for before the age of reason art was supernatural. Between the superreal and the supernatural there is only a difference of age, of evolution. The supernatural is associated with the mysticism of a religious view of life. But both agree in rejecting the 'real' or the 'natural' as the only aspect of existence. Supernaturalism, it is true, implies a dualism of spirit and matter; whereas super-realism implies a monism or identity of spirit and matter. Nevertheless, there is sufficient resemblance in the two attitudes to give more than a surface resemblance to their arts. Medieval religion required the plastic realization of irrational concepts. An angel or a devil could not be copied from a living model; the artist was compelled to use his imagination. Medieval sculpture, and above all medieval manuscripts, offer a wealth of material which it would be only too easy to call surrealist. I do not draw on this material, because I respect the difference of intention. Nevertheless, as an example of what I mean, we find that a subject like 'Christ in Limbo' is often treated in a manner recalled by Picasso's etching 'Minotauromachia'.

Between the end of the Middle Ages and the beginning of the Romantic Movement, painting and sculpture in England were almost completely dead: a significant fact. Interest begins again with Gainsborough and Blake. Blake I will leave aside for the moment; I shall have something to say about him here in another connection, and I have written about him elsewhere. The early paintings of Gainsborough have a naïve spontaneity which brings them close to the Douanier Rousseau; as he increased in technical efficiency, he scarcely added to his aesthetic appeal. At least, his dullest works were done to rival the academic standards of Reynolds or to flatter the bourgeois desire for 'finish'. The same

Surrealism and the Romantic Principle

is true of Constable, and the history of Turner is actually the history of the emancipation of a great artist from the fetters of naturalism. Turner is certainly a subject for revaluation; from the first the victim of Ruskin's enthusiasm, and in our own day the blind spot of influential critics like Roger Fry, this painter actually transformed the topographical canvas which he had inherited into a veritable torch of sensational fury. A little dogged in spirit, he lacked the final courage to take leave of his senses—the vacation which every hard-working artist owes to himself. But he remains a very significant figure—far more significant than any of the French Impressionists, the compeer of Delacroix and Cézanne. There are other painters to be rescued from the dustbin of the nineteenth century: Samuel Palmer and John Martin; but the most serious task is a reconsideration of the Pre-Raphaelites. I doubt if any Englishman—at least, any Englishman still so near to them—can approach these artists with the freshness and freedom that Salvador Dali, for example, brings to their revaluation. But certain truths may be admitted. First, the Pre-Raphaelites were integral artists; like the surrealists, they had a philosophy of life which embraced painting, poetry, philosophy and politics. They were also convinced of the imbecility of most of their contemporaries, and reacted in the strongest possible way to the academic naturalism of the time. They were not afraid to experiment with their sensations; they acknowledged the primacy of the imagination. But they were incapable of a really comprehensive reaction—a revolution. They had no dialectic, no scientific method, no real energy. In a word, they were sentimentalists. They should have developed romanticism from the stage where Coleridge left it; instead, they developed nostalgia. They read the *Ancient Mariner* and Keats and Blake, and merely indulged in the easy path of repetition. They might have read instead the *Biographia Literaria* and even Hegel, and produced a more vital movement of thought. One has only to contrast Morris with Marx, contemporaries almost, to measure the failure of the Pre-Raphaelites and their followers.

Their followers degenerated into soulful weavers, mock-medieval craftsmen, bookbinders and harpists. English plastic arts had to wait for the inspiration of Picasso to show any real revival. In the last twenty years we have produced potentially great artists—Wyndham Lewis is the typical example—but they have suffered from a disastrous form of individualism. The

126

Surrealism and the Romantic Principle

English sin has always been eccentricity; by which I do not mean a lack of conformity, but simply a lack of social coherence. Surrealism does not, like Communism, call upon artists to surrender their individuality; but it does insist that artists have common problems to solve and common dangers to avoid, and that a certain coherence, even a certain mutuality, is one of the conditions of the efficacity of art.

The fact that the surrealists inherited from the dadaists a certain scorn for the 'formalism' and 'purism' of the later stages of impressionism has led to some misunderstanding of their attitude towards the technique of art. Surrealists are opposed to any intellectualization of art—to any preference, that is to say, for rational as opposed to imaginative elements. Nothing, in their opinion, could be more futile and unnecessary than an art exclusively concerned with the rendering of some aspect of natural fact—effects of light, of space, of mass or solidity. This seems to them to be a purely mechanical or muscular preoccupation, and the result entirely without artistic interest. Was it not Monet who painted the same haystack in thirty-two different degrees of light? Well, there is always a haystack to be seen somewhere at whatever time and in whatever light you like. It does not seem worth recording at immense pains the passive mutations of such a banal object. It would be just as interesting to record the artist's reaction to thirty-two different degrees of toothache. Even the preoccupation of a Cézanne, though it invested nature with a structure that in actual appearance it lacks, and to that extent contributed a mental and even an imaginative element; and though this preoccupation led to the discovery of perfect relations between intellectual order and sensuous colour; yet even such an art is deceptive if it does not extend our sensibility on more than a sensational level. Cézanne himself seemed to realize this, and was not satisfied with his apples. The series of 'Baigneuses' which he painted at the end of his career marks the wider imaginative range of his genius. Seurat is a special case, too complex and too unresolved to dogmatize about—we must not forget that he died at the age of thirty-two; but obviously, in paintings like 'Le Cirque' and 'La Parade', he was creating a new world, a world of imagination or fantasy which owed no more than its primary elements to the world of objective vision. Since their day, painters not so great as Cézanne or Seurat have seized on one part of their achievement, and that the least interesting part, and have elaborated it into an exclusive method. They have made painting an ocular exercise; a decorative variation on the data of physical vision. Against such an art it was necessary to protest; and the best protest, which should have been final in its effect, was the invention of the collage by Picasso or Braque— the work of art made of any old pieces of string or newspaper but which, nevertheless, in spite of its complete lack of the fiddling kind of finesse that threatened to become the sole aim of painting, was undeniably a work of art. Max Ernst, taking rubbings from the surfaces of wood and other natural materials, went a step further and reproduced *mechanically* the actual effect of sensibility so much prized as a personal quality by bourgeois amateurs. In this manner the physique of art was seen in its proper proportions; not as a thing which could be dispensed with or despised, but as an instrument subordinate to the sovereign power of the imagination.

The surrealist, therefore, by no means denies or ridicules aesthetic values as such. To him, no less than to any other sensitive creature, there is good art and bad art, good painting and bad painting, *good surrealism and bad surrealism*. He has a scale of values and these values are aesthetic. But aesthetic values are not necessarily objective values—in painting they are not necessarily what the Germans call *malerisch* or painterly values: they do not belong so much to the paint as to the person. Like the pitch of a voice, the 'hand' in handwriting or even the gait in walking, they are the expression of a personality—a mentality. Dali's neat, tight Vermeerish *facture* has its aesthetic as well as Picasso's bold, plangent, viscous brushwork. There is no one style of using paint, no one criterion of perfection: the artist is using a medium to express certain sensations or ideas and he is not to be judged by the manner in which he uses the medium but by the success with which he conveys the sensations or ideas (I do not suggest that in practice there is any possibility of making the distinction). This is even true of so-called 'abstract' art, where the ideas are contained within the formal relations: are, that is to say, the direct expression of formal relations. The alternative which must otherwise be admitted is an art tending towards one uniform standard of perfection: a form of idealism contradicted by history no less than by common sense.

This explanation made, it will perhaps be seen how certain 'found objects' which are not the work of human artists, but the products of natural (or unnatural) forces, come to be cherished by surrealists. If I am walking along the beach and my eye catches a sea-worn and sun-bleached knot of wood whose shape and colour strongly appeal to me, the act of identification (which may in any case have a psychological explanation) makes that object as expressive of my personality as if I had actually carved the wood into that shape. Selection is also creation. Nothing is so expressive of a man as the fetishes he gathers round him—his pipe, his pens, his pocket-knife—even the pattern of his suit. Art in its widest sense is an extension of the personality: a host of artificial limbs.

To the plastic objects which we find by the aid of our eyes correspond, on another plan of consciousness, the images found in dreams. The direct use of dream imagery has not been frequent in the past, for the good psychological reason that the conscious mind is a jealous guardian of the secrecy of this world. But now we turn to the dream with the same confidence that formerly men placed in the objective world of sensation, and we weave its reality into the synthesis of our art. It is possible that in the integral dream—the dream as entire myth rather than as a series of fragmentary symbols—the work of synthesis is already done. In most dreams we find elements that are merely the casual residues of the day's anxieties; but we find also the day-world transformed, and occasionally this new reality presents itself to us as a poetic unity. But to make this distinction clear I will relate the history of an experiment.

Hitherto poets and critics have shown singularly little curiosity about the actual mechanism of poetic inspiration. There are, of course, many disjointed statements which throw light on the subject, such as Wordsworth's quasi-psychological description of emotion recollected in tranquillity, and Keats and Rilke have observed themselves to some profit. Not long before his death A. E. Housman disconcerted his academic cronies by confessing that inspiration was most often induced in him by a pint of beer; that in any case it had physical symptoms. My own suggestion is that poetic inspiration has an exact parallel in dream-formation. In what respect the two processes differ can only be shown by the analysis of a particular case of inspiration, which is what I propose to undertake. But first I must make sure that the reader has a clear picture of the process of dream-formation as described by Freud.

Surrealism and the Romantic Principle

In his latest 'Revision of the Theory of Dreams' (*New Introductory Lectures*, 1933, chapter 1) Freud gives the following schematic summary of the process:

'The introduction: the wish to sleep, the voluntary withdrawal from the outside world. Two things follow from this: firstly, the possibility for older and more primitive modes of activity to manifest themselves, i.e., regression; and secondly, the decrease of the repression-resistance which weighs on the unconscious. As a result of this latter feature an opportunity for dream-formation presents itself, which is seized upon by the factors which are the occasion of the dream; that is to say, the internal and external stimuli which are in activity. The dream which thus eventuates is already a compromise formation; it has a double function; it is on the one hand in conformity with the ego ("ego-syntonic"), since it subserves the wish to sleep by draining off the stimuli which would otherwise disturb it, while on the other hand it allows to a repressed impulse the satisfaction which is possible in these circumstances in the form of an hallucinatory wish-fulfilment. The whole process of dream-formation, which is permitted by the sleeping ego, is, however, under the control of the censorship, a control which is exercised by what is left of the forces of repression.'

What is allowed to emerge as a dream—that is to say, what is remembered as a dream—Freud calls the dream-text or the *manifest* dream; but what the analyst suspects to lie beyond the dream, its motive force, these are the *latent* dream-thoughts. 'Their dominating element is the repressed impulse, which has obtained some kind of expression, toned down and disguised though it may be, by associating itself with stimuli which happen to be there and by tacking itself on to the residue of the day before.' The rest of Freud's description should be followed with close attention, because its bearing on the process of poetic inspiration is direct and immensely significant:

'Just like any other impulse this one presses forward towards satisfaction in action, but the path to motor discharge is closed to it on account of the physiological characteristics of the state of sleep, and so it is forced to travel in the retrograde direction to perception, and content itself with an hallucinatory satisfaction. The latent dream-thoughts are therefore turned into a collection of sensory images and visual scenes. As they are travelling in this direction something happens to them which seems to us new and bewildering. All the verbal apparatus by means of which the more subtle thought-relations are expressed, the conjunctions and prepositions, the variations of declension and conjugation, are lacking, because the means of portraying them are absent; just as in primitive grammarless speech, only the raw material of thought can be expressed, and *the abstract is merged again in the concrete from which it sprang*. What is left over may very well seem to lack coherence. It is as much the result of the archaic regression in the mental apparatus as of the demands of the censorship that so much use is made of the representation of certain objects and processes by means of symbols which have become strange to conscious thought. But of more far-reaching import are the other alterations to which the elements comprising the dream-thoughts are subjected. Such of them as have any point of contact are *condensed* into new unities. When the thoughts are translated into pictures those forms are indubitably preferred which allow of this kind of telescoping, or condensation; it is as though a force were at work which subjected the material to a process of pressure or squeezing together. As a result of condensation one element in a manifest dream may correspond to a number of elements of the dream-thoughts; but conversely one of the elements from among the dream-thoughts may be represented by a number of pictures in the dream.'

This spate of quotation is already too long, but there are two further refinements in the process of dream-formation which are still relevant. The first is *displacement* or transference of accent. The individual ideas which make up the dream-thoughts are not all of equal value; 'they have various degrees of affective tone attached to them, and, corresponding to these, they are judged as more or less important, and more or less worthy of attention. In the dream-work these ideas are separated from their affects; the affects are treated separately. They may be transferred to something else, they may remain where they were, they may undergo transformation, or they may disappear from the dream entirely. *The importance of the ideas which have been shorn of their affect reappears in the dream in the form of the sensuous vividness of the dream-pictures*; but we notice that this accent, which should lie on important elements, has been transferred to unimportant ones, so that what seems to be pushed to the forefront in the dream, as the most important element in it, only plays a subsidiary rôle in the dream-thoughts, and conversely, what is important among the dream-thoughts obtains only incidental and rather indistinct representation in the dream.'

The other refinement in the process is, from our point of view, perhaps the most important of all. 'After these operations on the dream-thoughts the dream is almost ready. There is still, however, a more or less non-constant factor, the so-called secondary elaboration, that makes its appearance after the dream has come into consciousness as an object of perception. When the dream has come into consciousness, we treat it in exactly the same way that we treat any content of perception; we try to fill in the gaps, we add connecting links and often enough we let ourselves in for serious misunderstandings. But this, as it were, rationalizing activity, which at its best provides the dream with a smooth façade, such as cannot correspond to its real content, may be altogether absent in some cases, or only operate in a very feeble way, in which case the dream displays to view all its gaps and inconsistencies . . .'

To trace the parallel between dream-formation and poem-formation it is necessary to analyse a particular poem, and of necessity such a poem must be one of my own (or otherwise I should have to conduct a long and searching analysis of another poet). The poem I shall take is actually based on a dream. On December 31, 1935, I was present at a family gathering in York-shire, and at midnight we celebrated the passing of the Old Year and the birth of the New Year by drinking a rum-punch (I am, it will be seen, about to confirm Housman's diagnosis). I retired to bed and dreamt a vivid dream. It was still vivid to me when next day I travelled by train back to London, and since, like several poets of my acquaintance, I have always found the rhythm of a train journey conducive to poetic composition, I began to transfer to paper the haunting images of my dream. The following poem was the result—I will explain the significance of the italics presently:

> The narrow labyrinth has light
> which casts our shadows on the wall
> as in extremity of flight
> I follow one whose face I have not seen.
> The walls are white
> and turn at intervals to make a screen
> on which our racing shadows rise and fall
> *like waves against the bleached cliff.*

> Anxious to make my mentor turn
> I lift my hands and make a pass
> which casts upon the facing wall
> a silhouette hovering like a baffled bird.
> But on he leads unmoved
> and fatally I follow till at last
> we leave the labyrinth and I find myself
> alone, upon a plinth.
> The houses in the square below
> stand newly built, brick-rough, bright
> bathed in some *Castilian* light.
> In the unpaved area a few children play.
> This must be a foreign land, I say,
> and gaze about with eager eyes.
> Then suddenly know that it is *Heaven*
> to which *Death* has led me in disguise.

What I described in this poem was, of course, the *manifest* content of my dream; the *latent* content could only be elicited by analysis, and is of no immediate interest. But our poetic analysis of the poem should begin by asking to what extent I succeeded in conveying the manifest content. Is the poem efficient merely as the narrative of an experience? As far as the events of the poem are concerned, I think it is only towards the end that I myself am conscious of any failure. I fancy that in the dream the identity of the unknown figure was revealed to me, and that immediately I awoke—in the process of awaking—this identity slipped from me and I was left with a sense of being baffled. The notion of suddenly finding myself in a Heaven was present in the dream, but identifying the figure with Death was a subsequent rationalization; it did not, if I can trust my memory, occur to me until I began to write the poem.

Let us now examine the images in the poem. In the dream the labyrinth was real; an intricate maze always turning at right angles and full of an evenly diffused white light; the figure, clad rather like a harlequin in close-fitting tights, never turned. I made the pass by lifting my hands above my head and making a shadow on the wall in the manner of the shadow-game played by children; the image of the baffled bird—the fluttering shadow like a bird beating against a window-pane—*occurred to me in my dream*. In this it differs from the wave-image I have used to describe the shadows of our bodies on the walls of the labyrinth, which is a conscious image produced in the process of writing the poem; I would on that account call it a metaphor rather than an image. In a similar way the word 'Castilian', used to describe the peculiar light which was diffused over the square, is an epithet derived from my conscious experience; the nearest equivalent in my memory being certain effects of sunlight in Spain. I have not conveyed exactly enough the vivid impression I have of the effect of this dream-light on the houses; I have a distinct sensuous image of the porous quality of the brick into which the light seemed to soak, as if absorbed. The children in the square (it was a new square, not yet paved or laid out in any way, rough and uneven) seemed to be self-centred, detached, in a different perspective to the rest of the scene; an effect which Salvador Dali often conveys in his paintings.

It will be observed that there are several rhymes, but no regular rhyme system; these rhymes were not sought by me, but came unconsciously in the act of writing the poem. If I had sought for rhymes I should inevitably have been compelled to distort my narrative and my imagery, and to that extent to be false to my inspiration. And such, indeed, has always been my practice in writing poetry. I neither seek rhymes nor avoid them, for either attitude would involve a too conscious control of my expression—would defeat the desirable automatism. But this does not prevent me from recognizing that when there is no total inspiration—when a poet is writing line by line—the search for rhymes may lead to the discovery of surprising images. That is merely a different method of composition; a mosaic as opposed to a reflection. If a poet wishes to remain faithful to a myth—a myth presented to him integrally—he cannot afford to go off in pursuit of surface ornaments.

Perhaps the most important distinction which this analysis reveals is that between images and metaphors—a distinction which has already been made by Pierre Reverdy and which I have referred to before (Breton also quotes it in the First Surrealist Manifesto):

'L'image est une création pure de l'esprit.

'Elle ne peut naître d'une comparaison mais du rapprochement de deux réalités plus ou moins éloignées.

'Plus les rapports des deux réalités rapprochées seront lointains et justes, plus l'image sera forte—plus elle aura de puissance émotive et de réalité poétique . . .'

Surrealism and the Romantic Principle

In my poem the metaphor of the waves against the bleached cliff, though to my mind accurate enough as description, has not the same force as the image of the baffled bird; and actually, of course, the whole content of the poem—labyrinth, square, light, children—is a series of images, but of images whose counterpart is not manifest, and which therefore we call symbols.

The metaphor may have its associational significance within the psychological unity of the poem; if it is purely intellectual in origin it is apt to stick out of the poem like an irrelevant ornament.

This type of poem, then, we might describe, to adopt Freud's terminology, as the manifest content of a dream whose latent thoughts have been turned into sensory images or visual scenes; the abstract, that is to say, is merged again in the concrete form from which it sprang. * Certain of the dream-thoughts have been condensed into images or symbols, whose latent significance resists any analysis, but which nevertheless, *and perhaps precisely on that account*, have extreme poetic force. Then, to disguise any gaps or incoherency, the conscious mind of the poet has worked over the poem, and given it that smooth façade which is generally demanded by the literary conventions of an age, and which in any case makes for ease of communication.

It is not every poem that has the integral character of a dream, but every authentic image is conceived in the unconscious; that is to say, the two realities of which Reverdy speaks, though more or less distantly separated, cohere as an image and gain their emotive power from the presence in the unconscious of a hidden connecting link. There is no need, in any poetic analysis, to reveal that repressed connection; the poetic reality lies in the evident power of the image, and is no stronger—indeed, may be much weaker—if its latent meaning is made manifest. The whole irrationality of art, and the surrealist defence of irrationality, is

* *Compare* Vico's theory of poetry, especially the following passage: '(So for us) the whole art of Poetry reduces itself to this, that anyone who wishes to excel as a poet must unlearn all his native language, and return to the pristine beggary of words; by this necessity he will express the feelings of his mind by means of the most obvious and easily perceived aspects of things; he will, by the aid of the senses and the imagination, paint the most striking and lovely images of things, manners and feelings; and just as anyone who wishes to be a philosopher must first purge himself of the prejudices of children and common people, so anyone who would write a poem must feel and think entirely according to the childlike and common views of the world. In this way he will become really imaginative, and will compose at once sublimely and in accordance with the popular understanding.' *De Constantia Philologiae*. (Trans. by H. S. Davies.)

explained by the Freudian theory of regression. An unconscious impulse creates the poem no less than the dream; it provides, that is to say, the mental energy required for its formation. That impulse seeks in the poem, no less and no otherwise than in the dream, its desired satisfaction. The latent ideas or thoughts are turned into visual images, are dramatized and illustrated, are finally liberated in the hallucinatory reality of the poem.

That the actual choice of words—the poet's language as distinct from his imagery—is formed by a similar process of unconscious association, would seem to be a fair deduction from the evidence of psychoanalysis. In the degree that they are poetic such words are automatic associations of an aural rather than a visual nature. It may be that some poets search the dictionary of their conscious memory for the apt epithet, and in that way display an inventive wit; but such a faculty—the faculty of a Pope or a Dryden—is not the essentially poetic gift. The poetic image, to adapt a saying of Picasso's, is found, not sought. It emerges, perhaps not easily but at any rate directly, from the well of the unconscious. It may be elaborated or distorted by the exercise of conscious skill, but there is no evidence at all to show that as a result the poem ever gains in its specifically poetic power.

We are so uncertain of the limits of mental activity—its actual range and effectiveness—that even as materialists we must not exclude the possibility of hitherto unsuspected modes of operation. For example, psychoanalysis has already been compelled to admit the scientific possibility of thought-transference or telepathy. On the analogy of such 'occult" phenomena, it is possible that the mind of the poet or painter, during the course of its ordinary activity, picks up and transmits 'messages' in a wholly unconscious manner. I think it is possible that such 'messages' are always in the form of 'images'—that is to say, the ideas they deal with are not verbalized. In this way, for example, the 'residues' of the day's activity, in their least unimportant and unobserved details, are taken up and 'used' in the course of the dream activity. A pattern on a wall, a patch of lichen, or any abstract pattern which I have for a moment stared at, may in this way sink into my mind and determine the form of my unconscious images, which when called up in the activity of painting, emerge in this apparently inexplicable and illogical shape. That process is comparatively easy to understand; but in the contrary direction it is also possible that ideas, with which we may have been obsessed during the activity of thought, may, when conscious thought is for the time being superseded by instinctive modes of expression, so guide such expression that it corresponds to the latent thought. Salvador Dali relates how a splash of paint on his palette had assumed *unknown to his conscious mind* the shape of a distorted skull which he had consciously and vainly been trying to discover. It is another aspect of automatism; and all that it is necessary to admit is the superreality, the something-more-than-conscious naturalism, which encompasses all our actions. At this moment I have an intimation that I shall find in Blake a verse or a sentence bearing on this question. I take the book from the shelf, it opens at page 562 and I read:

'. . . Condens'd his Emanations into hard opaque substances,
And his infant thoughts & desires into cold dark cliffs of death.
His hammer of gold he seiz'd, and his anvil of adamant;
He seiz'd the bars of condens'd thoughts to forge them
Into the sword of war, into the bow and arrow,
Into the thundering cannon and into the murdering gun.
I saw the limbs form'd for exercise contemn'd, & the beauty of
Eternity look'd upon as deformity, & loveliness as a dry tree.
I saw disease forming a Body of Death around the Lamb
Of God to destroy Jerusalem & to devour the body of Albion,
By war and stratagem to win the labour of the husbandman.
Awkwardness arm'd in steel, folly in a helmet of gold,
Weakness with horns & talons, ignorance with a rav'ning beak,
Every Emanative joy forbidden as a Crime
And the Emanations buried alive in the earth with pomp of
    religion,
Inspiration deny'd, Genius forbidden by laws of punishment,
I saw terrified. I took the sighs & tears & bitter groans,
I lifted them into my Furnaces to form the spiritual sword
That lays open the hidden heart. I drew forth the pang
Of sorrow red hot: I work'd on my resolute anvil:
I heated it in the flames of Hand & Hyle & Coban
Nine times . . .'   *Jerusalem*, i, 9.

Thus Blake labours in hope that Enthusiasm and Life may not cease. In the whole of his writings I feel the presence of an instinctive dialecticism which is of the greatest interest. I know that some surrealists have important reserves to make about Blake; they are suspicious of his obscurity, which wears the too obvious mask of mysticism. I am equally suspicious; but I must confess that the more I have studied Blake the more these mists have dispersed. It would be absurd to call Blake a materialist (it would be absurd to call the surrealist anything but a *dialectical* materialist); nevertheless, in works like *The Marriage of Heaven and Hell* and *Jerusalem* there is a realization of the fundamental contradictions of reality, and a movement towards a synthesis which is anything but idealistic.

From much the same point of view the metaphysical element in Shelley should be re-examined. In Shelley's case there is no doubt of the point of departure—a materialistic determinism of the most antitheist type. But it is generally assumed that Shelley abandoned his early antitheism and ended in the clouds of neo-platonic idealism. But actually he too arrived at a dialectical synthesis of the real and the unreal, actuality and hallucination, as the following quotation from his *Speculations on Metaphysics* will make clear:

'Thoughts, or ideas, or notions, call them what you will, differ from each other, not in kind, but in force. It has commonly been supposed that those distinct thoughts which affect a number of persons, at regular intervals, during the passage of a multitude of other thoughts, which are called *real* or *external objects*, are totally different from those which affect only a few persons, and which recur at irregular intervals, and are usually more obscure and indistinct, such as hallucinations, dreams, and the ideas of madness. No essential distinction between any one of these ideas, or any class of them, is founded on a correct observation of the nature of things, but merely on a consideration of what thoughts are most invariably subservient to the security and happiness of life; and if nothing more were expressed by the distinction, the philosopher might safely accommodate his language to that of the vulgar. But they pretend to assert an essential difference, which has no foundation in truth, and which suggests a narrow and false conception of universal nature, the parent of the most fatal errors in speculation. A specific difference between every thought of the mind, is, indeed, a necessary consequence of that law by which it perceives diversity and number; but a generic and essential difference is wholly arbitrary.'

In an essay of this kind I am mainly concerned with presenting the positive aspects of surrealism; all that necessary part of a critical activity which consists in removing misunderstandings and replying to criticism made on the basis of such misunderstandings may be left to more fugitive forms of publication. But one form of attack may be mentioned here because it is of a serious nature and because it will serve to introduce an aspect of surrealism which yet remains to be dealt with. During the London Exhibition Mr J. B. Priestley was commissioned to write an article for an evening paper famous for its betting news. Now, that Mr Priestley should be made to feel, as he confesses, 'not too comfortable', in fact, 'profoundly disturbed' by surrealism is exactly as it should be. But when he goes on to ascribe to the surrealists in general all kinds of moral perversion, he is merely indulging in the abortive vituperation of his kind:

> As if a man should spit against the wind;
> The filth returns in's face.

The surrealists, he said, 'stand for violence and neurotic unreason. They are truly decadent. You catch a glimpse behind them of the deepening twilight of barbarism that may soon blot out the sky, until at last humanity finds itself in another long night.' In that fuliginous perspective, and knowing what a man of Mr Priestley's prejudices means by decadence, the surrealists might willingly stand. But that is not the end of Mr Priestley's insinuations. 'There are about far too many effeminate or epicene young men, lisping and undulating. Too many young women without manners, balance, dignity—greedy and slobbering sensation-seekers. Too many people who are steadily lapsing into shaved and powdered barbarism. . . . Frequently they have strong sexual impulses that they soon contrive to misuse or pervert.'

Mr Priestley no doubt feels none too comfortable on his bed of roses, and sympathy for the under-dog flows in a copious if somewhat muddled stream from his generous heart. But Mr Priestley is not personally acquainted with the surrealists, in this country or any other; and as a novelist he ought to have enough penetration to realize that the least repressed of people are generally the most moral; or, as Huysmans puts it, 'au fond . . . il n'y a de réellement obscènes que les gens chastes'. As a matter of fact, the surrealists are no less aware than Mr Priestley of undesirable elements in their midst; but they are not themselves to be identified with such elements. It is true that they cannot protest against the perversions of a moral code for which they have no

respect. But they despise the kind of people who indulge in perversion just as much as they despise people who indulge in
hypocrisy. They despise any kind of weakness, any lack of personal integrity. Their principle of liberty allows to each the free
exercise of his natural propensities so long as this does not infringe
the equal rights of others. On the subject of homosexuality, for
example (a subject which the evening papers do not mention,
though it is one of the most acute questions of the day), the surrealists are not in the least prejudiced; they recognize that inver-
sion is an abnormal condition due to a certain psychological or
physiological predisposition for which the individual is in no way
responsible. But they protest when such individuals form a
sodality or freemasonry for the purpose of imposing their special
ethos upon the social and intellectual life of the day. It leads in
particular to an intolerance for women which is certainly no
part of the surrealist creed.

In short, the surrealists admit the disciplinary truth that, if
you have to attack a diseased body for the purpose of healing it,
your own body should be in a healthy state. The kind of insult
which Mr Priestley hurls at the surrealists is the kind of insult
that used tobe insinuated about the early Bolsheviks until the purity
and disinterestedness of their lives could no longer be disguised.

The surrealist is opposed to current morality because he con-
siders that it is rotten. He can have no respect for a code of ethics
that tolerates extremes of poverty and riches; that wastes or
deliberately destroys the products of the earth amidst a starving
or undernourished people; that preaches a gospel of universal
peace and wages aggressive war with all the appendages of horror
and destruction which its evil genius can invent; that so distorts
the sexual impulse that thousands of unsatisfied men and women
go mad, millions waste their lives in unhappiness or poison their
minds with hypocrisy. For such a morality (and these are merely
its most general features) the surrealist has nothing but hatred
and scorn.

His own code of morality is based on liberty and love. He sees
no reason why the frailties of the human race should be erected
into a doctrine of original sin, but he realizes that most men are
born imperfect and are made less perfect still by their circumstances. Such evils and imperfections cannot wholly be eradicated
in any conceivable span of human development. But it is his
belief that the whole system of organized control and repression

which is the social aspect of present-day morality is psychologic-
ally misconceived and positively harmful. He believes, that is to
say, in the fullest possible liberation of the impulses and is
convinced that what law and oppression have failed to achieve
will in due time be brought about by love and fraternity.

The surrealist is not a sentimental humanitarian; the superrealism of his art has its counterpart in the realism of his science.
He is a psychologist of the strictest type, and if he uses words like
'love' and 'fraternity', it is because his analysis of the sexual and
affective and of the economic life of man has given him the right
to use such words cleanlily, without the least surplus of sentimentality. Art, we conclude, is more than description or 'reportage'; it is a dialectical activity, an act of renewal. It renews
vision, it renews language; but most essentially it renews life
itself by enlarging the sensibility, by making men more conscious
of the terror and the beauty, the *wonder* of the possible forms of
being.

The renascence of wonder—I remember this as the title of an
essay by Watts-Dunton, the friend of Swinburne. I should not be
afraid to adopt such a grandiloquent phrase to describe the general
aim of surrealism, as I conceive it. Just as curiosity is the faculty
which drives man to seek out the hidden structure of the external
universe, thereby enabling him to build up that body of knowledge which we call science, so wonder is the faculty which dares
man to create what has not before existed, which dares man to
use his powers in new ways and for new effects. We have lost this
sense of the word 'wonderful'—it is one of the most outworn
clichés in the language. But actually 'wonder' is a better and
more inclusive word than 'beauty', and what is full of wonder has
the most compelling force over the imagination of men. 'We
cease to wonder at what we understand,' said Dr Johnson, a man
indifferent to the cost of complacency. It would have been much
more to the point to have observed that understanding ceases
when we cease to wonder, that, as Pascal, a less complacent man,
observed, 'there are reasons of the heart of which Reason knows
nothing'.

III

7

Paul Gauguin

We must first distinguish between the art and the legend. To thousands, perhaps millions of people, the name of Gauguin signifies something typical, even something heroic. He is the stockbroker, the ordinary middle-class salaried man, who threw up a good job to devote his whole time to 'art'. More than that, he is the artist who revolted against the ugliness and deceptiveness of modern civilization and went to the South Seas, to warmth and colour, innocence and naïvety. Novels and plays, and biographies that read like novels, have been written round his romantic life-story, until the facts, which are not quite so romantic, have been forgotten. So ubiquitous, so answering to some deep longing in our breasts, is this legend that the art, the paintings to which Gauguin devoted all his energies and all his thoughts, no longer seem to exist in their own rights, but to have become part of the iconography of the legend.

We must try to recover the facts—or rather, to correct the emphasis given to the facts in the public imagination. The facts are not in doubt—they have been presented in two collections of letters*, in the biography by his son Pola†, and in numerous volumes of reminiscences by his contemporaries. In so far as these facts concern the personal character of Gauguin, we may be tempted to exercise our moral judgment. Gauguin deliberately deserted his wife and four young children, left them to fend for themselves as best they might, and for twenty years remained indifferent to their fate. That is the brutal aspect of the facts. There is, however, another aspect. Once his decision was taken, Gauguin made no concessions to himself. All his property, including the proceeds of his choice collection of pictures, he gave to his

* *Lettres à Daniel de Monfreid*. Précédées d'un hommage par Victor Segalen. Paris, 1919. New edition (Librairie Plon), 1930.—*Lettres de Gauguin à sa femme et à ses amis*. Recueillies et préfacées par Maurice Malingue. Paris (Grasset), 1947.

† *My Father Paul Gauguin*. London (Cassell), 1937.

wife. He loved his children—so much so that he took his eldest son, Clovis, to share his poverty in Paris—perhaps, from the point of view of the child, not the kindest thing he could have done. In Tahiti he kept a journal for his daughter Aline, and when she died his grief was expressed in two letters to his wife, one so bitter that she destroyed it, the other sentimental enough to have survived ('I have lost my daughter, I no longer love God. Like my mother, she was called Aline—everyone loves after his own fashion, for some love is exalted in the presence of death, for others . . . I don't know. Her grave there, with its flowers, is all an illusion. Her grave is here by my side; my tears are its flowers, living flowers.') These were the last letters he ever wrote to his wife, and her comment shows to what depths of bitterness she had been driven: 'His ferocious egoism revolts me every time I think of it.'

Egoism it undoubtedly was, and nothing was ever to move Gauguin from the dedication of his life to what he conceived to be an end justifying the renunciation of all human bonds. Such fanaticism in another milieu is held to be saintly, and though from a religious point of view there could be no greater heresy, Gauguin had substituted the love of Beauty for the love of God, and his life only makes sense when this is realized. Nevertheless, when he made his great decision he was actuated, not only by a blind faith in his own destiny, but by a confident hope that once all his time and energy were devoted to painting, his reputation would be secured, his paintings would sell, and he would still be able to support his family. But, of course, his paintings did not sell—he was merely able to produce more and not necessarily better unsaleable paintings. His savings disappeared in eight months. He retreated to Copenhagen, to sponge on his wife's parents for a further eighteen months. He made himself so disagreeable to everyone there that finally he had to return to Paris, where for six months he lived in conditions of terrible poverty and distress. The rest of his life is to be interpreted, not so much as a flight from civilization, but rather as a desperate search for the lowest possible cost of living. He went to Brittany, not because he had any love for the country or the seaside, but because he heard that at the *pension* of Marie-Jeanne Gloanec in Pont-Aven one could live for £2 or £3 a month. When he found that he could not earn even that small amount by his painting, he began to think of those tropical islands where the food grew on

Paul Gauguin

trees and where even clothing was not a necessity. 'May the day come', he wrote to his wife, 'and soon, when I shall go and bury myself in the woods of an island in Oceania, live there joyfully and calmly with my art. Far from my family, far from this European struggle for money. There, in Tahiti, I shall be able, in the silence of the lovely tropical nights, to listen to the soft murmuring music of the movements of my heart in loving harmony with the mysterious beings who surround me. True, at last, without money troubles, I shall be able to love, sing, and die . . .'*

We, who know that atomic bombs have been dropped on 'an island in Oceania', can be wise after the event. We know now that there is no escape from 'this European struggle for money'; and, if we are artists of some sort, we can see that we are caught in a trap from which there is no escape. We either sacrifice our art to stockbroking or some similar occupation and keep ourselves and our families in a reasonable state of comfort; or we repeat Gauguin's mistake in a world where innocence and naïvety no longer exist, where currency restrictions and exit-visas effectively deprive us of even Gauguin's illusion of liberty. Our immobilization is our rectitude, and I am suggesting that it is not a good ground for the criticism of Gauguin's moral failure. Let us turn to the art for which Gauguin endured everything, sacrificed everything and everybody.

It does not seem that Gauguin had any idea of becoming a painter before, at the age of 23, he entered a stockbroker's office and there met Emile Schuffenecker, a fellow employee who was an enthusiastic amateur painter. It was 'le bon Schuff' who first inspired him and always encouraged him. The pupil immediately revealed innate gifts and made rapid progress. Within four years he had had a painting accepted for the Salon. That was in 1876. The first impressionist exhibition had been held in 1874—it included, along with the work of artists now forgotten, paintings by Degas, Cézanne, Monet, Berthe Morisot, Pissarro, Renoir and Sisley. Gauguin became an enthusiast of the new school—he began to collect their paintings and to study the theories that inspired them. He cultivated the friendship of Pissarro, who could claim to be a Dane, having been born in the Danish West Indies, and was therefore a compatriot of Gauguin's wife.

* Trans. by Robert Burnett, in his *Life of Paul Gauguin*. London (Cobden Sanderson), 1936, p. 106.

Paul Gauguin

Pissarro introduced Gauguin to his fellow-impressionists, and he gradually became one of them, exhibiting with them for the first time in 1880. He was later to renounce impressionism, and to quarrel with most of the impressionists; but there is no doubt that for about ten years he was committed to the theory and the practice of this school. Degas remained his most admired master (and Degas repaid his admiration with a faith in Gauguin that survived the disappointment of most of his friends of this time); but Pissarro was the most direct influence to which he submitted. Late in 1883 Gauguin went to Rouen to be near Pissarro, and he carried his discipleship to the length of sitting side by side with Pissarro and painting the same subject*. These impressionist paintings of Gauguin's are not often seen by the public—they are mostly in Scandinavian collections—but they have considerable merits and give some substance to the view, which Pissarro among others held, that Gauguin was later misled by the false theories of art he adopted. A nude of 1880 now in the Carlsberg Glyptotek, Copenhagen, drew from Huysmans the declaration that no contemporary painter, not even Courbet, had rendered the nude with such vehement realism. Huysmans' description of the picture is in itself a piece of vehement realism.

The decisive change in Gauguin's style—it is not too much to call it a transformation—took place quite suddenly in the year 1888, and must be attributed to his meeting with a painter called Emile Bernard, already a friend of Van Gogh and a young man of great charm, fine sensibility and prodigious intelligence. At the age of twenty, as he then was, Bernard had already evolved a theory of art based on his passion for medieval stained glass, 'images d'Epinal' (coloured broadsheets), peasant art, Japanese woodcuts—a theory to which he gave the name 'synthetism'. It is based on the idea that the imagination retains the essential form of things, and that this essential form is a simplification of the perceptual image. The memory only retains what is significant— in a certain sense, what is symbolic. What is retained is a 'schema', a simple linear structure with the colours reduced to their prismatic purity. Maurice Denis, who became one of the adepts of the new theory, adds this useful gloss: 'To synthetize is not necessarily to simplify in the sense of suppressing certain parts of the object: it is to simplify in the sense of rendering intelligible.

* Reproduced (pls. 6 and 7) in *Camille Pissarro: Letters to His Son Lucien*, edited by John Rewald. London (Kegan Paul), 1943.

Paul Gauguin

It is in fact to . . . submit each picture to one dominant rhythm, to sacrifice, to subordinate, to generalize.'

It has been argued that Gauguin had arrived at these principles before he came under the influence of Bernard, and certainly some of the pictures he painted in Martinique in 1887 show a new emphasis on linear design, a greater simplicity of composition, and an increasing richness of colour. But they are still 'true to nature'—there is nothing schematic about them and no trace of the symbolism which makes a sudden appearance with paintings like *The Yellow Christ* and *Jacob wrestling with the Angel* (painted in 1888 and 1889). There can be no doubt that the influence of Bernard on Gauguin was profound and decisive. It completely obliterated the influence of the impressionists. Pissarro's comment, in a letter to his son Lucien, is a sad recognition of this fact:

'According to him [Albert Aurier, who had written an article on Gauguin in the *Mercure de France*], what in the last instance can be dispensed with in a work of art is drawing or painting; only ideas are essential and these can be indicated by a few symbols.—Now I will grant that art is as he says, except that "the few symbols" have to be drawn, after all; moreover it is also necessary to express ideas in terms of colour, hence you have to have sensations in order to have ideas. . . . The Japanese practised this art as did the Chinese, and their symbols are wonderfully natural, but then they were not Catholics, and Gauguin is a Catholic.—I do not criticize Gauguin for having painted a rose background nor do I object to the two struggling fighters and the Breton peasants in the foreground; what I dislike is that he copied these elements from the Japanese, the Byzantine painters and others. I criticize him for not applying his synthesis to our modern philosophy which is absolutely social, anti-authoritarian, and anti-mystical.—There is where the problem becomes serious. This is a step backwards; Gauguin is not a seer, he is a schemer who has sensed that the bourgeoisie are moving to the right, recoiling before the great idea of solidarity which sprouts among the people—an instinctive idea, but fecund, the only idea that is permissible.' *

This was written in April, 1891, about the time that Gauguin was embarking on the ship that was to take him to Tahiti—

* *Ibid.*, pp. 163–4.

before, therefore, the characteristic work of Gauguin that would justify such criticism had been painted. But in paintings such as the portrait of his friend Meyer de Haan (*Nirvana*, 1890—now in the Wadsworth Athenaeum, Hartford, U.S.A.) and *La Belle Angèle* (1898—now in the Louvre) he had already revealed the style based on the new theory, and all that Tahiti was to add was a more exotic, a more colourful subject-matter. The *Nirvana* of 1890 bears an astonishing resemblance to the *Contes Barbares* of 1902 (Folkwang Museum, Essen). When Gauguin met Bernard he had only fifteen more years to live: it is a period of complete consistency, of ideals once and for all conceived in their finality and carried through with an unrelenting power of will.

It will be noticed that Pissarro's criticism of Gauguin has two aspects—one is social and the other technical, and they remain the two aspects from which Gauguin's work can still be criticized. To what degree do we still feel them to be valid? There is no doubt that from the point of view of the 'socialist realist', Gauguin's later work represents a flight from reality; it is an escapist art. But I think it must be admitted that, on a large view of its history and development, one of the functions of art *is* to be 'escapist'. The world is apt to be 'too much with us', and we retreat into day-dreaming or fantasy as a natural reaction. Such reactions have a therapeutic value, a biological function; they are thus a part of the dialectical process of life itself. In this sense the landscapes of the gentle Pissarro are as much an 'escape' as the symbolic compositions of Gauguin. Gauguin's condemnation of modern society was as strong as Pissarro's and much more fiercely expressed. 'A terrible epoch is being prepared in Europe for the coming generation: the reign of Gold. Everything is rotten, both men and the arts. Here one is incessantly distracted.' Such were the reasons he gave (to the Danish painter Willemsen) for going to Tahiti. The mistake he made was to assume that 'there', in Tahiti, one could avoid the distractions of modern civilization. Unfortunately its evils are ubiquitous and Pissarro was right in believing that one has to fight it at the centre, with steadfastness and solidarity.

But the more serious criticism is the technical one. Pissarro was willing to accept the validity of a symbolic art, but the symbolism must be genuine (not taken over from past civilizations) **because only** a genuine symbolism could evoke in the painter the necessary 'sensations'—and without these sensations the painting would lack sensibility: it would be coarse and schematic. Admittedly Gauguin does not carry the research into the subtleties of sensation to the degree that Pissarro did, or Cézanne. That was not his aim. Nevertheless, carried away by the broad generalizations of criticism, it is easy to underestimate the purely 'painterly' qualities of Gauguin's work. A critic who in this respect was the most exacting I have ever known, the late Sir Charles Holmes, once pointed out that the best of Gauguin's works 'do very much more than combine formidable colour with striking and audacious design. They have real substance. The figures are admirably modelled in very low relief, and the paintings have a "complex" underlying their outward pattern. They seem haunted by some spell of savage magic and mystery, an indwelling spirit, which in this age of the sceptic and the materialist is naturally suspect. . . . Nor is his colour as simple as it seems. If we take the trouble to examine it closely we shall find that under its apparent crude force there are unexpected subtleties of gradation, the outcome of a deliberate refining process based on Gauguin's early Impressionist training. What looks like a vivid patch of pure yellow, for example, will prove to be modified towards one extremity by little touches of blue or green—at the other the modification may be red or orange. These interweavings, this ever-changing texture, give Gauguin's best works a subtlety which, added to his undeniable vitality and breadth, make him one of the men we should do well to consider seriously, whatever we may be told to his discredit.' *

I can add little to such an admirable summary. There is, however, in Gauguin's colour, a quality that might be characterized by the word 'resonance': it distinguishes him from all his contemporaries. When he was in Brittany he once wrote to his friend Schuffenecker: 'Quand mes sabots retombent sur ce sol de granit, j'entends le son sourd, mat et puissant que je cherche en peinture' ('When my sabots fall on this granite ground, I hear the heavy dull and powerful sound that I try for in painting'). Harmony is not confined to a restricted range of the colour-scale: it is not necessarily 'subdued' to a dominant tone—it can be keyed up to a vibrant pitch of primary oppositions, revelling in the richness of saturation rather than in a finesse of transitions. Finally, colour itself is (or can be) symbolic—as Gauguin realized

* *Old Masters and Modern Art: The National Gallery: France and England.* (Bell), 1927, p. 137.

(la couleur étant elle-meme énigmatique dans les sensations qu'elle nous donne, on ne peut logiquement l'employer qu'énigmatiquement). Colour no less than form has significance within the unconscious, and by a too conscious control (a 'scientific' control such as the Impressionist attempted) we may destroy its proper force.

The rhythmical quality of Gauguin's compositions is perhaps obvious enough, but it is one more technical accomplishment and, with the rest we have noted, disposes of the easy assumption that Gauguin was merely a 'literary' painter. Literary he certainly was—it was one of his deliberate aims to reinfuse painting with dramatic significance, but he never forgot that the drama must have form as well as substance. That he was a 'decorative' painter must again be admitted, and no doubt some of his qualities would have been better applied to monumental art rather than to the confined space of the cabinet-picture. 'Des murs, des murs, donnez-lui des murs,' cried his friend Albert Aurier.* Gauguin, like many another modern painter, would have been a greater artist if he had lived in a society willing and able to make use of his great gifts. But his fate was otherwise: he was condemned to live in an epoch that reserved for its artists all the most vicious instruments in its armoury of poverty and neglect.

* Quoted by Maurice Malingue: *Gauguin, le peintre et son oeuvre*. Paris and London (Les Presses de la Cité and James Ripley), 1948, p. 50.

8
Pablo Picasso

Pablo Picasso was born at Malaga on October 25, 1881. His mother's family had had in the past some connection with Genoa —hence the Italian form of the surname which Picasso eventually adopted. His father Blasco Ruiz y Etcheverria, was a drawing-master of Basque origin, and early taught Picasso the rudiments of the art. The family moved from Malaga to Pontevedra, to Corunna, and finally to Barcelona, where, at the age of fourteen, Picasso entered the School of Fine Arts. But his talent was already prodigious, and there still exist paintings done by him at this age which have all the sureness of a master's hand. After a few months at the Barcelona school, Picasso passed to the principal school of art in Spain at Madrid. In 1900 he made his first journey to Paris, and there, in the following year, he held his first exhibition. It was an immediate success. In 1904 he definitely took up his residence in Paris.

Picasso is not the first artist to shuffle out of the skin he was born in; artists in general have been rather prone to change their domicile. But such artists—an El Greco in Spain or a Holbein in England—have usually become in some degree naturalized, and have even, as in the case of El Greco, become exponents of some subtle aspect of the spirit of their adopted countries which hitherto had never been so well felt and expressed. When Picasso left Spain to settle in France, he did not become a Frenchman, but he ceased to be a Spaniard; he became a citizen of the world or, in the sense of that phrase, an artist of the world.

Up to this time, and until 1906, Picasso's work shows a certain consistency. It is usual to distinguish a 'Blue Period' lasting until 1904, and a 'Rose Period' lasting until 1906, but this is merely a distinction based on the predominant colouring of his paintings, and has no justification in method or form of composition. All his early work is manifestly traditional; that is to say, one can trace in it the influence of the great Spanish masters—Zurbaran, even

Pablo Picasso

Velazquez, and certainly Goya (as in the magnificent portrait of the Señora Ricard Canals in the Museum of Catalonian Art, Barcelona); and sometimes mingled with this strain, sometimes separate, the influence of the French Impressionists and Post-impressionists—the influence of Manet and Degas, and above all of Toulouse-Lautrec. The influence of Cézanne is not at first very decisive, but probably Picasso had not seen any of Cézanne's work before he first came to Paris in 1900, and may not have seen it in any quantity until 1904. Over the whole of this period the influence of Toulouse-Lautrec would seem to have been the most decisive. It shows itself above all in a predilection for the same subject-matter—types and genre-subjects from the music-halls, circuses and bars of Barcelona and Paris. Both in colour and com-position these paintings betray a psychological emphasis which some critics have not hesitated to call sentimental; and since there is a suggestion that the subsequent development of Picasso's style is in some sense a mask for this sentimentality, we must ask what such a criticism really implies.

Sentimentality is a desperate word to hurl at an artist of any kind, and nowadays we are all so sensitive about it, that the charge is very liable to produce inhibitions and distortions. We should, therefore, be quite clear what we mean by the word. It always implies some disproportion between an emotion and its cause. It is not suggested, for example, that the emotion of love is in itself sentimental; it only becomes sentimental when an object is unworthy of the kind and degree of love lavished upon it, as in the case of the English love of animals. Such a misapplication of love is due to a defect of judgment, and generally we may say that sentimentality is the display of emotion unchecked by rational judgment. Sentimental art in this sense is art which arouses these unchecked emotions, either directly or by association. Certainly some of Picasso's early pictures, those, for example, of blind men, and a well-known one, in the Chicago Art Institute, of an *Old Guitarist* (1903), come within range of this charge. The point to determine in any such case is, first, the validity of the emotion expressed, and, secondly, the aesthetic worth of the expression. If the aesthetic worth is nil, the question need not be discussed. If the aesthetic worth is considerable, as in the case of the *Old Guitarist*, then the only question is to what degree does the sentiment of the picture interfere with our aesthetic enjoyment. And that is probably a question for the individual; the normal person, I think, can stand a good deal of irrelevant sentiment, and even downright sentimentality, if the design and colour of the picture are of sufficient interest. But actually the question is more often than not automatically cancelled; for the great artist tends to become so absorbed in the purely aesthetic meaning of his picture, that he grows jealous of this subsidiary psychological interest, and gradually excludes it. This may not be true of all periods of art, but it is certainly true of modern art. Picasso, in this respect, merely repeats the development of Turner, Cézanne, or Matisse. Only the change, in his case, has a somewhat apocalyptic suddenness.

The years 1906–7 are sometimes called his 'Negro Period', and here and there, in the paintings and drawings of this time, one can trace the influence, more or less direct, of Negro sculpture, the artistic qualities of which were then becoming recognized. But such influences are completely absorbed in the general tendency towards abstraction of which Picasso was henceforth to be the leader. In a large canvas always discussed in books about Picasso, and now in the Museum of Modern Art, New York, *Les Demoiselles d'Avignon*, *'tableau capital de l'oeuvre de Picasso'*, painted in 1906–7, we have a broad flat design made up of five nudes and their fluttering draperies. The lines of their bodies and the folds of the draperies are angularized; the background and shadows are intensified to emphasize this geometric effect; the faces of the young ladies are a rather incongruous assembly of Negro masks. Apart from these masks, there is a complete disappearance of what I have called a psychological appeal, and even in the masks that appeal is disintegrating. The subject is meant to shock rather than to attract. But such a picture is only a transitional piece; more significant, for the future, are a series of still-lifes painted during 1907 and 1908, in which we see a patient simplification of the forms, tending towards an almost complete geometricization. In 1909 the process was applied to the human form. The logical end of this process was complete abstraction, and this was not an end that Picasso could accept.

The process was, of course, inherent in the practice of Cézanne, who had conceived the art of painting as the art of giving permanence and solidity to the immediate data of visual experience. Instead of catching the shimmering surface of appearances, the momentary effects of light and movement, Cézanne sought to reveal a permanent reality, to feel nature as eternal, and in this attempt he arrived, almost unconsciously, at something like a geometricization of objects; nature, he said, could be resolved into the cylinder, the sphere, and the cone. But that effect, with Cézanne, was a by-product of his primary aim, which was still to realize his sensations in the face of natural phenomena. Picasso, though he may have begun with a similar aim, and though some of his early cubist paintings succeed exactly as Cézanne's succeeded, carried the process a stage further. He found that the cylinder, the sphere, and the cone were satisfactory objects in themselves, and that out of such elements he could construct a design which conveyed all the purely aesthetic appeal inherent in any painting.

Though such a literal interpretation was novel, actually the theory which justifies such a step had been current for some time. Without, on this occasion, referring to its presence in Plato,* let me quote a paragraph from an essay written in England in 1877:

'Art, then, is thus always striving to be independent of the mere intelligence, to become a matter of pure perception, to get rid of its responsibilities to its subject or material; the ideal examples of poetry and painting being those in which the constituent elements of the composition are so welded together that the material or subject no longer strikes the intellect only; nor the form, the eye or the ear only; but form and matter, in their union or identity, present one single effect to the "imaginative reason", that complex faculty for which every thought and feeling is twin-born with its sensible analogue or symbol.'

Pater, from whose essay on *The School of Giorgione* this passage comes, has been so persistently misrepresented and misunderstood, that perhaps it is a mistake to resuscitate his theory, with all its melancholy aftermath of 'art for art's sake'. One does so in justice to Pater, and because his expression of the theory is not likely to be bettered. It is true that events since Pater's time have given a very different complexion to the theory, and probably he would not countenance the application we are now making. But theories, when they are logically incontrovertible, have the power of running away from their authors, and reaping whatever comes into their path. At the end of many centuries of critical consideration, and in virtue of a vast amount of accumulated wisdom, there seems no avoiding the conclusion, that if we

* Cf. *Art Now*, pp. 91-3.

are to keep our aesthetic judgments, whether in poetry, painting, or music, clear of all irrelevant facts, then those judgments must be based on the operative sensibilities, and on those sensibilities alone. No criticism that is not a criticism of form in its relation to subject-matter has ever advanced any of the arts a single step. The virtue of any art wholly inheres in its appeal to the senses and to the 'non-discursive' or 'imaginative' reason, and all other criteria, whether moral or sociological, are *aesthetically* irrelevant. It is criticism of a wider scope and a different kind that attempts to relate aesthetic values to their social environment—to explain the distortions which these values suffer in the historical circumstances of a particular period, and in the estimation of all succeeding periods. It is sometimes necessary, however, to maintain the antonomy of art, as of philosophy, however abstract and theoretical such an attitude may seem.

Such a distinction does not rest on the narrow basis of modern art. Any coherent conception of art extending beyond the Renaissance in Europe, and open to the appeal of Byzantine art, of Oriental art, of African art, of Palaeolithic art—indeed, of art wherever and whenever it issues from the clear perceptions and instinctive expressions of man, is based on aesthetic sensibility, and not on historical objectivity. Admittedly the word sensibility, in this context, includes such 'intellectual' reactions as are involved in the apprehension of formal relations; and art is a dialectical process which holds in suspense such 'identical opposites' as idealism and materialism, individuality and universality, reason and irrationality, romantic and classic—the whole logic of its intensity depending on such a resolution of conflicting elements.

Picasso's aim has always been to extend the material of the artist, to overcome the limitations of the normal equipment of the painter. From 1913 to 1915 he experimented in *papiers collés*, that is to say, in designs made up of coloured and printed papers, gummed on to a canvas or board, sometimes completed with details in oil or pencil. On the basis of these experiments we then have a series of paintings which create designs of a much more complicated structure and more varied texture. These were painted intermittently with a series of so-called neo-classic pictures, in which Picasso returns to a figurative or representational mode of painting, with classical themes as his subject-matter. Especially in the form of drawings and etchings, these exercises are strongly reminiscent of Greek vase paintings, or the engraved designs on Greek and Etruscan mirror-backs. Occasionally the themes are modern, as in the portraits of his wife and child, and of his friends and contemporaries, such as Stravinsky and Ansermet.

About 1925 Picasso began to paint a new type of abstraction, which calls for an entirely new theory of explanation. Such a theory is only offered to those who need an intelligent excuse for their aesthetic perceptions. Aesthetically, there is no difference between any of the forms art assumes, as Picasso himself has said. The only important distinction is that between nature and art, and once that distinction has been made, on the evidence of all art whatsoever, then the only difference between one form of art and another is the degree of conviction which it carries. 'From the point of view of art, there are no concrete or abstract forms, but only forms which are more or less convincing lies. That these lies are necessary for our spiritual being is beyond any doubt, because with them we form our aesthetic image of the world.'

This statement is taken from an interview which Picasso gave to a German art critic, Paul Westheim. The book in which it was published (*Künstlerbekenntnisse*: Berlin, Propyläen Verlag) bears no date, but from internal evidence it would seem that the interview was given before 1925, that is to say, before the decisive change in Picasso's style already mentioned took place. * But in this interview there is another statement of great psychological interest, which seems almost to anticipate the new style. Picasso says he cannot understand why so much importance is attached to the word 'research' in modern painting. Painting has nothing to do with seeking, but is concerned only with finding. 'Among the many sins charged against me, none has less justification than that which says the spirit of research is the most important element in my work. When I paint, I set about to indicate what I have found, and not what I am seeking. In art, to will is not enough. As we say in Spain: love is proved by deeds, not by arguments. What a man does is all that counts, not what he intends to do.

'We all know that art is not truth. Art is a fiction that enables us to recognize the truth—at least, such truth as is given to us to

---

* This 'interview' is based on a statement made in Spanish to Marius de Zayas and published in an approved translation in *The Arts*, New York, May 1923, under the title 'Picasso Speaks'. Cf. Alfred Barr, *Picasso: Fifty Years of His Art* (New York: Museum of Modern Art, 1946), pp. 270–1.

Pablo Picasso

understand. The artist must know her ways and means of convincing others of the truthfulness of his fictions. When his art only indicates that he has sought or investigated the best means of persuading other people to accept his fictions, then nothing is achieved.

'The idea of research has often led painting into error and forced the artist into fruitless lucubrations. This is perhaps the main fault of modern art. The spirit of inquiry has poisoned all those who do not fully grasp the positive and fundamental elements of modern art, for it has led them to wish to paint the invisible and therefore the unpaintable.'

At first this statement seems to be a complete denial of Picasso's practice during recent years. But all depends on what he means by the act of seeing. We see outwardly and represent the apparent nature of things; and we see inwardly and represent the world of the imagination. The mistake is to think, in the manner of the Impressionists, that there exists a more exact or more scientific mode of vision, which it is the business of the artist to exploit. Picasso's meaning is made quite clear from a later statement, reported by M. Zervos in *Cahiers d'Art* (1932). '*Je vois pour les autres*,' that is to say, as an artist he sees things which other people cannot see—he has visions, as we say—'*apparitions soudaines qui s'imposent à moi*.' He does not know in advance what he is going to put on the canvas, nor does he decide what colours to use. He does not will to do anything, he does not seek to do anything. He allows his sensibilities a free rein, paints in a trance—a trance which has all the acuteness, the visual definiteness of dreams. His only care is to be faithful to what is given, to what is found, to paint what he sees.

Those who are familiar with the paintings done by Picasso in this latest phase of his career will find any verbal description of them very inadequate, but in the absence of illustrations I must make some attempt to differentiate them from the normal type of abstract painting. The normal conception of an abstract picture is comparatively simple: it is the disposition, on a plane surface, of lines and colours in an aesthetically pleasing pattern. Logically, no further definition is necessary. The pattern may have some more or less remote relation to objects, but such a relationship is not necessary. The painting, like an eastern carpet, is a decorative design within a rectangular frame. As such it is completely justified as decorative art, but art gains an additional force if it expresses a subjective reaction to the objects of perception—if the artist adopts, as it were, an attitude of intellectual love towards the world of his creation. The transition from the decorative to the creative is not easy to explain in general terms: in Picasso's case it involved a renunciation of the will and a surrender to the promptings of the unconscious, which promptings, far from being decorative, are presumably symbolic.

The later pictures of Picasso differ from abstractions in that they have their origin in the observation of nature—they 'represent' something. This representation is often a strangely distorted female form; heads incomprehensibly interlocked or dislocated; swollen forms in which one can still distinguish a stretched mouth, an occluded eye; vague rhythmical shapes which can still be identified as a monstrous bust, a branch of leaves, a bowl of fruit, a guitar; gigantic sculptural figures built up with misshapen bones, or of bones with some complex function, like the bones of the ear; forms foetal and nightmarish, actual and vital. The colours in these compositions are clear and strident; the composition usually simple and architectural. More recently, as if not satisfied with the limitations of paint and canvas, Picasso has begun to model such conceptions in plaster, to cast them in bronze, to construct them in metals and any materials at hand.

Such works of art cannot be rationally explained without some theory of the unconscious origin of imagery. In the state in which he admittedly paints these pictures, Picasso is obviously in the condition of day-dreaming, perhaps a condition of self-hypnosis. Apart from any aesthetic considerations, the value of such art will depend on the significance of the imagery which he brings to the surface and transfers directly to his canvas. What can be affirmed, on the evidence of many people who have seen such paintings, is that their imagery has a very haunting quality. Whatever the nature of the vitality expressed by Picasso, it has an undoubted power of fascination. I do not think the purely aesthetic qualities in the paintings—their colour harmonies and formal arrangement —can be dismissed as unimportant in the total effect. Picasso is too essentially an artist ever to betray his innate talent for form and colour, and I should say that this talent is all the surer for being exercised under purely instinctive conditions.

The important qualification to make about such art—for Picasso's example in this respect as in all others has been quickly

Pablo Picasso

followed by a host of imitators—is that it should be involuntary. To will is not enough. Conscious research is fatal. The artist must paint what he finds; he must not seek for something he has not found. Not many artists are capable of observing those conditions; for they are the conditions of the rarest form of inspiration. 'The Genius of Poetry', wrote Keats, 'must work out its own salvation in a man. It cannot be matured by law and precept, but by sensation and watchfulness in itself. That which is creative must create itself.' That is true of all the arts, and Picasso, more abundantly than any of his contemporaries, has been creative, even to the extent of creating the art he practises.

Though he has extended the possible world of art, and brought within its scope material that was never thought of before, yet it is important to remember that Picasso retains all his previous conquests. The idea of an evolution in Picasso's art is, as he has declared, quite foreign to its nature. Extension is more than development. Everything Picasso creates comes from the same centre, a vital genius for all modes of plastic expression; even when, in the midst of painting the spectres of his unconscious intuition, he turns aside and makes a drawing which in grace and sensibility and objective truth not Ingres nor Raphael could excel. Every mode of expression is valid, and each is the man, who is to be accepted in all the fullness and complexity of his genius.

Picasso's protean diversity is, for his critics, one of his most baffling characteristics. No unprejudiced person can deny that in certain of his phases Picasso's talent as a draughtsman, as a painter, as a colourist, is unassailable. From his boyhood he has shown the prodigious infallibility of a genius. But a genius, say his detractors, can be perverse, and they claim the right to tell this genius when and where and why he is perverse.

This charge of perversity may be either moral or artistic. In most cases it is probably a confusion of the two—that is to say, the reaction is a moral one, for which the shocked (knowing their artistic manners) hasten to find an aesthetic sanction. But it is very difficult to find in this reaction any aesthetic criticism of a concrete technical kind. The composition of the paintings is not analysed and found wanting; there is no criticism of Picasso's colour harmonies, of his tones, of his painting technique. The criticism is all on a vague level of abuse—'extravagance',—'monstrous', 'hoax', 'insult', 'nonsense', 'nausea', 'presumptuous', 'horrors', 'freaks', 'tormented', 'bilious', 'squalid', 'corrupt': these

161

are the derogatory epithets actually used by the people who have taken the trouble to write to *The Times* about Picasso, and they are *the only kind* of epithets used by them. Such words do not belong to the vocabulary of art criticism—they are expressions of moral indignation.

There is one further point to notice about such controversy. People usually express their disapproval on a moral issue by 'cutting' the delinquent: they ostracize the guilty. But they do not 'cut' Picasso: they do not keep away from his degrading company. On the contrary, his 'corruption' seems to have an irresistible attraction for them, and they flock to his exhibitions in thousands.

This should put us on the track of a solution. We are attracted by the strange and the uncanny when it has some hidden significance for us. Whether it is the 'mystery' of religion, or the 'secrets' of a cult (devil-worship or freemasonry), there is always some appeal which overrides the rational faculties and makes contact with those mental layers which the psychologists call 'the unconscious'.

There is no doubt that Picasso, in one particular phase of his painting, is projecting images from his unconscious. We have already seen that he himself has given descriptions of his procedure in painting such pictures which show clearly that he paints in a state of trance, and that he accepts the images which he finds when his mind is in that state. Here, if they like, is legitimate ground for his critics to take their stand on. They can say that the artist should not indulge in such extra-rational or superrealist exercises. But let such critics be quite clear what they are saying and doing. They are issuing a moral command to the artist. They are saying that one part of reality is good and proper for depiction by the artist, another part taboo. In fact, the whole of this reaction has the character of a mass outcry against the offender against a taboo.

In my own opinion a painter should be at liberty to paint what he likes: if the public do not like what he paints, they need not take the trouble to look at it. Those who disapprove can ostracize the artist and leave those who approve his works to enjoy them in peace. But we who approve such works of art are quite willing to vouchsafe an explanation of our peculiarity. We do not all agree on the same explanation—why should we? I myself do not altogether agree with those critics who say that Picasso is expressing,

in these works painted 'between two charnel-houses', the reaction of a profoundly humanistic nature to the horrors and
cruelties that began at Guernica and continues in Korea. Picasso
naturally reacts powerfully to such events, but not so directly as
some of his exponents suggest. In these pictures he is not
merely a satirist.* Satire is an intellectual weapon and Picasso
is not an intellectual artist—he himself made that quite
clear in several published statements. But he is an artist who, by
intense concentration of his intuitive faculties, has gone very
deep beneath the surface of conscious perception, to explore the
terrain of the collective unconscious. It is in that terrain that we
find, according to the most profound psychologist of our time, the
specific symptoms of the psychic disorders of society. It is the
stresses and conflicts of that unassuaged chaos which find their
compensations in the physical horrors of war and persecution.
From that chaos Picasso has snatched his disturbing images—
images that are archetypal, spectres of the 'forest of the night' in
which we all wander, in which we are all lost unless saved by our
own powers of self-integration. Jung himself has said: 'We must
admit that the archetypal contents of the collective unconscious
often take a peculiarly grotesque and horrible form in dreams
and phantasies. Even the most rationalistic consciousness is not
proof against shattering nightmares, nor can it avoid being
obsessed by terrifying ideas.' (*Psychology and Alchemy*, Introduction.)

No wonder, then, that a public like the English, still to some
extent integrated on an ancient level of moral convention, should
profoundly resent these phantasies—they afflict their rationalistic consciousness. That consciousness is shaky now: its foundations have been eaten away and the flood of anxiety is rising.
Already the cry is heard: Every man for himself. We can only
save ourselves by contracting out of collective surrender: by an
integration of the personality. Part of the process of salvation is a
clear look into the abyss that opens up in front of the dis-
integrated, and that is precisely what Picasso has given us in these
works of 'fearful symmetry'.

---

* A recent (1951) painting of atrocities in Korea is an exception.

9
Paul Klee

Paul Klee was born in the German-speaking part of Switzerland
(at Münchenbuchsee, near Berne), on December 18, 1879. His
father came from Germany, his mother from Besançon in
France: the family was bilingual, and his mother claimed a
Mediterranean strain of which Klee seems to have been proud.
But Berne, where Klee went to school, is Germanic in its atmosphere (though it might be called specifically Swiss), and it was
to Munich that Klee, at the age of 19, went to study painting.
Thereafter, but for two intervals of five or six years,—the first
spent in travel, the second a consequence of the First World War
—he spent the whole of his active life in Germany. He was to die
in his native Switzerland during the Second World War, but it is
evident that, apart from any question of 'race', environment and
experience made Klee a German artist. Though the significance
of this fact must not be exaggerated, it is the first of three circumstances which determined the course of his development.

The second circumstance which we must take into consideration is a certain inherited talent. His father, Johann Wilhelm
Klee, was a musician and the descendant of musicians—a distinguished organist and conductor and teacher of singing. His
mother was also musical, and the whole social environment in
which Klee spent his early years was musical. Klee himself inherited the musical sensibility of his parents and was so gifted in
this art that until he left for Munich in 1898, it was uncertain
whether he would become a painter or a violinist. All his life he
remained an extremely talented violinist, a man to whom music
was a necessary mode of expression.

The third circumstance is a further contraction of the circle—it
is Klee's own temperament, which was psychically introverted,
and metaphysical in its modes of expression. The evidence for this
characteristic will be given presently, but let us first observe that
to be musical and metaphysical is to be consistently German, and
that it has often been suspected that these very qualities in the

Paul Klee

German race explain their relative deficiency in the visual arts. Whatever may be the value of such speculations within the range of such amorphous categories as nations, it is nevertheless certain that in the individual a disposition to express feelings and intuitions in concepts (that is to say, in *imageless* signs and symbols) is generally inconsistent with an ability to create plastic images of precision or vivid actuality. This is not to say that art cannot be created by conceptual types: there is metaphysical poetry, a fully recognized category; and there is metaphysical painting. The metaphysical poet—a Dante, a Donne, or a Shelley—succeeds in expressing thought in verbal symbols which have all the concreteness of images. There is a sense in which all great poetry is metaphysical, 'born', as Sir Herbert Grierson has so well said, 'of man's passionate thinking about life and love and death'. The point is, that if the thinking is passionate enough it succeeds in

> *Annihilating* all that's made
> To a green thought in a green shade.

Marvell's word, which I have emphasized, is exact. The images, in this kind of poetry, are fused to the thought: it is no longer a question of metaphor, or simile: the little word 'like', which separates whilst it compares, is abolished.

> My love is of a birth as rare
> As 'tis for object strange and high;
> It was begotten by Despair
> Upon Impossibility.

The metaphor can be unravelled, but it is not necessary: it is fused with the thought it expresses.

In a similar way, the metaphysical painter seeks to find some plastic equivalent, not for the content of the thought, but for its felt intensity. The 'idea' is not illustrated: the illustration is the idea.

Let us now try to trace Klee's development towards this type of expression.

Klee's earliest paintings were done under the immediate influence of his academic masters in Munich, from whom he derived no inspiration, no insight, no aesthetic revelation. Then came the visit to Italy—a transforming experience. Karl Nierendorf tells us* that 'Klee enjoyed life in southern ports such as Genoa, with its multitude of ships from all over the world. Siena and the old basilicas and cloisters, Byzantine and Christian art,

---

* 'Notes on Klee' in *Paul Klee: Paintings, Watercolours*, 1913–1939. Edited by Karl Nierendorf. (Oxford University Press. New York, 1941.)

Paul Klee

Coptic weaving and ancient calligraphy, all this gave him muc. more than the heroic monuments, equestrian bronzes, magnificent palazzi and Renaissance churches. An unforgettable and deeply moving experience was his visit to the famous Aquarium at Naples. . . . In a darkened room the unearthly world of the ocean appeared behind glass windows, close enough to make one feel the breath and the life of this monstrous fauna and weirdly demonic flora. How fascinating to watch a flower's transformation into an animal and to discover a rock to be a turtle or an old mossy fish.'

If Klee felt more attraction for such a living phantasmagoria than for the remains of a dead civilization, there is nevertheless evidence that he studied the art of the Renaissance to some purpose. The etchings which he did on his return show the decisive influence of fifteenth century engravings—the *Girl in the Tree* (*Dreaming*),* for example, a zinc etching of 1903, is based on Pisanello's *Allegory of Luxury* (a fact first pointed out by Miss Ruth S. Magurn of the Fogg Museum, Boston). In the next ten years Klee was to assimilate many such influences, but one must insist that assimilation means spiritual absorption and complete mental digestion. Goya, Blake, Redon, Ensor, Beardsley, Toulouse-Lautrec, Daumier, Doré, Munch, van Gogh, Cézanne, Matisse, Picasso—all these were successively his enthusiasms, and one could add other names which would not mean much to a public unfamiliar with German art at the turn of the century—Corinth, Slevogt, Klinger. But here we must make a distinction which is never sufficiently appreciated. There is a sense in which an artist can submit to only one influence and be so completely enslaved by it that his own personality is obliterated. And there is a sense in which an artist can submit to a multitude of influences and yet always remain himself. Klee is of this latter type.

This brings us to the necessity of defining Klee's personality. We must resort to Jungian psychology, and identify him as a representative of the introverted feeling type—that is to say, a type of personality whose mental functions are habitually based on feeling (rather than thought, sensation, or intuition) and whose relation to the perceptions which ensue is self-contained, introspective, subjective. In a type of this sort, the artist expresses himself in symbols which correspond to his inwardly apprehended feelings: he does not attempt to create symbols which correspond

* *The Prints of Paul Klee*, by James Thrall Soby. (New York, Curt Valentin, 1945, pl. 1.)

either to the objective correlates of his sensation (by imitating the appearance of what he sees), nor does he attempt to accommodate his feelings to a common language or convention. He creates symbols, as Klee once said, which reassure his mind. It is the typical form of musical expression, and that is why it came so naturally to Klee.

The evidence for this description of Klee's temperament can be found, not only in the whole of his work; not only in the descriptions of his character which have been given by his friends; but also in certain of his writings, which have survived and been published. Karl Nierendorf tells us that on his return from Italy Klee became completely absorbed in poetry and literature, 'consecrating himself to an intensive study of Poe, Baudelaire, Gogol, Dostoievsky, E. T. A. Hoffman and Byron'. Later the Voltaire of *Candide*, Aristophanes, and that poet of the absurd and the sinister, Christian Morgenstern. These writers have certain qualities in common: they are profound and at the same time light, philosophic yet sardonic, comically macabre. At the same time there is, in most of them, a lyrical element—I would not refuse that quality even to the author of *Candide*. These are precisely the qualities which Klee was to express in his paintings.

His mind finds further expression in the Diary published by Leopold Kahn in 1920,* but written in the years immediately following his return from Italy. This diary, which precedes in time all the outward manifestations of a revolution in art, is a clear expression of the inner necessity which was to lead, nearly ten years later, to the organized movements led by Kandinsky and Marc in Munich (*Der Blaue Reiter*), by Malevich and Tatlin in Moscow (Suprematism, Constructivism), by Picasso and Apollinaire in Paris (Cubism), Boccioni and Marinetti in Milan (Futurism).

In April, 1902, Klee wrote: 'A month has now elapsed since my trip to Italy. A review of my professional affairs is not too encouraging. I do not know why, but I am nevertheless still hopeful. Perhaps because criticism of my work, although almost totally destructive, now means something to me, whereas previously my self-deception admitted nothing.

'But by way of consolation, it is valueless to paint premature things: *what counts is to be a personality, or at least, to become one.* The domination of life is one of the basic conditions of productive

* *Paul Klee: Leben, Werk, Geist.* Potsdam (Gustav Kiepenheuer), 1920.

Paul Klee

expression. For me this is surely the case; when I am depressed I am unable even to think about it—and this holds true for painting, sculpture, tragedy or music. But I believe that pictures alone will abundantly fill out this one life. . . .

'I have to disappoint people at first. I am expected to do things a clever fellow could easily fake. But my consolation must be that I am much more handicapped by the sincerity of my intentions than by any lack of talent or ability. I have a feeling that sooner or later I shall arrive at something legitimate, only I must begin, not with hypotheses, but with specific instances, no matter how minute. If I then succeed in distinguishing a clear structure, I get more from it than from a lofty imaginary construction. And the typical will automatically follow from a series of examples.'*

This extract shows a very remarkable degree of self-realization for a young man of twenty-three, writing in the year 1902. The truth is that Klee had not succumbed to the classical tradition of Europe, as represented by all he had seen in Italy. He had had an oppressive sense of devitalization, of death. He felt the need for a new beginning, the need to cultivate the tiny seeds of a new organic life. In June of that same year he wrote:

'It is a great difficulty and a great necessity to have to start with the smallest. I want to be as though new-born, knowing nothing, absolutely nothing, about Europe; ignoring poets and fashions, to be almost primitive. Then I want to do something very modest; *to work out by myself a tiny, formal motive, one that my pencil will be able to hold without any technique*. One favourable moment is enough. The little thing is easily and concisely set down. It's already done! It was a tiny but real affair, and someday, through the repetition of such small but original deeds, there will come one work upon which I can really build.'†

These words, especially the sentence I have italicized, are prophetic: they do not describe the practice in 1902. For ten years Klee was to accumulate his little discoveries, his original needs, and only then did his pure and completely characteristic style emerge in all its integrity and originality. Will Grohmann has well said that there are no visible turning points in Klee's career; he lived and worked out of a fixed centre.‡ This centre was

* Trans. by Robert Goldwater and Marco Treves: *Artists on Art*. New York (Pantheon Books), 1945, p. 442.

† *Ibid.*

‡ *The Drawings of Paul Klee*. New York (Curt Valentin), 1944. German edition: Potsdam-Berlin (Müller und I. Kiepenheuer), 1954.

168

found in these early years of intense, quasi-mystical meditation. The outer rings are not so clearly marked—those uncertain experiences represented by his heritage of *Jugendstil* (*Art Nouveau*), by Expressionism (Munch, van Gogh), by Cézanne, by Cubism. When he joined the *Blaue Reiter* group in 1912, Kandinsky could still consider him 'at the beginning of his development'. He probably, at this time, found a considerable degree of intellectual support in the highly metaphysical theories of Kandinsky, whose *Art of Spiritual Harmony*, written in 1910, is the prolegomena to what, in this context, I am calling metaphysical painting. But Franz Marc and August Macke were equally capable of giving a theoretical exposition of basic ideas and intuitions, and it was during these years (1912–14) that Klee reached his full self-realization, his sureness of purpose and unfailing technical dexterity. In 1914 he and Macke went for a trip to Tunis, reaching Kairuan. To describe his stay in this fantastic city as a turning-point in Klee's life would again be wrong: it was rather that here he found the physical counterpart of that spiritual centre which he had already established within his being. The genius of the artist and the genius of the place coincided. The conformation of the houses and mosques, the battlements and the hills, the bright colours of the bazaars and the abstract Islamic calligraphy that everywhere met his eyes— these were the most exact expression of a vision that had hitherto been dreamlike or—if credence could be given to the legend of Arabic blood on his mother's side—some mental trace of an archaic heritage. The orientalism which had often been suggested unconsciously in his drawings and paintings could now be based on visual perceptions, on actual experience. So apocalyptic was this experience that a German art-historian, Wilhelm Hausenstein, made it the basis of a book on Klee which, although written twenty-five years ago, remains in many respects the most complete and understanding account of the painter and his work. *

Henceforth, save for the last few years, under the shadow of a Second World War, Klee's work was to be as effortless as speech or as calligraphy: a natural mode of expression once certain conditions were satisfied. Klee himself defined these—'The heart,' he said, 'must do its work undisturbed by reflective consciousness. To know when to stop is of the same importance as to

---

* *Kairuan, oder eine Geschichte vom Maler Klee und von der Kunst dieses Zeitalters.* Munich (Kurt Wolff), 1921.

know when to begin. To continue merely automatically is as much a sin against the creative spirit as to start work without true inspiration.' *

These are the conditions of all creative activity—in poetry, in music, in painting—even in science. But no man can live in a continuous state of inward communion, of such abstraction from practical affairs. Klee was to find a compensatory activity in teaching. †

* Quoted by Nierendorf, *op. cit.*, p. 25.

† Karl Nierendorf has given us a vivid picture of the life Klee was living before he became a teacher:

'It was in the spring of 1919 when I found out that he had the same address as Rainer Maria Rilke, who at this time was the idol of us all and whose poems we recited by heart. A house that could attract my two favourite artists should certainly have something of the unusual. I imagined it to have at least a kind of rustic charm or the patina of an old garden-house. But instead I found a rather average, unpretentious apartment house situated in Schwabing, the artists' quarter of Munich. The stairway was gloomy, prosaic and a little oppressive. Klee himself opened the door. He was of slight build and of solemn grace. His roughly woven brown suit only strengthened his resemblance to a young monk of Franciscan gentility, who once had guided me through the Roman Catacombs. That this association came to mind was not pure accident. Klee definitely had something of a monk, devout and kindly—an air which Hausenstein and others were obliged to term "near holiness". At this time Klee was very poor, and upon entering the semi-darkness of his studio, I recall Rilke's eulogy of the resplendent inner grandeur which poverty may bestow. It was late in the afternoon and the window facing the court did not provide much light, but the warm reflections of an invisible sunset cast its soft gold-tones into the room which strangely seemed to come to life with its own glow. There were primitive Bavarian paintings on glass, masks, collected nature objects, his own humorous figurines and constructions in wire, wood and plaster, a touching photograph of his mother in all her strange southern beauty, shining paint-tubes, opalescent shells, and a profusion of multi-coloured beloved little things. The dynamic spirit of the "Blue Rider" caught in these fanciful objects reached a crescendo of colour in paintings by Jawlensky, Kandinsky and other friends. The dark lustre of a grand piano balanced by contrast the smaller, brilliant notes and gave a solemn background to the most cherished of Klee's worldly goods, his precious old violin, enshrined in a silk-lined case. On top of the piano, it occupied the very centre of the room and thus seemed to polarize in its mild light all of the twilight's atmosphere which was vibrant with so much inner radiance.

'Fascinated and caught by the unexpected transfiguration I nearly forgot the presence of the artist. Yet there he was—quiet, in silence, as if reluctant to break the spell of the hour. The more the dusk deepened, the more translucent his pale bearded face emerged from the darkness. He seemed to be a part of the whole and yet to transcend it. The lights of his eyes and the burning embers of his pipe shone through the slowly floating clouds of smoke. He seemed to be completely absorbed in a kind of Bergsonian empathy with the universe of his own creation. Phosphorescent green orbs appeared and darted away again with the moving shadow of a large cat who found her final vantage point on the piano. From there she stared, transfixed, at her master's face.'

Paul Klee

In 1920 Walter Gropius invited him to join the staff of the Bauhaus, the school of design which was to have such a decisive effect on the development of architecture and the industrial arts in Europe. It was a happy choice—Klee proved to be an inspiring teacher, inspiring his pupils with enthusiasm and practical imagination. But once again we are brought up against the funamentally metaphysical strain in Klee's mentality. A lecture which he gave in 1924 has survived and has recently been published.* It is a work which only a German philospher could have conceived —full of that transcendental phraseology which defies exact translation into more concrete languages such as French or English. His main concern is to elucidate the part played by associative elements in art, which he rightly regards as the source of the most passionate misunderstandings between the artist and the layman. Though they may lead the layman astray, to a literary interest in art, they lead the artist into new worlds of form—to a kind of conceptual imagination which is capable of creating new worlds, or organic variations of the existing world. But these concepts can only be expressed in the concrete terms of line, chiaroscuro and colour. Klee describes the elements of composition as analysed by him in his classes at the Bauhaus, and all this part of the lecture is a clue to his own methods of composition. He lays particular emphasis on *mobility*, a quality which corresponds to the flexibility, or lability, found everywhere in nature; and on the patience and discipline necessary to discover the right formal

* *Uber die Moderne Kunst.* Bern-Bümpliz (Verlag Benteli), 1945. English trans. by Paul Findlay, London (Faber & Faber), 1948. The following paragraph from my Preface to this edition may perhaps be usefully repeated here:
'To explain art—that, for Klee, meant an exercise in self-anàlysis. He therefore tells us what happens inside the mind of the artist in the act of composition—for what purposes he uses his materials, for what particular effects gives to them particular definitions and dimensions. He distinguishes clearly between the different degrees or orders of reality and defends the right of the artist to create his own order of reality. But this transcendental world, he is careful to point out, can only be created if the artist obeys certain rules, implicit in the natural order. The artist must penetrate to the sources of the life-force—"the power-house of all time and space"—and only then will he have the requisite energy and freedom to create, with the proper technical means, a vital work of art. But "nothing can be rushed". Klee, with a clarity and humility not characteristic of many of his contemporaries, realized that the individual effort is not sufficient. The final source of power in the artist is given by society, and that is precisely what is lacking in the modern artist—"Uns trägt kein Volk". We have no sense of community, of a people for whom and with whom we work. That is the tragedy of the modern artist, and only those who are blind to their own social disunity and spiritual separateness blame the modern artist for his obscurity.'

171

means of representing the reality which underlies the confusion of impressions, and which is only to be seen in secret vision.

Klee's lectures at the Bauhaus were illustrated with sketches and diagrams which had all the subtlety and charm of his less pedagogical work: they serve to illustrate once more the fact that he was inspired by conceptual rather than perceptual processes. If any further proof of this fact is required it may be found in the importance which Klee attached to the titles he always gave to his pictures. He once confessed:*

'I do not think that the titles of my pictures are exactly what everybody would like them to be, but since for me the painting itself is primordial, since my subtitles illustrate my painting and I consequently do not make an illustration after a given text, it may very well be that such and such a person may see in one of my pictures something which I myself do not see at all.' This means that we are not to take the picture as an illustration, in the literal sense of the idea expressed by the title. The titles are often merely descriptive of the object represented, as *Temple near the Water*, or *Bathing Beach at St Germain*, but others more characteristically are clues to a state of mind, a metaphysical category or an imaginative invention—*Idiot Dwarf in a Trance*, *Visage of a Flower*, *The Vigilant Angel*. In this respect they are like the titles of modern poems: they provide an emotional *leit-motiv*, not a descriptive label.

Klee taught for twelve years at the Bauhaus, first in Weimar, then in Dessau. When the Bauhaus was suppressed in 1932, Klee went to Düsseldorf, where he taught for about a year. But the atmosphere in Germany had grown oppressive; Klee's friends were being driven into exile. His own work was condemned; he felt compelled to resign his post at the Düsseldorf Academy. He returned to his native Switzerland and lived modestly in the suburbs of Berne. But he was now a sick man and he died on the 29th June, 1940, at Muralto, near Locarno. His work in these last few years takes on a new quality—stronger, coarser, more powerful, more morbid. Klee's work, for all its fantasy and super-reality, was never an escape world: the threat of war, the dark emanations of the unconscious, the grotesque and the erotic, suffering and death, all find a place in his microcosm. And yet it is humour, sometimes sardonic, more often gay, that predominates.

* To Hans Schiess. See 'Notes sur Klee', Cahiers d'Art, 5–8, Paris, 1934. Quoted by Soby, *op. cit.*, p.v.

Paul Klee

It would not serve much purpose to divide Klee's work into categories. He used every conceivable technique and often invented his own. He combined these techniques in unexpected ways, so that often the cataloguer has to use the convenient phrase, 'various mediums'. He nearly always worked on a small scale —18 in. x 12 in. is probably the average. Some critics have considered this a limitation, as though genius were to be measured by a ruler. Great poetry does not need big print, nor does great painting need acres of canvas. It is the still small voice that is the most penetrating.

Klee is now recognized as one of the great masters of modern painting. Of all the groups which have contributed to that complete 'transvaluation of all values' which the modern movement in art represents, it seems to me that the four painters who came together in Munich in 1912 had the clearest realization of its philosophical basis. Marc and Macke were killed in the First World War. There is a consistency in the development of the two survivors, Kandinsky and Klee, which can only be explained by an inner certainty or conviction, the essence of which is their experience 'that what matters in the end is the abstract meaning or harmonization' of a picture. On that conviction—we may call it a dogma—the whole structure of modern art depends. Once it is understood and accepted, its manifestation in the work of an artist like Klee becomes an everlasting delight.

10
Paul Nash

i

After the passage of more than thirty years, during which we have endured the obliterating experiences of two world wars, nothing is so difficult to reconstruct as the hopes and aspirations of an age ignorant of all that was in store for it. It was an age of peace and security, of complacency and priggishness: and a young man who decided to become an artist in such an atmosphere was faced by problems which are no longer real to us, and which, even if we could revive them in all their urgency, would seem merely futile. The artist whose work we are now going to consider was born in 1889. After an unsuccessful effort to train for the Navy, and a short but aimless period at St Paul's School, he decided, in the year 1907, to become an artist, and went to the Chelsea Polytechnic to acquire the necessary skill. He sprang from a background which was typically English—the Navy, the Law, the Land, a substantial house in Kensington, a country retreat in Buckinghamshire.

Whistler was dead: art in England was dormant. It was a world in which the sprightly academicism of Augustus John could excite the cognoscenti. Ricketts and Shannon, Conder and the Rothensteins—these were the shimmering stars in a twilight through which the sinister figures of Oscar Wilde and Aubrey Beardsley still seemed to slouch. Walter Sickert was the closest link with reality—the reality of Degas and Manet, but Sickert was not then taken so seriously as of late. It may be a little out of proportion in an essay devoted to another artist, but I would like to quote a criticism of Sickert which George Moore wrote in that doldrum epoch: it will serve as well as anything to give us the atmosphere of the period.

'According to his aestheticism any grey tint will do for the sky provided the paint is nicely laid on, and with brown and a little Indian red the roofs and the shadows can be achieved. His one preoccupation is beauty of touch, and he gets it in the curve of the pavement. He has invented a formula which leaves out almost

174

everything, and is therefore suitable to his own talent and to the talents of a large following, principally ladies. For the last seven summers his pupils have been painting in our streets, and they have left London seeking gable ends in all the old English towns; they have spread over the continent; Dieppe has not a wall left unpainted; they have reached Venice, and St Mark's affords endless opportunities for their art; they have gone on to Constantinople and to Egypt, applying their method unembarrassed by the fact that in Egypt the relations of the sky and earth are the reverse of what they are here. . . But truth of effect does not trouble them. The strip of grey that sets off the tower in Smith's Square, Westminster, furnishes an equally truthful background for the domes and minarets of Egypt; and hundreds of small pictures of unvarying merit are brought back—faint designs in gold frames, inoffensive always, and sometimes soothing to the eye.' *

George Moore was trying to persuade young English painters that it was not necessary to trail to that mecca of the art student —Julian's studio in Paris: they should rather stay in England and study 'the naïve simplicity' of our own tradition. It is possible that Paul Nash heard this advice and took it to heart. He was, at any rate, to remain uncompromisingly English. He had a family link with Edward Lear, as English a genius as anyone could find, and he often, in the impressionable years, gazed at Lear's watercolours which hung on the walls in his aunt's house. But the artist's earliest efforts recall a simplicity still more naïve—the idyllic mysticism of Blake's wood-engravings. I do not think Paul Nash has ever lost that element—it is the substance of the charge that he is a literary painter, about which I shall have something to say presently.

The one revolutionary event in those precataclysmic days was the Post-Impressionist Exhibition held at the Grafton Galleries from November, 1910, to January, 1911, followed and reinforced by a second and more extreme exhibition held in the same place in the following autumn. When the history of English art in the early twentieth century comes to be written, a very interesting and very entertaining chapter will have to be devoted to the immediate reception and permanent effects of this demonstration†

* *Impressions and Opinions* ('Une Recontre au Salon').

† This has now been done by Benedict Nicolson in *The Burlington Magazine*, ol. XCIII (Jan., 1951), pp. 11-15.

—it was more than an exhibition: it was a campaign conducted with terrifying critical din. In a manifesto printed in the catalogue of the second exhibition Mr Clive Bell could cry: 'The battle is won. We all agree now that any form in which an artist can express himself is legitimate, and the more sensitive perceive that there are things worth expressing that could never have been expressed in traditional forms.' It was in this year of excitement that Paul Nash himself was first introduced to the world, in a modest exhibition of landscape drawings and watercolours at the Carfax Gallery. The forms seemed traditional enough, but the discerning critic could perceive a quality in some of the drawings which, though in no way related to the Post-Impressionist Movement, was too imaginative to be included within the academic conventions. The discerning critic, at this time, happened to be William Rothenstein, who bought a drawing in chalk, pen and wash, called *The Falling Stars*, which, however jejune it may now appear in view of the artist's later development, deserves to be carefully considered as a revelation of the artist's original tendency. It shows two contorted pine-trees moulded in ghostly moonlight against a night sky, across which two falling stars trace their burning way. The technique is summary—no striving after 'beauty of touch'. It is the technique of Blake, an art of imagination and outline, of imagination given visual precision.

The Carfax Exhibition was a considerable success for a young and unknown artist. Nash was now invited to exhibit with the New English Art Club, and his work for a time took on a 'New English' quality: that is to say, it became more precise, more objective, more decorative, more eclectic.

If the world of summer 1914 had not ended so dramatically, Paul Nash might have continued to paint pictures in the genteel idiom of the New English Art Club. But in September of that year he joined the Artist Rifles, was some time afterwards given a commission in the Hampshire Regiment, and eventually saw active service in France. Invalided home in the summer of 1917, he held a small exhibition of drawings he had made in the trenches, and this aroused so much attention that he was made an official war artist and returned to the Front in October. He made a large number of sketches and notes, and these formed the basis of a series of watercolours, lithographs and oil paintings which was exhibited at the Leicester Galleries in May, 1918.

Paul Nash

I had myself just returned from the Front, and it is perhaps worth recording that my interest in Paul Nash's work dates from this time. I was in no mood for any falsification of this theme: I wanted to see and hear the truth told about our hellish existence in the trenches. As I have recorded elsewhere,* I was immediately convinced by the pictures I then saw, 'because there was someone who could convey, as no other artist, the phantasmagoric atmosphere of No Man's Land'. Other artists were to depict the psychological horrors of war—especially the poets and novelists—but the aspect which Paul Nash revealed was the outrage on Nature—the Nature which had been so delicate and sensuous to New English eyes. The revulsion which we had experienced could not have been more violent. Here, for example, are the feeble words in which I myself had tried to convey our outraged feelings: they come from a narrative which I was writing at the Front about the same time that Paul Nash was making his sketches:

'All was black and upriven. In the valley the shell-holes were full of water and reflected the harsh cold sky. Devil's Wood was a naked congregation of shattered trunks, like an old broken comb against the skyline. An emotion—a sudden realization and anger —flushed his brain. This was his earth, earth of lithe green trees, earth of vigorous sap and delicate growth. Now riven and violated: a wide glabrous desolation: a black diseased scab, erupted and pustulous . . .' Such words defeat their purpose, simply because the reader does not believe in their objectivity. But Paul Nash's pictures were, as I have said, immediately convincing. There was selection and formalization, as there must be in all art. But there was the direct communication of truth, and therefore of emotion. Our experience had been recorded—recorded for as long as our civilization cared to preserve the historical truth. Luckily this was generally recognized at the time, and before the war ended Paul Nash had been commissioned to paint important panels for the Imperial War Museum and the Canadian War Records. And meanwhile the artist himself had emerged from relative obscurity to the front rank of English painters.

I have described these war paintings as formalized. There was formal composition in the traditional sense, but there was also evidence that the experience of war had not altogether obliterated

* *Paul Nash:* a Portfolio of Colour Plates with an Introduction by Herbert Read. London (Soho Gallery), 1937.

the experience of post-impressionism. The formalism tended towards certain simplifications and emphases of a geometrical nature which could only have their origins in the cubism of Picasso and Gris: perhaps also in the futurism of Boccioni and Severini. This cubist influence has persisted all through Paul Nash's development, but it was never stronger than in the period succeeding the war—a period which culminates in an exhibition held at the Leicester Galleries in 1924. Again one must try to re-create a mood—the mood of the artist suddenly released from the limitations and frustrations of war, facing the future in a spirit of new hope and aspiration. The realism of our experience had made us idealists at heart: we bounded forward with renewed confidence, founding magazines, organizing societies and exhibitions, relentlessly experimenting with new forms and techniques. Eliot's first poems had appeared, and Joyce's *Ulysses* was being serialized in *The Egoist*. For a time we were only too eager to forget the war—to bury our horrible memories. It was not until 1924 or 1925 that the war became a possible— or at any rate a popular—subject again. Meanwhile Paul Nash was casting round with restless energy for an appropriate activity. He began to design for the theatre and for textiles. (He was responsible for the scene and costumes in the fantasy Barrie wrote for Karsavina, which was produced with music by Bax in 1920; he also designed scenes and costumes for *A Midsummer Night's Dream* and *King Lear* in the Players' Shakespeare Series, edited by Granville Barker.) He found a sympathetic medium in wood-engraving and exploited his distinctive talent for book illustration (he illustrated the Nonesuch Press edition of *Genesis*, 1923—the first of a famous series of illustrated books—and made several drawings for T. E. Lawrence's *Seven Pillars of Wisdom*). But all these activities were subordinate to the main business of painting, and it was in the oils and watercolours of this period that his more profound intuitions found expression.

I use the doubtful word 'intuition' because what we are concerned with in the most distinctive work of Paul Nash must be called an intuition of the *genius loci*. That faculty of apprehension was already present in the war landscapes, though we do not willingly ascribe 'genius' to that particular 'locus'. But now that the artist was in England again, in woods and valleys from which the evil spirits had long ago absconded, the faculty could work with more joyful effect, to reveal the immemorial values in the

Paul Nash

natural scene. The first landscapes after the war are still deliberately formalized. The pattern of drooping boughs and fan-shaped foliage is sophisticated: it is imposed on the natural facts, not emergent from them. But between the landscapes of 1919 or 1920, and the *Pond* or the *Chilterns Under Snow* of 1923, a significant change has taken place. The formal element is still emphatic, as it is in Cézanne, in all 'intuitive' painters: there is still a trace of wilful arabesque: but in general the natural fact, in a word the truth, is in control. This achievement is all the clearer in a series of paintings made at Dymchurch in Kent in the year 1923. Superficially, these are among the most formal and geometric of the artist's works. Nevertheless, the form is inherent in the scene—in the long, low level stretches of the beach, in the linear perspective of the sea-wall. Here were natural elements which lent themselves without distortion to the tendency towards abstraction which the post-impressionist movement had inherited from Cézanne. In so far as the abstraction was inherent in the scene it might be said that the artist's task was made easy for him: he could get his abstract effect without too much distortion. But the ease of this particular solution only served to make clear to the artist that success depended on the reconciliation of form and fact; and when, after this enlightening experience, he began to range over a vastly wider variety of scene, he still carried with him the secret of that success.

The succeeding four years were as experimental as any that went before, but the search was for subject rather than treatment. The period begins with a five-months' stay in the south of France, during which material was collected which was to last for many bleak days in England. It is a period of widening contrasts. By the beginning of 1927, the tendency to abstraction seems to have given way entirely to a free 'painterly' style— almost to the aestheticism of 'touch', 'so soothing to the eye'. The first still-lifes belong to this period, and again show a restless experimentation—from the Cézannish *Still-life* in the Richard Wyndham collection by way of the plastic *Dahlias* and *St Pancras Lilies* to the autumnal *Swan Song* with its anticipations of a surrealist phase—all three paintings belonging to the same year, 1927. With the *Swan Song*—painted at Iden near Rye in Sussex —the way seems open to an imaginative freedom of treatment far removed from the artist's earlier style. But actually the geometric tendency was first to flare up again, and a series of still-lifes, of which the *Dead Spring* of 1928 is typical, was to intervene. At first sight these rigid architectural structures, in which instruments of precision sometimes make a symbolical appearance, are far removed from the irrational composition of *Swan Song*. But they can nevertheless be described as an attempt to carry the urge to abstraction into the realm of fantasy. The transit was successfully made in the drawings which Paul Nash made for the La Belle Sauvage edition of Sir Thomas Browne's *Urn Burial*, a book which will always be treasured, for it is one of the loveliest achievements of contemporary English art. In a drawing like *The Soul Visiting the Mansions of the Dead* Paul Nash evolved a completely original fantasy. It may seem to owe something to Chirico or Giacometti, but one has only to compare this drawing with the *Atlantic* which immediately precedes it to see that the fantasy actually emerges out of the objective observation of fact: and the ambivalence thus established was in effect a personal discovery of the essential truth which was at this time being advanced by the surréalistes in France—I mean their insistence on the contemporaneity of the rational and the irrational, of reality and the dream.

In the next few years Paul Nash was to travel a good deal, sometimes in search of health, sometimes for pleasure, and once, when he went to America in 1931 as member of the International Jury of Award at the Pittsburgh International Exhibition, *en mission*. In 1934 he spent a short time in Spain and Morocco, after a longer stay for medical treatment in Nice. But he was now too well launched on a voyage of imagination to be visibly affected by a change of terrestrial scene. He was now conscious of his course, of his artistic destiny. And it was a destiny which he felt to be peculiarly English. Early in this year, 1933, he had taken a leading part in the formation of a new group of English artists—painters, sculptors and architects—which adopted the name UNIT ONE. In a letter which appeared in *The Times* on June 2 he announced the formation of the group in terms which were not only uncompromisingly nationalist, but included a definition of purpose which showed how consciously representative our artist had become:

'Only the most stubborn can dispute that English art has always suffered from one crippling weakness—the lack of structural purpose. With few exceptions our artists have painted "by the light of Nature". . . . This immunity from the responsibility of design has become a tradition; we are frequently invited to admire the "unconscious" beauties of the British School—"so faithful to Nature". Nature we need not deny, but art, we are inclined to feel, should control.

'This precept is in danger of being forgotten. About every seven years English art goes back on her tracks. She has never forgotten that she invented Impressionism and Pre-Raphaelitism and, inevitably, she seeks to revive the favourite forms of expression. It may be observed that we are now heading for a new revival, either of one or both; in any case, the Nature cult in some form or other. Against this are opposed a few artists anxious to go forward from the point they have reached, instead of turning with the tide. The fact that some of them have come through many phases and arrived at a so-called abstract expression is not important; they have come through and wish to go on. This tends to isolate them from the majority of their contemporaries. They discover that what they stand for is decidedly at variance with the great Unconscious School of Painting; also, they seem to be lacking in reverence for Nature as such. These facts are frequently pointed out to them. Their answer is that they are interested in other matters which seem to them more engrossing, more immediate. Design, for instance—considered as a structural pursuit; imagination, explored apart from literature or metaphysics.'

Most manifestoes are read with embarrassment ten years after their appearance, but this one by exception still rings true. The Unit itself was doomed to early disruption: the causes had little to do with the principles it professed. Three years later it looked as though it had been completely submerged under a wave which had been gathering weight and force outside our shores—surrealism. Paul Nash accepted an invitation to participate in the Surrealist Exhibition of 1936, where design, considered as a structural pursuit, seemed to be the remotest of objectives. For a year or two the English tradition was lost in a cauldron of excitement—premonitory of the international chaos that was to be let loose in September, 1939. How, it may be asked, could an artist who had so recently declared himself in favour of a structural purpose in art, and of an imagination free from metaphysics, now subscribe so openly to the apotheosis of unreason? To answer that question we must look a little closer at the terms involved in such an apparent contradiction.

Paul Nash

I would say myself that there is no real contradiction between art, conceived as design, and the unconscious. The unconscious does, in fact, reveal design. Not only is the dream, when understood, a dramatic unity, but even in its plastic manifestations the unconscious possesses a principle of organization. This is too complicated a fact to demonstrate in an essay devoted to another subject, especially as the whole question is still incompletely explored and debatable. But it should be obvious that a declaration in favour of the structural principle does not necessarily exclude the intangible elements of the imagination. A painter so dedicated to the *genius loci* was never likely to compromise this aspect of reality.

At the end of his contribution to UNIT ONE, Paul Nash describes an experience and defines an attitude which fully anticipates any of the work which, during the next five years, was to be dubbed 'surrealist':

'Last summer I walked in a field near Avebury where two rough monoliths stand up, sixteen feet high, miraculously patterned with black and orange lichen, remnants of an avenue of stones which led to the Great Circle. A mile away, a green pyramid casts a gigantic shadow. In the hedge, at hand, the white trumpet of a convolvulus turns from its spiral stem, following the sun. In my art I would solve such an equation.' *

The art of these five years, 1934 to 1938, succeeds in solving such equations. The natural organic fact, the present life of flower and leaf, invades the animistic landscape, the habitation of familiar spirits. The shell, the fossil, the withered stalk, fungus, tree and cloud, are so many elements in a druidic ritual. The synthesis, the solution of the equation, is not literature: it is not metaphysics. It may be magic, but, if so, it is only reviving the first and most potent function of art.

These years had seen exhibition after exhibition, and full recognition in all the officially organized international events of the art world. Many public collections, at home and abroad, had acquired the artist's work, and it had indeed never been lacking in what might be called collector's appeal. At any time in the past fifteen years Paul Nash might have rested on his laurels, content with some arrested cliché of expression. That, indeed, is what the public likes, and only a few artists are sufficiently strong in will

* *Unit One: the Modern Movement in English Architecture, Painting and Sculpture.* Edited by Herbert Read. London (Cassell), 1934.

Paul Nash

and inspiration to drive on in restless imaginative research. A new war came and Paul Nash was inevitably selected as one of the first official artists. New subjects served as so many new facets in which the development of his artistic vision was reflected. His first war work was done for the Air Ministry, but there could be no question of subordinating imagination to reportage. The wrecked aeroplane was one more monolithic object, fallen unexpectedly from the sky, but endowed with an additional mystery, ominous and deathly. A dump of wrecked German planes fell into the geometrical design first extricated from the sea at Dymchurch, twenty years before: but this time it was a Dead Sea, metallic waves harbouring no life, for ever devoid of movement. But soaring in the clouds the aeroplane is animated, becomes an immense sword-fish or vulture, alive with the electric voracity of animals that inhabit the extreme elements.

In the midst of this specialized work the normal activity of the artist's imagination has continued. New equations have been solved. The artist's environment is still his pre-occupation: landscape his favourite theme. The watercolour technique has grown more subtle, the touch of the brush feathery, the colours falling on the paper as gently as snowflakes. It is the English idiom, which the artist himself has described as 'a pronounced linear method in design, no doubt traceable to sources in Celtic ornament, or to a predilection for the Gothic idiom. A peculiar bright delicacy in the choice of colours—somewhat cold, but radiant and sharp in key.' Paul Nash had passed his fiftieth year, but his art showed no decline of imaginative invention or of technical efficiency. Though often interrupted by illness, he showed a consistent devotion to his art, and the corpus of his work, in a wide range of traditional and experimental media, is impressive. It might be objected that the scale is seldom grandiose —a painting like *The Battle of Britain* (48×72) is exceptional. But the artist is often frustrated in this respect, for, however congenial to his talent and tempting to his ambition, the fact is that the grandiose in painting is not compatible with contemporary moods, nor with contemporary habits. Our expression is, as Paul Nash himself has said, 'almost entirely lyrical'.

I write, not as a painter, nor even as someone particularly knowledgeable about the technique of painting: I write as a poet, and that is perhaps why the art of Paul Nash has always had a special appeal for me. But it would be doing him a disservice if I allowed it to be assumed that this involves a limitation. Pictures are not made for painters, nor are poems written for poets, though a certain 'mystery' belongs to every craft. The appeal of any art is to the total sensibility: to the senses as the instigators of mind and emotion. To say of a painter that he is poetic is to describe a quality, not of his art, but of his imagination. The imagination is of many kinds, but 'poesis' is its creative or structural aspect. Poetry is intuition, invention, the active aspect of imagination: poetry can be translated into words, or into sound, or into form and colour. Poetry is the original quality of all the arts, and to describe a painter's work as poetic is to relate it to the source of all inspiration.

ii

The foregoing pages were written while Paul Nash was still alive (he died on July 11, 1946). But what is written whilst an artist is alive can sometimes be repeated with different emphasis when he is dead. It is not that the presence of the artist—in this case an intimate friend of the critic—affects the sincerity of what one may venture to say, either by way of praise or censure: that would be a miserable abdication of the rights of a friend no less than of the duties of a critic. It is simply that in one case the subject is vital and responsive: one writes with an eye on a living, developing personality. In the other case the subject has become historic, a part of that objective reality we call the Past. One must now judge rather than estimate: measure and classify rather than sympathize and encourage. Some writers welcome this freedom, but since it is the work of a man who was my friend that is to be the object of my dispassionate analysis, I confess to a certain reluctance.

I might, perhaps, begin with an example of a criticism which, during Paul's life-time, I expressed with reserve or even left unexpressed. The case was made more difficult because what I believed to be a limitation which, if recognized, was a source of peculiar strength, appeared to the artist as a reflection on his capability. It was the question of scale. Some artists are inevitably miniaturists—Paul Klee is an example in our time; Chardin or Corot will serve as obvious examples from the past. This limitation of scale does not, in my opinion, reflect the dimensions of the artist's genius. In discussing the relative merits of Corot and

Paul Nash

Courbet, for example, the question of mere size does not seem to me to be very relevant. In the arts major and minor in no way correspond to bigness and smallness. A bass is not necessarily more beautiful than a tenor—one sings with whatever voice one is born with. And so the painter—he works on the scale of his unique vision.

Paul Nash's scale was not monumental. The reason was perhaps merely a physical one. The asthma from which he suffered, and which was a consequence of the gas which he had inhaled while serving on the Western Front, made it difficult for him to work for long in a standing position. Works like *The Menin Road* prove that, while still strong, he could paint superbly on a monumental scale. But as time went on he found that he had to limit himself to works of a smaller scale, and he made a virtue of this limitation, and excelled in canvases of some 600 square inches. But he did not like to admit this fact—indeed, he vigorously denied it. One could only wonder why the perfect lyrist should aspire, if not to epics, at least to odes.

On the question of formative influences, often so delicate a point with artists, Paul Nash never betrayed any sensitiveness. His own personality was too positive to absorb other painters' traits unconsciously. What he did consciously is another matter. Like every genuine craftsman, he was curious to learn everything he could from the practice of other painters, past or contemporary. But the significant details of handling or 'facture' which constitute his style were his own discovery. He at some time may have learned a good deal from the study of water-colourists like Girtin and Cotman; but his handwriting was his own, formed unconsciously, as a direct expression of his own personality.

His vagaries were not of style but of subject-matter, and of corresponding form. Naturalism, cubism, surrealism—these phases or fashions of art are assumed by the responsive artist as naturally as the actor assumes different costumes in a play. The unity is in the playing, the art in the acting. There is a perfect coherence between the style of the war scenes, of the English landscapes, of the superrealist phantasies—the subjects change, the focus shifts, but the artist remains the same. He remains the same in his handwriting, as I have already said; but also the same in his mental furniture. All Paul Nash's work is distinguished by a certain concreteness, so that even in his most imaginative fantasies, the elements are objective—they are not abstractions, or distortions, or merely mental phenomena: they are bright images, surprising only in their metaphorical arrangement— their 'strange meeting'.

Like Gainsborough, and indeed many artists, Paul Nash would collect and have about him a number of curious objects— strangely shaped stones, streaked pebbles, dried lichens, fragments of bark, crystals, pressed leaves—objects which served as stimulants to his imagination. He could use these objects in very different ways. They would serve as referents or prototypes of natural forms—they were then used literally, or realistically. They could serve as objects to be arranged for a still-life—they were then used imaginatively, but still depicted in their natural forms. But finally, they could command or stimulate the imagination—they were the beginnings of a phantasy, which in its final form was no longer realistic—was, in fact, superrealistic. Paul Nash was capable of passing from one use to another of such natural objects (and not merely of those he collected about him, but of all the phenomena of his observation) without any effort, and in each phase of his creative activity, he remained the same personality, with the same recognizable signature. An English landscape, a cubist still-life, a surrealist vision—these were not so many dogmatic statements of irreconcilable 'schools'—they were manners, media, in which an artist could express his vision.

It may seem that I have assumed an attitude to my subject which is too defensive, but the public has an unreasonable prejudice in favour of unity of style in an artist. They like their poets to be lyrical *or* dramatic, and not to indulge in metaphysics or table-tennis; they like their actors to act off stage and their moviestars to be romantic in real life. The *variety* which an artist like Paul Nash exhibited arouses in them a feeling of mistrust. One or other of his styles must, they assume, be serious; the rest a recreation, an exercise in the gentle art of leg-pulling. The assumption of such people, of course, is that the most naturalistic style is the most natural to the artist; and that surrealism is rather a bad joke which the fellow was fond of.

Nothing could more falsely represent Paul Nash's character. He could be amusing—he loved his *little* jokes. But he always treated painting as a serious, even a sacred, activity; and the freer his fantasy became, the more firmly he held on to his technical diciplines. He never *botched* a thing—even his surrealist 'objets' were always immaculately mounted, presented as the precious objects they were in his imaginative valuation. His mind was not particularly philosophical, but he was fully aware of the theoretical background of a movement like surréalisme, and moved easily among the current aesthetic ideas. He spoke well in discussion, and with the authority of a man who had worked out his guiding principles.

Though he was not characteristically English in appearance—he might more easily have been taken for a Frenchman—Paul Nash was openly, even obstinately, English in all his instincts and predilections. If his early intention had been followed out, he would have been a naval officer, and he carried over, into his actual career, some of the swagger of the rejected career—art, for him, was to be a Senior Service. His clothes were not conventional, but they were always well-cut; his manners were perfect, even gallant; and his studio was as orderly as a chart-room. He always dominated his environment, building a grotto in his Hampstead garden, transforming with paint or botanical prints or *objets trouvés* the rooms he lived in. His work was a part of his environment—not an unrelated activity relegated to some graceless workshop.

I have just remarked that Paul Nash was obstinately English—his origins were perhaps Celtic rather than Saxon, but this does not affect the point I am about to make, which is, that Paul Nash was characteristically English in his style. He was fully conscious of the fact, and, one might say, proud of it. In that significant declaration which he contributed to the UNIT ONE volume, he asked: 'To what extent has contemporary art in England a national character? . . . Can we find in our short history of painting and of sculpture, qualities so peculiar as to identify their subjects beyond doubt, and, if so, do these qualities persist to-day?' An English genius in the plastic arts has never been allowed, he concluded, but 'that it does exist—a distinctive element, traceable through the whole history of our expression—becomes obvious upon any study of the subject beyond surface appearances. It would be ridiculous to claim for it a very powerful personality or a profound influence; that is not its character. It has never possessed the force which created a Shakespeare, or even some of the lesser figures of our literature, nor has it such sureness or spontaneity in expressing itself, except through occasional erratic channels. But, in essence, it is the same native spring.'

Then, after observing that 'in proportion as art becomes more abstract, so the nuances of national or racial distinction become more subtle and, consequently, more interesting to trace', he distinguished the particular tendencies which recur throughout the history of English art as 'a pronounced linear method in design, no doubt traceable to courses in Celtic ornament, or to a predilection for the Gothic idiom. A peculiar bright delicacy in choice of colours—somewhat cold, but radiant and sharp in key. A concentration, too in the practice of portraiture; as though everything must be a likeness rather than an equivalent; not only eligible persons and parts of the countryside, but the very dew, the light, the wind as it passed . . .'

Such characterization, he then remarked, does not help to explain what he had in mind. But let us note, before we touch the essential element, that of the three characteristics so far mentioned, Nash possessed two of them very clearly—a pronounced linear method in design, and colours cold, but radiant and sharp in key. He never developed the practice of portraiture, but a few pencil portraits do exist which show that he had great talent in this direction. He did not develop it, perhaps, because he thought that it would divert him from a more essential task, which he clearly defined in this same contribution to UNIT ONE. 'There seems to exist', he wrote, 'behind the frank expressions of portrait and scene, an imprisoned spirit: yet this spirit is the source, the motive power which animates this [English] art. These pictures are the vehicles of this spirit, but, somehow, they are inadequate, being only echoes and reflections of familiar images (in portrait and scene). If I were asked to describe this spirit I would say it is of the land; *genius loci* is indeed almost its conception. If its expression could be further designated I would say it is almost entirely lyrical'. And then, at the conclusion of this article, he expressed his own faith, his own conception of the task awaiting the contemporary movement in England, and himself as a leader of this movement.

'We, today, must find new symbols to express our reaction to environment. In some cases this will take the form of an abstract art, in others we may look for some different nature of imaginative research. But in whatever form, it will be a subjective art.'

And he then ended with that poetic image already quoted, in which his whole aim is expressed more clearly than is possible in any critical explanation.

Paul Nash

Paul Nash was to develop his theory of the *genius loci* in further essays (in 'Aerial Flowers', for example), and above all in his autobiography, *Outline*.*

There also exist certain analyses or explanations of his paintings which he wrote from time to time, either for his dealer, or for a purchaser. One of these I would like to quote because, precisely because not written for publication, it is somewhat incautious, and therefore exceptionally revealing. It refers to the painting *Sunflower and Sun*:

'This is the second of a series of paintings of the same conception. The idea behind the design is the mystical association of two objects which inhabit different elements and have no apparent relation in life. In the first picture called *Pillar and Moon*, the pale stone sphere on top of a ruined pillar faces its counterpart the moon, cold and pale and solid as stone. No legend or history attaches to such a picture: its drama is inherent in the scene. Its appeal is purely evocatory. That is to say, its power, if power it has, is to call up memories and stir emotions in the spectator, rather than to impose a particular idea upon him. Even so, the animation of such a picture lies in its ruling design. Not only does this dictate the nature of the drama; it also expresses by its forms and colours the nature of its mystery. Thus in the second picture, *Sunflower and Sun*, over a scene of wooded landscape dominated by twin hills, crowned with clumps of dense trees, a shaft of sunlight breaking through the cloud falls across the form of a giant sunflower bowed by the wind. I cannot explain this picture. It means only what it says. Its design was evolved from the actual landscape under much the same atmospheric conditions. There was such a sunflower and some such effect of sunlight. All the elements of this picture were present in more or less degree. But the drama of the event, which implies the mystical association of the sun and the sunflower, is heightened by the two opposing ellipses and by the other echoing forms of the sky which retaliate with the same apparent movement of outspread wings made by the leaves of the flower.'

The echoing of forms in a painting is, of course, one of the commonplaces of composition—there can be no rhythmic structure without it. But normally such echoes have only a spatial or physical significance. In a painting by Poussin or Cézanne, for

* *Outline: an autobiography and other writings*. London (Faber & Faber), 1949.

example, one might discern a recession of cubes which are in effect the architectural structure upon which the composition depends for its coherence. The ellipses and leaf-forms serve a similar function in *Sunflower and Sun*, but apart from this the forms are in themselves significant. Without seeking any explanation in psychology (though Jung has shown what significance this particular form, the *mandala* or almond-shaped ellipse, has in the history of culture), one might discover a biological analogy—it is a typical seed-form, for example, and therefore might serve as a symbol of germination. To describe such associations as 'mystical' is, in my opinion, a misuse of the word—there is nothing mystical in forms that can be explained in scientific terms (and have been so explained by Sir D'Arcy Thomson, for example). But Paul Nash would not have insisted on this word—he would, I believe, have willingly substituted the word 'poetical'. What deserves more emphasis, however, is what he called 'the drama of the event'. He was not satisfied with what might be called the *passive* landscape of a Constable; he certainly preferred the fury of a Turner. But Turner's diction (to continue the dramatic metaphor) was too rhetorical; Nash was essentially a metaphysical painter, which explains why he found no difficulty in associating himself for a time with the surréaliste movement. But he was not in any true sense of the word a mystical painter—he was not a visionary like Blake or Palmer, seeing in landscape 'the symbols of prospects brightening in futurity'. I cannot find any apt parallel among the painters of the past. Among his contempories, the nearest parallel was perhaps Chirico, also at one time called a 'metaphysical' painter. But Chirico never had the same intimate relationship with landscape, in the sense of a *genius loci*. A *genius*, yes; but the 'locus' was always cerebral rather than pastoral.

This metaphysical element was present in Paul Nash's painting from the beginning—a somewhat naïve presence, perhaps, in an early drawing like *Vision at Evening* (1910). Even in his most grimly realistic work, the drawings made on the Western Front in 1917–18, there is a formal element which expresses, not so much the drama of war, but rather the drama of the landscape, of the 'event' created by light and shade and natural forms. I can testify, as one who often traversed it in those days, that *The Menin Road*, for example, is, as a realization of the scene, completely authentic. But in the painting we are also conscious of the drama created by shafts of sunlight falling athwart the denuded tree-trunks, the formal 'echoes' in duck-boards and blocks of concrete, the play of reflections in the flooded shell-holes. To create this 'drama', and yet remain faithful to the *genius loci*— that, it seems to me, was the peculiar achievement of Paul Nash, and I do not know any other artist who has succeeded in quite the same way.

Faith in a 'genius loci' imposes a particular kind of sensibility, an awareness of 'atmosphere', and this Paul Nash had in a very vivid degree. The basis for such a sensibility no doubt lies in a person's physical disposition: the feeling comes from the acuteness of certain sensations, particularly colour sensations. That Nash's reactions to colour were exceptional is evident from his writings no less than in his paintings. A passage from a letter, written to his wife from the Western Front in February, 1917, illustrates this 'gift' in a remarkable manner:

'As we were about to enter the village there was a cemetery on the left side perched up on the higher ground outside the village. It was a wonderful sight, little wooden shrines over each grave filled inside with some sort of wire wreaths and small flowering trees, a little bower pale blue and green in colour, and always there was floating a little cherub doll upon a thread. Wind and weather had washed white shrines to a moist delicate grey— had faded the bowers to a mysterious pale blue. The wind passing through the place set the cherubs flying gently over the wire trees and flowers—set the foliage whispering and the little doors that had swung open, creaking. Never have I seen such curious beauty connected with graves and burials, the uncompromising slabs, a brown coloured marble, rise before my mind, monstrous piles, a hopeless grey blank granite with chiselled words in gold of some vapid hymn, the circular glass cases filled with white wax flowers, the poison-berried yews, all conveying the idea of death for death's sake. I turned from this to the windy churchyard of waving trees and shrubs and little happy tinkling shrines . . .'

The whole of Paul Nash's 'vision' is in this word-picture, not only his characteristic colours, but even his characteristic symbols. Years later he was to find an echo of this vision in Sir Thomas Browne's *Urn Burial*, a book which inspired some of his most beautiful designs. If this letter had not survived from an earlier period, it would have been all too easy to have concluded that Nash's imagery was derived from literary sources like the *Urn Burial*; whereas, in fact, Nash brought to the task a sympathetic imagination of his own. He found in Sir Thomas Browne a kindred spirit, and I know of no parallel so exact as the work of these so widely separated but each so characteristically English artists. Browne, of course, moved in a whole world of thought which is alien to a visual artist like Nash; but we may say of Nash, as Coleridge said of Browne, that 'so completely does he see everything in a light of his own, reading nature neither by sun, moon, nor candlelight, but by the light of the faery glory around his own head'. Nash's feeling for earthmounds and megaliths is quite in the spirit of the author of *Hydriotaphia*, and bearing in mind Nash's echoing forms, to which I have just referred, how exactly similar is the method of Sir Thomas, as described by Coleridge: 'There is the same attention to oddities, to the remoteness and *minutiae* of vegetable terms—the same entireness of subject. You have quincunxes in earth below, and quincunxes in the water beneath the earth; quincunxes in deity, quincunxes in the mind of man, quincunxes in bones, in the optic nerves, in roots of trees, in leaves, in petals, in everything.' *

Paul Nash was a poet no less than a painter. This does not imply merely that he was a painter with a poetic style: he would, rightly, have repudiated any confusion of aims. He remained faithful, always, to what might be called the primacy of plastic values. If a painting of his is poetic, it is because it is first of all a good painting. In this respect it seems to me that he is more genuinely a painter than even Blake, the predecessor to whom, by inspiration and practice, he is most nearly allied. That Nash had, in the literary sense, a poetic gift is evident from his autobiography and certain related writings; but it was a gift which he did not develop to the extent of menacing the strictly plastic basis of his painting.

Outline is primarily the portrait of an artist, and it would, I think, be otiose to add any touches to that self-portrait. It has, as the artist himself says in his Preface, a curious 'inevitable' character, meaning not that it is faultless, but that the lines were already traced by destiny, and all that was required of him was a certain fidelity to the record so far unrolled. But he was underestimating his gifts if he supposed that such fidelity is a natural

* *Miscellaneous Criticism*. Ed. T. M. Raysor. London, 1936, p. 271.

or even a frequent possibility. It is, as a matter of fact, miraculously rare, and no category of literature is so poor in masterpieces as autobiography. It is not only that such a mode of writing requires an uncommon degree of honesty (which is more than modesty), but it depends for its virtues on a particular kind of memory—a memory unobscured by prejudice, passion, pride, caution—by half the armoury of the common mind! The painter is, perhaps, more likely to possess this kind of memory than most people—he is trained to keep a vivid record of his visual impressions, and the practical nature of his craft does not normally lead to the acquisition of cloudy conceptions of life in general. But there is more in it than that—there is, after all, a literary art, and we are fully aware of its presence on the very first page of *Outline*. Henry James himself might have envied the opening of Chapter I. We are immediately in possession of a precise environment, its form, its colour, its fantastic and fascinating detail. To visualize a scene in all its concreteness is already a considerable advantage for a writer, but if he can then place within his scenery living and breathing personalities, then nothing is lacking in his narrator's equipment. As soon as the scene is set, Mr Dry and Aunt Gussie step on with perfect assurance, and they are followed by a long sequence of *dramatis personae*, until the stage is full, and the illusion of a time recreated is complete. Note, too, how with every shift of the scene the colours change, always recorded with subtle accuracy—the path, for example, which, as it entered the twilight of a wood, 'changed from a bright resilient tone to a purplish brown. Its surface now became heavy, damp and unsure, its form confused by dead leaves or encroaching undergrowth.' And a little later 'the colour of faded, rotting paling in the pure distilled beams of the winter sun . . .'. The whole narrative has the vividness we associate with Dorothy Wordsworth's *Journals*. All the senses of this growing boy, this awakening artist, were alert, and with the passage of time their harvest was stored in the mind, to feed the imagination at need.

These early chapters are the most delightful. As the young Nash enters the social world of London the interest inevitably shifts from places to persons, and the persons are no longer anonymous figures in a landscape—they belong to history, the history of English art in the early years of the century. But how they come to life again in these pages—Selwyn Image, Will Rothenstein, Gordon Craig, Gordon Bottomley, Henry Tonks, and finally his contemporaries of a brilliant phase at the Slade. Perhaps the most nostalgic pages are those which recall a Chelsea, not one but two world wars away—a Chelsea in which eccentrics were still at home, and a new artist might any day be 'discovered'. Paul Nash himself was to be discovered there, and works of art themselves now enter into the story. His beginnings, his first experiments, his tentative approach to pundits and impresarios—all this is perhaps a familiar story, but it has rarely, if ever, been told with such a balance of intimacy and amused detachment.

The last chapter to be written was called 'End of a World' and the next was to be called 'Making a New World', but that new world was never to take visible shape. As he approached a second war, and finally became involved in it, Paul Nash felt an increasing reluctance to expend his energies in the resurrection of a past that might have no future. And his energies were engaged on so many sides—not only by his work, and his increasing involvement in public life, but more desperately in fighting the affliction of asthma. The scheme for the whole work was complete in his mind, and the headings were jotted down in tantalizing brevity. How bitterly we must regret those lost portraits of Rupert Brooke and Edward Thomas, of Arnold Bennett and Sickert. Occasionally a phrase is illuminating—for example, 'Roger Fry, the Quaker Jesuit'. The book, in its completeness, would have been the inner history of an epoch in English art and letters. As it is, it must always be quoted as an important chapter in that history.

One returns, for a final emphasis, to Nash's fidelity to a certain nativeness, a quality representing the historic English tradition in English art. I have often characterized this as 'lyricism': it is a quality which we find in the delicate stone tracery of an English cathedral, in the linear lightness and fantasy of English illuminated manuscripts, in the silvery radiance of our stained-glass. It returns, after an eclipse, in our interpretation of classicism—in our domestic architecture, in our furniture and silver, in Chippendale and Wedgwood. The same quality is expressed, distinctly, in our poetry and our music. It is not a conscious tradition: it is perhaps an emanation of our soil and our climate, as inevitable and as everlastingly vernal as an English meadow.

11
Henry Moore

i

The art of sculpture is notoriously difficult to appreciate. To the Greeks it was the supreme art, the one which called for the highest talent in the artist and the subtlest sensibility in the spectator. The Renaissance, for reasons which I shall discuss presently, depreciated sculpture and gave the highest place to painting. Leonardo, who practised both arts, stated bluntly that sculpture is 'less intellectual' than painting, in that it calls for less skill in the artist. Certainly, to the Renaissance artist (and that means to all artists for about five centuries) sculpture seemed a clumsy and inferior method *of arriving at an identical result*: the representation of natural appearances. But it was precisely the restriction of sculpture to this aim which brought about first its supersession by the art of painting, and then its complete degeneracy.

Painting, essentially a two-dimensional art, was for centuries dominated by the effort to achieve tri-dimensionality—or, more strictly, an 'aerial' or spatial perspective within which tri-dimensional objects can be given a position. Since the painter can thus within his frame control and 'fix' his conditions of lighting and atmosphere; and since he has, moreover, the whole range of colours at his service, he can achieve an infinite number of natural 'effects' beyond the capacity of the sculptor, who is limited to a few materials like stone, wood and metal, and has then to abandon his completed work to a lighting and environment which he can no longer control. It is true that a painting may equally suffer by being badly hung; but when it is properly seen a painting, in the Renaissance conception of art, is an extension of nature, a world into which we completely enter and by which we are imaginatively 'enclosed'; whereas a piece of sculpture is objectively external to us, an object sharing our realistic environment. So conscious were Renaissance artists of this supposed limitation of the art of sculpture that they made what must

195

be regarded as grotesque efforts to overcome it, compelling sculpture to imitate the effects of painting as in the bronze reliefs of Ghiberti and Brunelleschi. *

Sculpture begins as a three-dimensional art; that is the 'speciality' it shares with architecture, the art most nearly related to it. But sculpture is solid, whereas architecture is hollow. Architecture becomes more sculptural as it tends to neglect its inner spatial functions, as Greek and Egyptian architecture did. Sculpture, on the other hand, is never in any true sense architectural. That is one of the misunderstandings which has led to its undoing. Architecture must have a base—a bed or plinth from which it rises, and to which it is inevitably bound. Sculpture suffers no such necessity; it can be free, and perfectly free. The earliest known piece of sculpture, the prehistoric ivory statuette from the Grotte de Lespugue, has no base; is valid from any angle, from any point of view. Sculpture can be something to hold in the hand, or carry in the pocket, like a Japanese *netsuke*. It can hover in the air, like Barlach's war memorial at Güstrow, or rest on a pivotal point, like Brancusi's *Le Commencement du Monde*. The American sculptor Alexander Calder has perfected a form of sculpture which *moves*; proving that even in the contemporary craze for 'animation' sculpture is not to be outdone by the cartoon.

The 'basic' prejudice is easy to understand. The earliest types of sculpture were probably votive: symbolic figures associated with religious cults and preceding, in evolution, religious temples and monuments. But when the temple had been evolved, it was natural to associate symbolic sculpture with it, and eventually to combine the symbolic with the structural. Thus arose the caryatides or columnar figures of the Erectheion and of Chartres. But even apart from such an evolutionary explanation, it is a natural instinct to give an object a base; even a painter generally seeks his horizon line, or some reference to solid ground. The sculptor has the very practical consideration of stability; that is to say, if he is a naturalistic sculptor, and wants his figure to stand, he must

---

* This aim is revealed very clearly in Ghiberti's own 'Commentaries' which have survived in a mutilated condition (see Julius von Schlosser: *Lorenzo Ghibertis Denkwürdigkeiten*, 2 vols., Berlin, 1912). The third commentary is a collection of texts on optics and perspective interspersed with Ghiberti's own observations, and the whole document, which is of outstanding importance for the early history of Renaissance sculpture, shows Ghiberti's preoccupation with securing, in sculpture, those same illusions of natural appearance which were being achieved by the painters of the time.

replace the muscular tensions which keep the living model on its feet by a solid block of some sort to which the figure's feet are securely attached. This may seen a trivial observation, but it is a fact which has distorted the whole development of sculpture in its naturalistic phase. For the base has inevitably shifted the centre of gravity of the sculptured object; indeed, the object has in itself lost its true centre of gravity and in the physical sense becomes merely a protuberance from a substantial mound of some sort.

The art of sculpture was for centuries enslaved by this naturalism, this pinning-down to a base, to a single line of ponderation. There is no intrinsic reason for such a limitation. Sculpture is the creation of solid forms which give aesthetic pleasure. There is an infinite variety of such forms, and they arise, and are proliferated, by laws which are formal and not representational. As an art, sculpture has nothing in common with painting, and Leonardo, in comparing the two arts, was guilty of a paralogism. Nothing, in the history of art, is so fatal as the representational fallacy; nowhere, in the history of art, is that fatality so inevitable as in the evolution of sculpture. Repeatedly the art dies of this disease. It has never, hitherto, been in the power of a civilization to recover the art. An attempt is now being made.

ii

That attempt began with Auguste Rodin. We do not today sufficiently appreciate the greatness of this artist. The task accomplished by his contemporaries, the great Impressionists and Cézanne, was immense; but they at least had immediate precursors, like Constable and Turner, who pointed the way. Rodin, as a sculptor, inherited a piece of waste land, and in the half-century of his active life he literally rediscovered a lost art. 'I have invented nothing', he once said, 'I only rediscover and it seems to be new because the aim and the methods of my art have in a general way been lost sight of. People mistake for innovation what is only a return to the laws of the great statuary of antiquity. It is true that I like certain symbols. I look at things from a symbolic point of view, but it is nature that gives me all that. I do not imitate the Greeks, but I try to put myself in the state of mind of the men who have left us the statues of antiquity. The schools copy their works, but what is of importance, is to rediscover their methods.'

Henry Moore

By rediscovering the methods of the Greek sculptors, Rodin did not mean the technical methods by which they achieved their sculptural effects; as a matter of fact, he was comparatively indifferent to these. He meant rather the attitude which the Greek sculptor had adopted to his subject. It did not seem to him that European sculpture had degenerated for lack of technical capacity or craftsmanship—there were no secrets of this kind to be rediscovered. Methods are always subordinate to aims, and it was the aims of the Greek artist which had remained such a mystery. Since the Renaissance the aim of the artist, expressed in one word, had been *beauty*; and few people, even today, would question that aim. But Rodin saw that nothing is so fatal as to strive too directly or too officiously for an abstract quality like beauty. Beauty, he said in one of his best-known aphorisms, is not a starting-point, but a point of arrival, and that expressed the tragedy of five centuries of misdirected effort. 'A thing can only be beautiful if it be true'—a fact which gives us a starting-point, not in academic rules and aesthetic abstractions, but in nature. 'By following Nature one obtains everything. When I have a beautiful woman's body as a model, the drawings I make of it also give me pictures of insects, birds and fishes. That seems incredible and I did not know it myself until I found out. . . . There is no need to create. To create, to improvise, are words that mean nothing. Genius only comes to those who know how to use their eyes and their intelligence. A woman, a mountain, or a horse are formed according to the same principles.'

The reader should memorize these sentences, for they are an epitome of the modern movement in sculpture, and all that one can do, by way of patient exegesis, is to show their implications, or rather, the implications of this return to a true naturalism—a naturalism of realities instead of appearances; of physics rather than of optics. On the same occasion Rodin also wrote: 'I am not a dreamer, but a mathematician, and my sculpture is good because it is geometrical'. He also said: 'I find the cubic factor (*la raison cubique*) everywhere, so that plane and volume seem to me to be the laws of all life and all beauty'. All these, and many other statements one could quote, show that Rodin had an understanding of the art of sculpture comprehensive enough to include all the developments that have taken place since his time. If his art does not satisfy us fully today, it is because he did not completely realize his own ideals. I think it would be possible to show

198

that as a matter of fact Rodin's work somewhere or other does foreshadow all the subsequent phases of modern sculpture, but as a whole it is undoubtedly too idealistic, too symbolic, too 'psychological', for the modern taste. This reaction was first represented in sculpture by Aristide Maillol, who, with specific reference to Rodin, expressed his desire for *formes plus stables et plus fermées.* The diversity of the human personality cannot, of course, be reduced to a single artistic formula, and the distinctions between 'open' and 'closed' form, impressionism and realism, romanticism and classicism, etc., etc., reduce in the end to differences of psychological type. All psychological types, all phenomenal variations whatsoever, are equally 'natural', and the realities of art, as they must be expressed in any criticism which pretends to be more than the expression of personal prejudices, must relate to the normal, the fundamental, what Rodin called *le vrai*, rather than to the 'accidentality' or 'incidentality' of the formulation of such principles. The cabbage is just as natural as the crystal, and the natural laws underlying these phenomena are essentially identical. For this reason we should not make too much of the different modes of expression represented by Rodin and Maillol, or the different *methods* of expression represented by the techniques of modelling and carving.

In the too limited consideration which I gave to this problem in an earlier introduction to Henry Moore's work,* I hinted that the quarrel between the carvers and the modellers belonged to the sphere of ethics rather than to that of aesthetics. 'Truth to material' is, of course, as much an aesthetic injunction as 'truth to nature'; it is the preference for stone, as against clay, or for the chisel as against the naked fingers, which is an emotional prejudice. 'The complete sculptor', I said in my first essay, 'will be prepared to use every degree in the scale of solids, from clay to obsidian, from wood to steel', and that, I still think, expressed the simple truth of the matter. You might with equal justice limit the musician to an instrument like the pianoforte as the sculptor to a material like stone, or to tools like the hammer and chisel. What is important is that the effects of one set of tools on one kind of material should not be imitated in another material by another set of tools.

The modern sculptor, from Rodin onwards, was to be increasingly involved in a dilemma, but in so far as it was posed in the

* London (A. Zwemmer), 1934.

form of modelling versus direct cutting, it was a false dilemma. The real dilemma is illustrated clearly enough in various types of contemporary sculpture, but it was already present in Rodin's consciousness of the geometrical basis of natural forms. If we carry the analysis to nature to the limits, we are left with an antithesis which can be formulated as mind/matter, but equally as intuitive apprehension (idea)/rational measure (number), and scores of other antinomies which only represent the binomial aspects of a fundamentally isomorphic reality. The artist, in his search for a starting-point in the chaos of natural appearances, will tend to select one or other term of the antithesis. The finishing-point is to be beauty—something not given in nature; it is a romantic prejudice to imagine that nature itself is beautiful. Beauty is a human creation. Animals have no sense of beauty; the nightingale's song is the automatic repetition of an instinctive cry. Beauty begins with intelligence. It is man's sensuous apprehension of the godlike; the result of his assumption of a *constructive* function. In nature (which is what is given to man) the artist finds measure, which is a reality he has learned to express in number. One form of art, one point of arrival in beauty, consists in the manipulation of measure, the constructive expression of numerical relationships. This point of arrival, known to the Greeks since it is obvious in their architecture and was made explicit in Plato's aesthetics, has been rediscovered in our own time; it was rediscovered by Cézanne and Seurat in painting, and by Rodin and Maillol in sculpture; it has reached its logical conclusion in that phase of modern art known as constructivism.

Another form of art, equally natural and fundamental, has its point of departure in idea, in the intuitive apprehension of the object. It does not reject measure (any more than the first mentioned point of departure ignored idea), but it prefers to follow the path indicated by organic or biological evolution. Nature has been selective in its manipulation of geometrical data; growth is not amorphous, but restricted by a limited number of physical laws. These might be called environmental laws; the laws which determine the inter-relations of chemical substances. The egg is not an arbitrary shape; it is determined, as we say, by physical laws.

The second type of artist follows a path determined by these same physical laws. His matter is moulded like the egg or the apple *in an organic fashion.* * The organism and the construction are two derivations from the same source; elaborations of distinct aspects of the same reality.

To prefer the organic to the constructive (the usual reaction) is merely to express a prejudice. The constructive principle, whether in architecture or in sculpture, or in any other art, is a perfectly legitimate derivation from natural premises; so is the organic principle. The most one can say is that for purely practical or functional reasons, one principle may be preferred to the other in a particular art. The constructive principle has generally seemed more appropriate to architecture, though even here the organic principle has its relevance—a fact upon which Frank Lloyd Wright has always insisted. Where a functional purpose is not in question, the choice becomes a personal one, determined by personal predilections or *tastes*. The story of modern sculpture between Rodin and Henry Moore is the story of a wholly unintelligent strife between these two principles—a strife which sometimes takes place within the conscience of the artist. Brancusi,† Archipenko, Lipschitz, Laurens, Duchamp-Villon,

* To be quite specific: The form of the envelope of an egg (see D'Arcy Thompson, *On Growth and Form*, p. 941, 1942 edn.) can be expressed in an equation as follows: $p_n + T(1/r + 1/r^1) = P$, where p_n is the normal component of external pressure at a point where r and r^1 are the radii of curvature. T is the tension of the envelope, and P the internal fluid pressure. The artist can imagine variations in T and P and produce an object which is egg-like to the extent that represents the same equation with different 'values'. This is the 'organic' type of art. But the artist might also accept the given values of this equation in a particular egg and use the numerical proportions he thus derives from nature in the construction of entirely different forms—the body of an aeroplane, for example or a purely imaginary or non-functional object. It is really a choice between applying the values of a particular formula, or varying the values of a general formula. It is only necessary to add that the artist, even if he is a constructivist, proceeds by intuitive rather than calculative methods.

† Brancusi has a special place in the movement, a position of relatively serene detachment. Henry Moore has paid his own tribute to this sculptor: 'Since Gothic, European sculpture had become overgrown with moss, weeds—all sorts of surface excrescences which completely concealed shape. It has been Brancusi's special mission to get rid of this overgrowth, and to make us once more shape-conscious. To do this he has had to concentrate on very simple direct shapes, to keep sculpture, as it were, one-cylindered, to refine and polish a single shape to a degree almost too precious. Brancusi's work, apart from its individual value, has been of great historical importance in the development of contemporary sculpture. But it may now be no longer necessary to close down and restrict sculpture to the single (static) form unit. We can now begin to open out. To relate and combine together several forms of varied sizes, sections and direction, into one organic whole' (*The Painter's Object*, p. 23). These last two sentences define precisely enough the difference between the stages of historical development represented by Brancusi and Moore.

Henry Moore

Giacometti, Arp, Schlemmer, Tatlin, Pevsner, Gabo and Barbara Hepworth are the names of some of the participants in this confused movement, from which, however, the antithesis of organic and constructive does finally emerge in all its clarity and inevitability.

I have explained the scientific justification for both terms of the antithesis, but in the appreciation of art we tend to dispense with theory, and rely on the obvious and apparent differences. No one is likely to confuse the 'constructive' with the 'organic' if faced with typical examples of both types of art; and however much we may insist that the constructive work is no less justified in nature than the organic work, there will always be a tendency to associate the organic with the vital and therefore with the human. We have seen that constructive elements underlie all natural phenomena; that organic growth follows laws, and involves structures, which are as geometrical, or mathematical, as anything created by a constructive artist. Everything, in the world of human thought and invention, is in some sense 'organic'—everything, in human physique and natural organisms, is in some sense 'constructive'. The division which used to be made between the organic and the inorganic in science has been abandoned by science itself, but nevertheless a distinction which is popularly associated with the phenomenon of 'life' does exist, and Henry Moore himself has suggested that *vital* rather than 'organic' might therefore be a better word to describe the art which is the antithesis of constructivism. But vital is also an ambiguous word, for we are apt to call anything vital which forcibly impresses our senses. Our whole language is riddled with analogies and metaphors drawn from the organic world, and it is almost impossible to speak and make one's self understood about motor cars, for example, and machines generally, without drawing on such a vitalistic vocabulary. Constructive art is often associated with the machine; nevertheless, in describing its qualities of movement and rhythm, we are compelled in just the same way to rely on a vitalistic vocabulary. The constructive artist himself, seeking for a word to describe his creation, will often choose a word from the vocabulary of the organic world.

What still remains to be explained is why the artist who frankly resorts to vital or organic forms, does not literally reproduce them, but recombines them or distorts them in an apparently wilful manner.

Henry Moore

I think the answer to this important question (which refers directly to the work of Henry Moore) involves something more than aesthetics. It involves a certain philosophy of life. Modern civilized man regards that faculty which attributes spiritual or vital qualities to inanimate objects as the mark of a primitive stage in human development; and it would be a mistake to identify modern art with any revival of such 'animism'. But modern man at his most 'civilized' (the modern scientist) has restored a degree of animation to matter, which a short time ago was regarded as merely inert. Common sense still maintains a strict division between the quick and the dead, even between things which wax and wane and things which merely accrete and erode. But if we require monuments, stable symbols, to represent our religious or emotional ideas, it no longer seems either necessary or appropriate to choose anthropomorphic forms. The mystery of life is too ubiquitous, too diffused, too cosmic to be subordinate to such human vanity and egocentricity. Some part of our life is superpersonal, even if it is not transcendental, and this collective unconscious, as the psychoanalysists have called it, is best represented by images from the same region of our mental personality. How these images arise in the consciousness of the artist is a problem perhaps unsolvable, and certainly outside the scope of this essay.

Henry Moore, in common with artists of his type throughout the ages, believes that behind the appearance of things there is some kind of spiritual essence, a force or immanent being which is only partially revealed in actual living forms. Those actual forms are, as it were, clumsy expedients determined by the haphazard circumstances of time and place. The end of organic evolution is functional or utilitarian, and, spiritually speaking, a blind end. It is the business of art, therefore, to strip forms of their casual excrescences, to reveal the forms which the spirit might evolve if its aims were disinterested.

But there is still a choice before such an artist. He may, for example, imagine that all forms should strive towards one canon of form, which he will call beauty, and all his efforts will be directed towards reducing the forms of nature to this one type. Such was the classical ideal of art, and we must remember that this ideal also represents a distortion of actual appearances. It is only because we have become so habituated to such types as late Greek sculptors evolved that we do not realize how far they actually depart from the casual forms of nature. The acanthus motive, for example, is so stylized that scholars actually cannot agree as to which particular plant it was based on. In the decadent period of Greek sculpture (by which I mean anything later than about 500 B.C.) there seems to have been an attempt to reduce the canon of beauty to rigid laws of geometric proportion, and these laws were revived in the Renaissance period. But an artist like Henry Moore regards such a procedure as merely escaping from one kind of false imprisonment (truth to appearance) to another kind of false imprisonment (truth to type). The kind of fidelity he seeks is of an altogether different kind.

It is a kind of fidelity represented by Greek sculpture before 500 B.C. by certain kinds of Egyptian sculpture and very definitely by Mexican sculpture of the Aztec period, but perhaps originally and with the greatest sureness by early Chinese sculpture and by the long tradition which spread from the East and permeated the North and West known to art historians as the Animal Style. It is so called because it finds its most characteristic expression in the representation of animal forms. In such representations there is no attempt to conform with the exact but casual appearances of animals; and no desire to evolve an ideal type of animal. Rather from an intense awareness of the nature of the animal, its movements and its habits, the artist is able to select just those features which best denote its vitality, and by exaggerating these and distorting them until they cohere in some significant rhythms and shape, he produces a representation which conveys to us the very essence of the animal. The same significant vitality is developed, perhaps from the same origins, by the Romanesque and Gothic sculptors of Northern Europe.

It is from such a point of view that we must approach the sculpture of Henry Moore. But since we live in a much more complicated age than, say, that of the nomad tribes of Central Asia, we must expect in a modern sculptor reactions more complicated than any found in the sculpture of the Animal Style. In modern Europe we cannot avoid certain humanitarian preoccupations. We live in cities, and even in the country animals no longer play a predominant part in our economy. The modern sculptor, therefore, more naturally seeks to interpret the human form; at least, this has been the normal tendency of sculptors for many centuries, and in this respect Henry Moore is normal. In his case the tendency has been modified by a desire to relate the human form to certain universal forms which may be found in nature—an aspect of his work which I will deal with presently. But first I wish to emphasize the fact that Henry Moore's sculpture, like that of his great predecessors, is based primarily on the close observation and study of the human form. As a student he drew and modelled from life for many years, and he still periodically returns to life drawing. It is so important to stress this fact, that I would like to quote his own words to me:

'Every few months I stop carving for two or three weeks and do life drawing. At one time I used to mix the two, perhaps carving during the day and drawing from a model during the evening. But I found this unsatisfactory—the two activities interfered with each other, for the mental approach to each is different, one being objective and the other subjective. Stone as a medium is so different from flesh and blood that one cannot carve directly from life without almost the certainty of ill-treating the material. Drawing and carving are so different that a shape or size or conception which ought to be satisfying in a drawing will be totally wrong realized as stone. Nevertheless there is a connection between my drawings and my sculpture. Drawing keeps one fit, like physical exercises—perhaps acts like water to a plant—and it lessens the danger of repeating oneself and getting into a formula. It enlarges one's form repertoire, one's form experience. But in my sculpture I do not draw directly upon the memory or observations of a particular object, but rather use whatever comes up from my general fund of knowledge of natural forms.'

That is to say, the artist makes himself so familiar with the ways of nature—particularly the ways of growth—that he can out of the depth and sureness of that knowledge create ideal forms which have all the vital rhythm and structure of natural forms. He can escape from what is incidental in nature and create what is spiritually necessary and eternal.

But there is just this difficulty; most of the forms of natural growth are evolved in labile materials—flesh and blood, tender wood and sap—and these cannot be translated directly into hard and brittle materials like stone and metal. Henry Moore has therefore sought among the forms of nature for harder and slower types of growth, realizing that in these he would find the forms *natural* to his carving materials. He has gone beneath the flesh to the hard structure of bone; he has studied pebbles and rock formations. Pebbles and rocks show nature's way of treating stone—smooth sea-worn pebbles reveal the contours inherent in stones, contours determined by variations in the structural cohesion of stone. Stone is not an even mass, and symmetry is foreign to its nature; worn pebbles show the principles of its asymmetrical structure. Rocks show stone torn and hacked by cataclysmic forces, or eroded and polished by wind and rain. They show the jagged rhythms into which a laminated structure breaks; the outlines of hills and mountains are the nervous calligraphy of nature. More significant still are the forms built up out of hard materials, the actual growth in nature of crystals, shells and bones. Crystals are a key to geometrical proportions assumed naturally by minerals, whilst shells are nature's way of evolving hard hollow forms, and are exact epitomes of harmony and proportion. Bones combine great structural strength with extreme lightness; the result is a natural tenseness of form. In their joints they exhibit the perfect transition of rigid structures from one variety of direction to another. They show the ideal torsions which a rigid structure undergoes in such transitional movements.

Having made these studies of natural form (and always continuing to make them) the sculptor's problem is then to apply them in the interpretation of his mental conceptions. He wishes to express in stone his emotional apprehension of, say, the human figure. To reproduce such a figure directly in stone seems to him a monstrous perversion of stone, and in any case a misrepresentation of the qualities of flesh and blood. Representational figure sculpture can never be anything but a travesty of one material in another—and actually, in most periods, sculptors have tried to disguise the stony nature of their representations by painting or otherwise colouring their statues. It is only in decadent periods that the aim has persisted of trying to represent the qualities of flesh in natural stone. *The aim of the sculptor like Henry Moore is to represent his conceptions in the forms natural to the material he is working in.* I have explained how by intensive research he discovers the forms natural to his materials. His whole art consists in effecting a credible compromise between these forms and the concepts of his imagination. A similar aim has characterized all the great periods of art; a confusion arises when we seek to identify this aim with a particular ideal of beauty. Henry Moore has dared to say that beauty, in the usually accepted sense of the term, is not the aim of his sculpture. As already noted, he substitutes the word *vitality*. The distinction is so important for an understanding of his work, and, indeed, for an understanding of many phases of modern art, that his words should be carefully pondered:

'For me a work must first have a vitality of its own. I do not mean a reflection of the vitality of life, of movement, physical action, frisking, dancing figures and so on, but that a work can have in it a pent-up energy, an intense life of its own, independent of the object it may represent. When work has this powerful vitality we do not connect the word beauty with it.

'Beauty, in the later Greek or Renaissance sense, is not the aim in my sculpture.

'Between beauty of expression and power of expression there is a difference of function. The first aims at pleasing the senses, the second has a spiritual vitality which for me is more moving and goes deeper than the senses.

'Because a work does not aim at reproducing natural appearances it is not, therefore, an escape from life—but may be a penetration into reality, not a sedative or drug, not just the exercise of good taste, the provision of pleasant shapes and colours in a pleasing combination, not a decoration to life, but an expression of the significance of life, a stimulation to greater effort of living.'*

These are the words of an artist—an artist who has had no truck with metaphysics or aesthetics, an artist who speaks directly out of experience. But they point with precision to the crux of a great debate which extends far beyond our immediate subject. The terms of the debate need careful definition, but obviously the whole scope of art is altered if you make it, instead of the more or less sensuous symbolization of intellectual ideals, the direct expression of an organic vitalism. No doubt intellectual elements will enter into the choice and elaboration of the images which the intellect selects to represent its ideals; but the difference is about as wide as is humanly possible.

iii

This is as far as I can carry a general explanation of the aims of Henry Moore. I would now like to make a short analysis of the

* *Unit One*, p. 30 (1934).

artist's evolution which will show how he has gradually realized these ideals. The artist, whether a sculptor, painter, poet, or musician, does not generally set out with a neatly defined set of aims. He is full of vague intuitions, sensations derived from nature and from his own physical experiences, suggestions given to him by the form and texture of his materials and his tools. He sets out on a voyage of exploration, takes many false turns, retreats occasionally, but always persists, always moves, and gradually approaches his destination. But long before he gets near to that destination he has, as it were, been carried away by a momentum of his own creating. The forms he has gradually realized and perfected have taken on a life of their own, and pursue a logical development which the artist could not change if he would—short of giving up the adventure.

There are, in fact, two sources of inspiration. As we have already seen, one of them is found in what, with certain qualifications and definitions, we can call *nature*. The other is in the work of art itself. That is to say, having taken his cue or theme or motif from nature, the artist finds that he has in contemplation, not a dead and fixed idea, but one which, as we say, is full of suggestions. The form lives, moves and has its being; like a cellular organism, it divides and sub-divides, multiplies and re-combines in an almost endless series of variations. (The process is, of course, familiar enough to the musician who has never had to compromise with the dictates of realism.) There is, that is to say, not only a form of life (form derived from nature) but also a life of forms. In the history of art, in the development of an individual artist, the typical forms develop out of one another and, even when most abstract, are most vital.

This aspect of the nature of art has been described in a work which is one of the few classics of our subject—the late Henri Focillon's *Vie des Formes*.* Professor Focillon's argument is expressed with a logical precision which does not easily lend itself to summary and quotation, but his main point is the one which concerns us now—namely, that once the forms found in nature (the relationships between forms which we call 'natural life') are transferred to the plastic world of art, they are subject to 'the principle of metamorphosis, by which they are perpetually renewed'. 'Organic life designs spirals, orbs, meanders, and stars,

* Paris, 1934. Now translated as *The Life of Forms in Art* by C. B. Hogan and G. Kubler. New York (Wittenborn, Schultz, Inc.), 1948.

and if I wish to study this life, I must have recourse to form and to number. But the instant these shapes invade the space and the materials specific to art, they acquire an entirely new value and give rise to entirely new systems.'

A particular illustration of this vitality is seen in the tendency of vital art to avoid symmetry. Symmetry leads to the cliché, to the mechanical (or at best merely logical) repetition of the same form. It may be argued that symmetry is found in nature, but as Moore himself has pointed out, * 'Organic forms, though they may be symmetrical in their main disposition, in their reaction to environment, growth and gravity, lose their perfect symmetry.' Asymmetry is, in fact, more 'organic' than any geometrical formula. It is for this reason that a full three-dimensional realization of form, such as Henry Moore seeks, must be a non-symmetrical mass. 'Sculpture fully in the round has no two points of view alike. The desire for form completely realized is connected with asymmetry. For a symmetrical mass being the same form both sides cannot have more than half the number of different points of view possessed by a non-symmetrical mass.'

Nowhere is this 'life of forms' so clearly demonstrated as in those notebooks and sheets of drawings in which Henry Moore is seen exploring the plastic possibilities of a given shape. A painter, in making a similar series of sketches, would explore the effects of attitude, of light and shade, above all of expression; the sculptor is feeling a round object, its bumps and depressions, tracing the contours and cutting imaginary sections. Expression is subsidiary to structure; flesh to bone. The process is essentially the same when the theme is less recognizably naturalistic—where, for example, the 'Mother and Child' theme is reduced to its cubic elements, to an embryonic unity. It is a process of crystallization —form emerging incidentally from the data of perception. But in later drawings an almost opposite process takes place; a given form is broken down, allowed to suggest associative forms and fantasies. If the first process may be called *crystallization*, this might be called *improvisation*. It is another aspect of the opposition between constructivism and superrealism which our artist is always seeking to synthetize. The synthesis achieved is the *style* of the artist. We seem to be concerned with the 'demented existence', as Focillon calls it, of a single, simple form. But just as, in its widest application, the same 'life' can be seen evolving

* *Unit One*, p. 29.

throughout the historical transformations of a period, constituting its 'principle of evolution', so we shall find a similar logical sequence within the evolution of any really vital artist. There are artists, of course, who never develop beyond a fixed point; their form is frozen, academic, and their life-work consists of a wearisome repetition of the same cliché. But in the work of a vital artist we find not only forms taken from nature, the necessary source of renewal, but for each form thus taken, an indefinite number of variations and transformations which are, however, held together by the artist's sense of 'style'. The academic artist, having no style, can only hold on desperately to the given forms; the organic artist, by virtue of his style, can take up, exhaust and discard as many forms as nature can suggest and his mind digest.

Moore began with life-studies of a normal type, though even here we can already distinguish his special quality. The early (1928-30) drawings from life are traditional, but they already have something of the power of a Masaccio for suggesting not merely the tridimensionality but even the solid mass and weight of the subject. But it would be a mistake to give the impression that the artist began with a relatively academic style, acquired in the schools, which he then progressively modified. Earlier than these drawings, and the sculpture contemporary with them, are certain figures and masks in stone, terracotta, concrete, and wood, which show the wide range of influences—Mexican, African and Egyptian—which he assimilated in his years of apprenticeship. It is as if, after exhausting the formal lessons of these exotic works of art, he returned to the European tradition before venturing to express himself in a wholly personal idiom. In 1928 the architect, Dr Charles Holden, had the courage to commission the then comparatively unknown artist to execute one of the decorative panels for the exterior of the new Headquarters of the Underground Railway at St James's, London. This figure of the *Northwind*, though it is a relief and therefore in the artist's own words, 'foregoes the full power of expression in sculpture', which is only given in the round, is nevertheless his first fully mature work. Onwards from this point his mastery of his material is assured, and the work never falters as a realization of a sculptor's formal conception. The period of ten years that follows is full of experimental variation, but there is a recognizable stylistic affinity between the extremes, and a sustained continuity throughout all the intermediate stages. The variations are stretched between a near-naturalism and an almost non-representational cubism; and between the forms appropriate to stone, terracotta, wood and metal. The forms given to the figures in an extensible material like lead are inconceivable in figures carved in a brittle crystalline material like marble. A Bernini will take pride and pleasure in making his marble resemble any texture or material. Only a narrow mind (more strictly speaking, a blinkered sensibility) will condemn such virtuosity; but between the limited objective of such technical skill and the plunge into the psychic depths of the organic process represented by the discoveries of Henry Moore there is all the difference that lies between a conventional symbol and the living image.

It is important to realize that Moore's figures are never, strictly speaking, symbolic. Therefore he never gives his sculptures literary titles; they are always 'figures', 'compositions', or simply particular and individual existences—a mother and child, never Maternity. The nearest he has come to a symbolic content is in the *Madonna and Child* commissioned for the church of S. Matthew, Northampton. But in a leaflet which was issued to celebrate the Jubilee Festival of this church in September, 1943, there is a quotation from a letter of the sculptor's which shows how cautiously he approaches the task of giving an ideological significance to his work:

'When I was first asked to carve a *Madonna and Child* for S. Matthew's, although I was very interested I wasn't sure whether I could do it, or whether I even wanted to do it. One knows that religion has been the inspiration of most of Europe's greatest painting and sculpture, and that the Church in the past has encouraged and employed the greatest artists; but the great tradition of religious art seems to have got lost completely in the present day, and the general level of church art has fallen very low (as anyone can see from the affected and sentimental prettinesses sold for church decoration in church art shops). Therefore I felt it was not a commission straightway and light heartedly to agree to undertake, and I could only promise to make note-book drawings from which I would do small clay models, and only then should I be able to say whether I could produce something which would be satisfactory as sculpture and also satisfy my idea of the "Madonna and Child" theme as well.

'There are two particular motives or subjects which I have constantly used in my sculpture in the last twenty years; they are the "Reclining Figure" idea and the "Mother and Child" idea. (Perhaps of the two the "Mother and Child" has been the more fundamental obsession.) I began thinking of the *Madonna and Child* for S. Matthew's considering in what ways a "Madonna and Child" differs from a carving of just a "Mother and Child"— that is, by considering how in my opinion religious art differs from secular art.

'It's not easy to describe in words what this difference is, except by saying in general terms that the *Madonna and Child* should have an austerity and a nobility, and some touch of grandeur (even hieratic aloofness) which is missing in the everyday "Mother and Child" idea. Of the sketches and models I have done, the one chosen has I think a quiet dignity and gentleness. I have tried to give a sense of complete easiness and repose, as though the Madonna could stay in that position for ever (as, being in stone, she will have to do).'

The qualities which the sculptor suggests as desirable in such a work, destined for a specifically Christian function (qualities such as 'austerity', 'grandeur', 'quiet dignity and gentleness', 'complete easiness and repose') are all qualities which can be immediately related to formal values; to angles and geometrical proportions. In other words every intellectual virtue or emotional tone must be given an aesthetic justification. There are some types of religious art for which this has always been a normal consideration for the artist; in a Giotto or a Piero della Francesca, for example. Sentimentality or decadence sets in once the balance of these values is lost. The function of art in religion is precisely to give a formal structure to vague emotions; it is, in an almost literal sense, a process of crystallization.

In this sense, the work of an artist of Henry Moore's seriousness is always religious: though it is not necessarily Christian or sectarian, but rather mystical (the theological word *numinous* would be more exact). Moore himself has confessed that he is 'very much aware that associational, psychological factors play a large part in sculpture. The meaning and significance of form itself probably depends on the countless associations of man's history. For example, rounded forms convey an idea of fruitfulness, maturity, probably because the earth, women's breasts, and most fruits are rounded, and these shapes are important because they have this background in our habits of perception.'* This, of

* *The Painter's Object*, p. 29.

course, is near to the symbolic conception of art, but the concepts involved (fruitfulness, etc.) are really too generic, in a sense too naturalistic, to be comparable to the dogmatic beliefs and ideological sentiments which are the usual basis of symbolic art. It is really the difference between the conscious ideas of human intellect and the deeper intuitions of what psychologists have called the collective unconscious. 'There are universal shapes', Moore has noted, 'to which everybody is subconsciously conditioned and to which they can respond if their conscious control does not shut them off.' * It might be more exact to say that there are universal ideas or archetypal images for which the artist finds the appropriate plastic representation. It is in this sense that Moore's 'shapes' are as archetypal as the 'idols' which primitive men carved to represent their notion of the unseen powers of the universe.

This analysis cannot be carried much further. We are dealing with a living and developing talent, and cannot therefore complete the outlines of its achievement. The outbreak of war in 1939 gave a sudden check to the sculptor's work. As the war progressed the materials of his craft became unobtainable. Even if a block of stone could be found, it was impossible to find transport to move it. But one outlet was left to the artist—his drawings. Even before the war this aspect of Moore's work had begun to take on an independent existence. Carving is a slow process; in the course of a year even under the most favourable circumstances not more than a dozen pieces of average size can be executed. A major work may take six months of concentrated effort. Meanwhile ideas flash through the artist's mind; he must catch them on the wing, and the rapid annotation of pencil and brush is the only means. The rate of inspiration is infinitely greater than the rate of execution. If, therefore, execution becomes an impossibility, it is only natural that the artist should seek to give more permanence to his sketches—to make them adequate substitutes for the inevitable casualties of war. The question has its economic aspect, too, for the artist must live. As a direct consequence of the war, energy was diverted into this medium which might otherwise not have been to spare for it; and though the relative value of such drawings against the sculpture that might have been is perhaps not in dispute, one result is that a far larger number of people have been able to enjoy and possess some example of the artist's work than would otherwise have been the case.

* *Ibid*, p. 24

Henry Moore

The effect of the war on Henry Moore's work was not merely of this accidental nature. He was deeply moved by its tragic aspects, particularly by his experiences during the air-raids on London. He saw the pathetic crowds of homeless people in their underground shelters, huddled in casual but monumental groups, abandoned to their misery, and he felt impelled to record what he had seen. The result was a series of 'shelter drawings' which constitute the most authentic expression of the special tragedy of this war—its direct impact on the ordinary mass of humanity, the women, children and old men of our cities.

For the achievement of this purpose there was no question of abandoning his established style—there is no sense of discontinuity between the shelter drawings and their predecessors, or their successors. They are an integral part of his artistic evolution. Moore has surrendered nothing in his endeavour to express this human tragedy; he has, on the other hand, proved the inherent humanism of his earlier work. But since these are no longer drawings for sculpture—though they remain the drawings of a sculptor—considerations of the materials into which the sketches for sculpture would normally be translated become irrelevant, and the drawing can exist in its own right, more cursive, more colourful, and more dramatic. The figures in such drawings are no longer isolated ideas; they are elements in an integral composition. *

The shelter-drawings were followed by a smaller series of mine-drawings. The sculptor revisited the scenes of his boyhood, went down the pits and recorded the activities of this underground army, no less heroic than any of the forces that fight in other elements. But the scope is more limited, the space more restricted, with little light and no colour. Nevertheless, this series has a grim and powerful beauty, and has the unique interest of showing the artist's treatment of the male body.

iv

The years since the war have seen the consolidation of Moore's reputation, and a leap forward into new ranges of creative activity. As materials became available again the sculptor returned to his major craft, and a series of large-scale figures and groups

* Cf. my article on 'The Drawings of Henry Moore' in *Art in Australia*, pp. 10–16, No. 3 (1941).

was carved in wood or stone. It included a reclining figure for the garden at Dartington Hall, Devon, and a group for the Village College at Impington, Cambridgeshire. The first of these pieces was conceived for a landscape-setting already determined and known to the artist, and its particular rhythms are related to its environment. In the case of the Impington group, some of the same considerations which influenced the conception of the Northampton *Madonna and Child* were again present—a specific symbolism was required by the terms of the commission, and the artist, like his medieval predecessors, willingly accepted the 'direction' given to him. In this way Moore took a further step towards the solution of a major problem of our time: the social assimilation of the idioms of modern art. These idioms arise out of the spiritual crisis of our time, but to a disturbing extent they remain a private language shared perhaps by a happy few, but not accepted by the public. The sculptor, however, has always been essentially a public artist. He cannot work in privacy, like the poet, or even like the painter. Least of all can a sculptor of Henry Moore's scope confine himself to the bibelots which are all that are within the reach of the individual patron of our egalitarian age. The sculptor must come out into the open, into the church and the market-place, the town-hall and the public park; his work must rise majestically above the agora, the assembled people. But it is no less necessary to point out that the people should be worthy of the sculpture. There is a long distance to be travelled before there exists between art and the people that spontaneous give-and-take of inspiration and appreciation which is the fundamental factor in a great period of art. One of Moore's latest and most ambitious works—a group of three standing figures—has been presented by the Contemporary Art Society to the London County Council for exhibition in a public place. In its dignity and monumentality it has every requirement of a public statue, and it conveys those qualities of beauty and of magic which are the artist's personal interpretation of the spirit of the age. It will not be accepted without protest— no great work of art was ever unveiled in an atmosphere of placid assent. But the great work of art subdues its spectators. As Keats said of a Grecian urn, it teases us out of thought 'as doth eternity', and all worldly emotions, like scorn, envy, and scepticism, suffer defeat.

12

Ben Nicholson

The plastic virtues: purity, unity, and truth, keep nature in subjection.
Guillaume Apollinaire.

Ben Nicholson is the leading representative in Great Britain of
that tendency in art which has been called *abstract*, and it might
therefore be best to begin with some account of the historical
origins of this tendency. We may then approach the work of our
artist equipped with some understanding of its stylistic significance.

It should be realized in the first place that the tendency to
abstraction in art is by no means specifically modern. It has re-
curred repeatedly throughout the history of art, and was already
recognized as an historical phenomenon, and called 'abstract',
before the modern movement came into being. As I have
already noted (see page 100) Wilhelm Worringer's essay on
Abstraktion und Einfühlung was written in 1906 and published
in 1908, and in this essay all the features which distinguish
abstract art as such are clearly recognized. Indeed, it is possible
that the *theory* of abstract art not only preceded the practice of it
in modern times, but actually inspired and influenced its development. Worringer's essay was published in Munich, and in the
first two years of its publication three editions were issued. In
Munich at this time lived Wassily Kandinsky, a Russian painter
who was to become the most consistent exponent of abstract art
in Europe. His first paintings in this style date from 1910, and in
the same year he wrote *Ueber das Geistige in der Kunst* (Concerning the Spiritual in Art), which is the earliest exposition of abstract art from the point of view of a practising painter.* The
Cubist movement in Paris was taking shape at the same time,
though it is doubtful whether anything as intransigeantly abstract in tendency as Kandinsky's *Improvisations* of 1910 was

*An English translation, under the title *The Art of Spiritual Harmony*, was
made by Michael Sadleir and published in London in 1914. A new translation
from a revised text under the title *Concerning the Spiritual in Art* was published
in New York (Wittenborn, Schultz, Inc.) in 1947.

painted before that year (it was in the summer of 1910 that Picasso, in the Catalan village of Cadaqués, 'brought cubism nearer than ever to an art of abstract design').* It will be part of my argument that the abstract movement in modern art corresponds to a certain psychological necessity which is widely diffused in the world today, and it is therefore idle to speculate on priorities in the formulation of a modern abstract style. But one more significant fact might be mentioned—it was to Munich that in 1909 came Naum Gabo, a medical student from Russia who was to become one of the founders of the abstract movement in Moscow known as Constructivism, and Gabo met Kandinsky the next year.

Worringer's famous essay has never been translated into English, but a very adequate summary of it was made by T. E. Hulme in a lecture he delivered in 1914, published later in the collection of his writings entitled *Speculations*.† An extensive quotation from this summary will give the reader the main outline of Worringer's argument.

After pointing out that there are two kinds of art, geometrical and vital, absolutely distinct from one another, and that these two arts are not modifications of one and the same art, but pursue different aims and are created for the satisfaction of different necessities of the mind, Hulme (closely following Worringer's text) goes on to define the tendencies underlying each type. Vital art, he writes:

'as contrasted with geometrical art can be broadly described as naturalism or realism—using these words in their widest sense and entirely excluding the mere imitation of nature. The source of the pleasure felt by the spectator before the products of art of this kind is a feeling of increased vitality, a process which the German writers on aesthetics call empathy (Einfühlung). This process is perhaps a little too complicated for me to describe it shortly here, but putting the matter in general terms, we can say that any work of art we find beautiful is an objectification of our own pleasure in activity, and our own vitality. The worth of a line or form consists in the value of the life which it contains for us. Putting the matter more simply we may say that in this art

* Cf. *Picasso: Fifty Years of His Art*. By Alfred H. Barr, Jr. New York (Museum of Modern Art), 1946. Page 73.

† London (Kegan Paul), 1924, pp. 75–109.

there is always a feeling of liking for, and pleasure in, the forms and movements to be found in nature. It is obvious therefore that this art can only occur in a people whose relation to outside nature is such that it admits of this feeling of pleasure in its contemplation.

'Turn now to geometrical art. It most obviously exhibits no delight in nature and no striving after vitality. Its forms are always what can be described as stiff and lifeless. The dead form of a pyramid and the suppression of life in a Byzantine mosaic show that behind these arts there must have been an impulse the direct opposite of that which finds satisfaction in the naturalism of Greek and Renaissance art.

'This is what Worringer calls the *tendency to abstraction.*

'What is the nature of this tendency? What is the condition of mind of the people whose art is governed by it?

'It can be described most generally as a feeling of separation in the face of outside nature.

'While a naturalistic art is the result of a happy pantheistic relation between man and the outside world, the tendency to abstraction, on the contrary, occurs in races whose attitude to the outside world is the exact contrary of this. This feeling of separation naturally takes different forms at different levels of culture.'

These different types of abstract art (and, indeed, different types of naturalistic art) can be illustrated from various historical periods. There is the 'abstraction' of peoples who live in a world whose lack of order and seeming arbitrariness must inspire them with a certain fear (the art of the Neolithic period, or of primitive races whose low technological abilities leave them at the mercy of drought, famine and other 'visitations'—the Australian aborigines, for example). There is also the 'abstraction' of highly developed civilizations such as the Egyptian, Indian and Byzantine, where the feeling of human separateness has a metaphysical or religious basis. Hulme contrasts the primitive and Byzantine attitudes. 'There is a certain likeness and a certain unlikeness in relation to man and the outside world. The primitive springs from what we have called a kind of mental spaceshyness, which is really an attitude of fear before the world; the Byzantine from what may be called, inaccurately, a kind of contempt for the world. Though these two attitudes differ very much, yet there is a common element in the idea of separation

Ben Nicholson

as opposed to the more intimate feeling towards the world in classical and renaissance thought.'

Worringer, who to some extent based himself on earlier philosophers of art like Lipps and Riegl, elaborated his theory, as I have already pointed out, before the 'tendency to abstraction' made its appearance in modern art, and it may well be asked how and why such a tendency should have made its appearance in our own time, and whether the same theoretical hypothesis will serve for both the historical types of abstract art in the past and those of the present day. I have already suggested that Worringer's theories may have been a direct inspiration of the modern tendency, but I doubt if what may have begun in this artificial way would have assumed the proportions of a world-wide movement affecting all the arts (for the music of a composer like Schönberg comes into comparison, as well as the main trend of modern architecture) unless there had been some underlying and urgent need for this type of expression. As a matter of fact philosophy had for many years been preparing the ground for such a development, and to Worringer's *Raumscheu* or space-shyness corresponds Heidegger's *Angst* or dread, which is merely space-shyness (fear of 'nothingness') in cosmic dimensions. In this connection I find it highly significant that it has been men of the metaphysically anguished races (Russian, German, Dutch) who have developed abstract art to its logical extremes, while artists who belong to the races who in the past were exponents of the naturalistic tradition (Picasso, Chirico, Severini) have consistently shyed away from pure abstraction. Picasso in particular has more than once violently affirmed the naturalistic basis of his art.

Existentialism is by no means a universal philosophy, and we cannot assume that an abstract art giving perfect expression to this metaphysical attitude will ever be generally accepted in any country (though a decay of modern civilization involving such a universal pessimism is not inconceivable). At present the adoption of such an attitude, whether in philosophy or art, is a matter for individual choice. But here we come upon a final complexity, not foreseen by Worringer or Hulme. They did, indeed, acknowledge the co-existence, in past epochs, of abstract and naturalistic styles, and Worringer's *Egyptian Art*,* for example, is a consideration of some of the problems suggested by this phenomenon.

* Trans. Bernard Rackham. London (Putnam), 1928.

But the social and psychological conditions associated with these styles are considered as the collective reactions of a particular social group or economic class. What we must now affirm is the possibility, not merely of an individual reaction, but even of the alternation, within the individual consciousness, of both attitudes. In a superficial sense, this may be interpreted as no more than an alternation of optimistic and pessimistic moods. Admitting the existentialist analysis of man's position in the universe, it is still possible for the individual to react positively or negatively, with despair or with courage, with fear or with confidence. In certain cases it seems possible for an individual to alternate between the extremes represented by this polarity—to tend in one psychological phase towards an affirmation of the world which results in a naturalistic style, and in another psychological phase to tend towards a rejection of that world which results in an abstract style of art. Ben Nicholson is an artist of this complex type.

ii

To describe Ben Nicholson as a 'complex' artist immediately introduces a paradox, for in another sense no artist could be more free from the introspective self-consciousness implied by such a word. He is in no sense an intellectual or metaphysical painter. All his development has proceeded from the play of a native sensibility with the materials of his craft. No painter could be less ideological, in the sense of using his craft to illustrate a thesis. Art for him has been a continuous process of exploration and discovery, and each conquest of a new territory has served as the base for a new expedition. He will often call these discoveries 'ideas', but an idea is something 'to work on', a concrete material of sensation to mould or manipulate sensuously. Certain symbols remain constant: for example, a jug which appears in an early naïve painting of 1911 reappears repeatedly, and is still present in his latest works. Colour, too, is a constant factor—the candid gay colours of fruits, playing cards, fishing floats and glazed pottery. Chiaroscuro is eliminated, or reduced to precise limits, as in a Byzantine mosaic. But with these constant factors the artist creates infinite variations, and it is in the exploitation of these variations that he quite naturally, without conscious deliberation, arrives at the extremes of realism and abstraction. Such contemporaneous contrasts represent, not a contradiction, not a dichotomy of any kind, but the same sensibility reacting with a different visual 'resonance'. The distinction is not one that can be usefully related to the historical categories of 'analytical' and 'synthetic' cubism. The abstractions, in any such comparison, are in no sense derived from a given subject, nor is a subject imposed on a predetermined architectural structure (in the manner of Juan Gris). The formal relations may emerge from the objective world—from the summary representations of walls, windows and doors, for example; and something very near, in a geometric sense, to these derivative forms, may appear in an abstraction (compare the paintings illustrated on plates v and vi). But the similarities are merely due to the limitations of geometrical formulas, from which the artist rarely frees himself. In general one might say that the artist always moors his sensibility to a geometrical pier—he is never merely an impressionist content to record some hazy and fleeting aspect of the visible world. He always seeks the utmost clarity and precision, but succeeds in combining these qualities with the complexity demanded by the polar tension (realism: abstraction) already mentioned.

The simplicity and fewness of the formal symbols employed by this artist do not constitute a limitation on his powers of invention—on the contrary, he revels in the multiplicity of the variations he can command with these limited means, for like all great artists he realizes that beauty is a product of self-imposed difficulties. In this respect his work may be compared with certain types of ornament—Celtic, Romanesque and Moslem—where the same richness emerges from a similar limitation. Some words of Henri Focillon's may be quoted in this connection:

'The most rigorous rules, apparently intended to impoverish and standardize formal material, are precisely those which, with an almost fantastic wealth of variations and of metamorphoses, best illuminate its superb vitality. What could be more removed from life, from its ease and its flexibility, than the geometric combinations of Moslem ornament? These combinations are produced by mathematical reasoning. They are based upon cold calculation; they are reducible to patterns of the utmost aridity. But deep within them, a sort of fever seems to goad on and multiply the shapes; some mysterious genius of complication interlocks, enfolds, disorganizes, and reorganizes the entire labyrinth. Their very immobility sparkles with metamorphoses.

Ben Nicholson

Whether they be read as voids or as solids, as vertical axes or as diagonals, each one of them both withholds the secret and exposes the reality of an immense number of possibilities. An analogous phenomenon occurs in Romanesque sculpture. Here abstract form is both stem and support for a strange, chimerical image of animal and human life; here monsters that are shackled permanently to an architectural and ornamental definition are yet endlessly reborn in so many different ways that their captivity mocks both us and itself. Form becomes a *rinceau*, a double-headed eagle, a mermaid, a duel of warriors. It duplicates, coils back upon, and devours its own shape. Without once trespassing its limits or falsifying its principles, this protean monster rouses up, and unrolls its demented existence—an existence that is merely the turmoil and the undulation of a single, simple form.' *

This paragraph, I believe, beautifully describes the 'internal logic' of the art of Ben Nicholson, but it may be thought that it lays it open to the charge of *mere decorativeness*, a charge which does not gain in intelligence by being repeated by critics who ought to know better. Apart from the truth of Ruskin's assertion, that all art is decorative in the degree that it is art, it is demonstrable that Ben Nicholson's painting is not even decorative in the sense implied by the derogatory use of the word. In this sense 'decorative' is descriptive of two-dimensional patterns without any fundamental content. But form, as Focillon remarks, is never 'the catch-as-catch-can garment of subject matter' (the mistake made by Juan Gris); 'form has a meaning—but it is a meaning entirely its own, a personal and specific value that must not be confused with the attributes we impose upon it'. In this sense, the formal values of Ben Nicholson's paintings have the same values as the forms of Poussin or Rembrandt or Cézanne. They are constructions in space and matter, with all the attributes which such constructions can possess—rhythm, balance, chiaroscuro and concrete finality. What such critics presumably mean is that such works of art are devoid of mythical content, of poetic 'story'. One must admit that this is true, but at the same time ask whether the critic is prepared to exclude from the highest categories of art a painting of bamboo shoots by Wu Chen or of apples by Cézanne, equally devoid of mythological content. It is not possible to accept certain still-life compositions of Ben

* *The Life of Forms in Art.* Trans. by Charles Beecher Hogan and George Kubler. 2nd edn. New York (Wittenborn, Schultz, Inc.), 1938, p. 6.

Ben Nicholson

Nicholson's and at the same time reject his severe abstractions without confessing to a prejudice which has nothing to do with the essential qualities of art. Nicholson himself, in some 'Notes on Abstract Art',* speaks of the 'poetic idea' as distinct from the 'literary content' of a painting. In the same sense one might say that one should never confuse the poetry and the iconography of a painting. There is no art without poetry, but iconography is irrelevant, except as a promoter of poetry.

iii

Sensibility is a physical endowment, inherited rather than acquired, and in this respect Ben Nicholson was born with a silver spoon in his mouth. His father, Sir William Nicholson, was one of the most distinguished representatives in our country of Whistlerian subtleties, of a tradition at once sensitive and intelligent, if a little lacking in poetic invention. But on the maternal side there are affinities no less significant, for the romantic rhetoric of his uncle, James Pryde, though never a direct influence, indicates perhaps the source of a dynamic energy which has driven the scion of such a formidable stock to new growths. Apart from these hereditary factors, the favours of fortune were prolonged in an early environment of accepted aesthetic standards, of activities and conversations which all tended to preserve and educate the natal endowments. Academic education was perfunctory; the real education was an apprenticeship in artists' studios, in travel, in visual experience. Then came the fruitful friendship with Christopher Wood, an artist equally endowed with sensibility, sympathetic in outlook and aims. Together they worked out certain simplifications of landscape, experimented in colour, made contact with some remnants of folk art in remote fishing villages. Later came the impact of the School of Paris—the still-lifes of Picasso and Braque, the *collages* of Juan Gris, the formal simplifications of Hans Arp and the fantasy of Joan Mirò. Distinct, and not less important, was an understanding of the sculptural vision of Barbara Hepworth, and finally and most decisively the plastic purity of Piet Mondrian. Mondrian's 'neo-plasticism' was a search for what he called 'a clear vision of true reality', an impersonal art 'unconditioned by subjective feeling

* Reprinted in the volume to which this essay originally served as Introduction. London (Lund Humphries), 1948.

and conception'. There are many works of Ben Nicholson which conform to the strict canons of neo-plasticism, and they now spread over a period of at least fifteen years, and continue to be produced. But as I have already explained, they represent only one particular resonance of the artist's sensibility. Mondrian had a vivid 'life of forms' within his impersonal, non-figurative, anti-naturalistic convention; but he remained fixed at one extreme of the existential axis. Ben Nicholson has never accepted such an extreme position, but has expressed the whole diapason of aesthetic vibrations encountered by an open sensibility in its vision of reality. Mondrian's search for a 'true' reality was a search for the philosopher's stone; but there is no sense in which reality is 'true'—that is a kind of philosophic idealism which has been thoroughly discredited in our time.* Rational constructions, definitions of truth, may be useful for logical discourse; but art requires concreteness in all its irrationality, its inconsequence and illogicality. Those concrete elements may be merged in some transcendental unity; but the artist lives and has his being in immediacy, in intuition, in a certain 'animal faith'. Art is a subjective process of individuation, and its products are meta-morphic. Art is variety; art is adventure.

It would be presumptuous to express any judgment on the work of a painter who is still intensely active, but his achievement is already considerable, and the consistency of that achievement, its unfailing revelation of a faultless sensibility and its fountain-like projection of varied forms from a seemingly in-exhaustible source, require us to recognize in Ben Nicholson one of the major artists of our time. It is not necessary to claim for him virtues which belong to natures essentially different—there are qualities, like monumentality and humanism, which his genius does not encompass. That his art serves as a prototype for monumentality, as an illustration of architectonic virtues, is evident from the interest it has always held for contemporary architects; and humanism is a prejudice which the modern artist can afford to ignore, as it was ignored before the Renaissance. As for the social relevance of such art as Ben Nicholson's, it has the overwhelming relevance of any extension of the visual faculty. 'It is the social function of great poets and artists continually to renew the appearance nature has for the eyes of men. Without poets, without artists, men would soon weary of nature's

* Cf. footnote, p. 226.

monotony', wrote Apollinaire. It is impossible to underestimate the biological significance of that intensity of perception, that renewal of the sensibility, which springs from the creation and appreciation of original works of art. In this sense the work of Ben Nicholson is peculiarly significant in that with relatively simple and direct means it produces the intensest vibrations of the aesthetic sensibility.

13

Constructivism
The Art of Naum Gabo and
Antoine Pevsner

Lieben Brüder, es reift unsere Kunst vielleicht,
Da, dem Jünglinge gleich, lange sie schon gegärt,
Bald zur Stille der Schönheit . . .

Hölderlin.

However much we allow for the speed of modern communications, we must nevertheless be struck by the apparent spontaneity with which a new and totally distinct type of art arose in several European countries during the five years preceding the First World War. In France, in Germany, in Russia, in Holland, in Italy, in Spain, even in England, movements were born which, though bearing different banners inscribed with the words Cubism, Suprematism, Neo-plasticism, Futurism, Vorticism, etc., agreed in their fundamental attitude, which was a complete rejection of *realism (naturalism)** in art, and an attempt to establish *an art of pure form.*

Many explanations, more or less profound, can be sought for this historical phenomenon. Most simply, we can regard it as an inevitable development within the technical tradition of European painting. Immediately precedent was the art of Cézanne. It is possible that French cubism, as developed by Braque and Picasso under the genial tutelage of Apollinaire, was based on a superficial aspect of Cézanne's work. Cézanne himself was

* The ambiguity of the word 'realism' as used in aesthetics and the philosophy of art is inescapable in this essay, where 'realism' in its metaphysical sense must also be used. One can avoid the ambiguity occasionally by using the word 'naturalism', but this word, with its nineteenth century literary associations, is no less ambiguous; it connotes the normal or average, even the superficial (impressionism), but does not include those realistic styles in art (e.g., expressionism) which are anything but naturalistic. This ambiguity is, of course, merely a reflection of our general inability to agree on the nature of 'reality'.

certainly a realist, and there is nothing in his career or statements which would sanction the theoretical or practical extremes of an art of pure form. We can be quite sure that he would have been revolted by the academic cubism of a Gleizes or a Delaunay. Realism is, in fact, something which is not renounced without a profound spiritual conversion—a conversion which painters like Picasso and Braque have never experienced.

There is, apart from the immediate example of Cézanne, a tradition of much wider historical significance to which the anti-realist can appeal. Disregarding the remote examples of Neolithic and Celtic art, there is the tradition of Eastern art in general, which penetrated Europe in the Byzantine period. The Russian Constructivists, Gabo in particular, do not hesitate to link themselves with the Russian ecclesiastical style in art, with its universal tendency to abstraction; and with the later and more secular style of the so-called Symbolists (in particular with the work of Vrubel who flourished in the eighties and nineties of the last century).

Two further explanations may be offered for the contemporary revolt against naturalism. The years before the First World War were years of increasing distrust, of spiritual and intellectual insecurity. A volcano was about to erupt from the ground under our feet, and its subterranean rumblings were being felt. Social tensions were acute; and since we are here concerned with two Russian artists, there is no difficulty in picturing to ourselves the political atmosphere of the last years of Tsarism.

Underneath these social and political tensions lay the wider and deeper disease of a civilization which was rapidly losing its dogmatic assurance. Christianity was in a rapid decline, and the philosophies which provided some sort of substitute (Bergsonism, Pragmatism, Nietzscheism) created by their emphasis on change, on plurality, on eternal recurrence, an atmosphere of flux and impermanency. The inevitable reaction to such an atmosphere, in art, is away from any associations with the organic, the biologic, the natural, and towards abstraction.

This general 'weltansichtlich' tendency was re-enforced by a more concrete influence—the rapidly increasing *mechanization* of civilization. We cannot go on inventing machines, constructing machines, using machines, without in some degree being mentally influenced by machines. The extent to which a machine-imagery already dominates, for example, the minds of our children is not sufficiently realized. The machine is the universal and coercive symbol of our age. It was a resolve to admit this fact, and to accept the consequences, which in the year 1913 brought together in Moscow a group of architects, engineers and painters who gave themselves the name of Suprematists. There were four animators of this group: Kasimir Malevich (*b.* 1878; *d.* 1935), Vladimir Tatlin (*b.* 1885), Antoine Pevsner (*b.* 1886), and Naum Gabo (*b.* 1890).

This group was united in its anti-realism, which at first took the form of a simple revolt against easel-painting, which was regarded as the idiom of a pre-industrial age. The new medium was to be, not paint, but rather steel; the new method not composition on a plane surface, but rather construction in space. The form to be achieved was not necessarily harmonious or beautiful, but rather dynamic, and quasi-functional. The work of art, that is to say, was to have the expressive qualities of an efficient machine. If the house, in Corbusier's famous phrase, was to be a machine to live in, the suprematist work of art might be described as a machine to live *with*.

The limitations of this aesthetic were soon to become apparent, and were to involve the disruption of the group. But first a few years of formative discussion, of ideological aggression, of practical construction, were to be lived through. It must be remembered that these were years of war, culminating in revolution. The years before the Revolution (1913–17) were years of united action against the established academicism of the old order; the years after the Revolution were years of expansion, triumph, crystallization and separation. This second phase came to an end with the first exhibition of post-revolutionary Russian art held in Berlin in 1922.

The inner history of these years must be related by the participants—the documentary evidence does not exist on which an objective account can be based. But one thing is certain: the history of this inner struggle among the artists of Moscow is an epitome of one of the most decisive conflicts in the evolution of modern Europe. The point at issue was the relation of the artist to society, and it was not the artists who were allowed to decide it. Nor was it left to the judgment of the people. The Communist Party, in its political capacity, condemned the modern movement in art in principle and in practice, and insisted on a restoration of the pictorial realism which had prevailed under the old order.

The Art of Naum Gabo and Antoine Pevsner

Once the political revolution had triumphed in Russia, the immediate problem for progressive artists like the Suprematists had been to extend the revolution into academic and educational spheres. This is never so automatic as a logical conception of revolution would seem to require. Institutions like universities and academies have a way of riding revolutionary storms, and of maintaining within a new political system the reactionary ideals of the old epoch. Revolutionary leaders at the same time are generally men of limited and even naïve cultural outlook; they think in terms of politics and power, and are slow to perceive the necessary unity of a revolutionary change. Lenin was no exception to this rule, and was little disposed to interfere in the politics of art. But the revolutionary artists themselves were of a different opinion, and in the first flush of victory they literary evicted the members and officers of the Imperial Academy and other art institutions. They created new institutions, the Vchutemas, or Art Workshops, which in their programme and practice anticipated the Bauhaus which some years later was to become the focus of similar ideals in Germany.

This triumph of the revolutionary artists was, however, short-lived. The academicians were to find unhoped-for allies among the orthodox Marxists. A fierce debate occupied the years 1919–22. The revolutionary artists themselves were divided, Tatlin, Rodschenko and Stepanova protesting their orthodoxy; Gabo and Pevsner maintaining the integrity of their aesthetic ideals. In 1920 both parties issued their separate manifestoes. For a year or two the debate was to continue, but there was no doubt on which side the all-powerful influence of the Party weighed. Influence, in such a case, implied action. Pevsner, Gabo and their associates were deprived of their membership of the Central Soviet of Artists, which meant in effect that they were deprived of all possibilities of making a living by the practice of their art. The only choice was between conformity and exile. Gabo and Pevsner chose exile. Tatlin and his associates remained in Russia, but it may be doubted whether their fate was more fortunate. For the real victor in this struggle was not any form of revolutionary art, marxist or other, but the bourgeois academicism of the nineteenth century.

The marxist accusation against Gabo and Pevsner, as against artists of a similar persuasion in poetry and music, can be summed up in the word *formalism*. According to their marxist critics, the Constructivists, as they had called themselves since their manifesto of 1920, were guilty of creating an art which had no basis in 'socialist realism'. This phrase, which has no sanction in the writings of Marx or Engels, implies that the artist, instead of attempting to create a self-sufficient or 'pure' work, should use his talent to interpret the phenomenal world (which is the general aim of realism in art) and in particular should interpret this 'reality' in a way which furthers the official conception of the social order. At its crudest this dogma exacts a rigid adherence to a propagandist purpose in painting and sculpture; in the more arcane debates of the Moscow artists of 1920 it implied a generalized functional art. The constructivist artist, that is to say, might find an outlet in functional architecture, engineering, etc., but apart from such outlets he must become a realist and paint in a pictorial idiom within reach of the more or less illiterate masses of the Soviet Union.

This debate, of course, has not been confined to the USSR, and it is still necessary to define and explain the principles for which artists like Pevsner and Gabo have suffered much persecution, and which still baffle the understanding of many people of good will all over the world.

The fundamental argument is a metaphysical one, and is as old as philosophy itself. It shifts its ground from time to time, and the antithetical terms do not always correspond. But there is always present a distinction between 'what is' and 'what is seen', between idea and image, between reality and appearance. There are extremists who deny such a distinction, and argue either that everything is an illusion presented by the senses, or that everything is a physical reality, even the mental operations of the brain which result in ideas. It is obvious enough that quite distinct philosophies can be founded on these arguments: what is not so obvious to most people is that quite distinct types of art can have similar bases. In epochs which were not, so far as we know, specifically metaphysical, the distinction was expressed merely as trust or mistrust in the face of nature—trust inspiring a mimetic or naturalistic art, mistrust inspiring an abstract or geometric art. In the history of art these two tendencies present extremely complicated reactions, largely because the motivation behind them is completely unconscious. Elements from both traditions may be mingled along the shifting frontiers of the two types of civilization—the evolution of Gothic art derives its complexity from this very fact.

The Art of Naum Gabo and Antoine Pevsner

What has happened in our own time is simply that artists have based themselves consciously on one or the other of these metaphysical outlooks. To the dialectical materialist, any form of idealism is anathema; and 'realism' (in the scholastic sense of the word, which is also the Constructivist sense) is regarded as a form of idealism. An art which deliberately denies the self-sufficiency of the phenomenal world is, for such philosophers, as perverse as a religion which assumes a life beyond the grave. But everything in this argument turns, of course, on our definition of the word 'reality'. The dialectical materialists seem to confine its meaning to the immediate data of sense perception. To the great majority of philosophers that has always seemed a very jejune attitude. A comparison of these data soon discovers similarities or identities from which emerge, not merely the general laws which constitute the body of science, but universal concepts to which the sense-data always conform, and which therefore may be regarded as the bases of reality. These concepts are not, as the materialist assumes, illusory or idealistic. We cannot have final knowledge about them, but we are aware of their concrete manifestations. They are inseparable from matter: unimagined outside matter. They describe the forms which matter universally assumes—the way matter behaves.

Now let us turn to the principles which Gabo and Pevsner opposed to the materialists, and to which they gave precise expression in their Manifesto of 1920. In that Manifesto they declared:

1. To communicate the reality of life, art should be based on the two fundamental elements: space and time.
2. Volume is not the only spatial concept.
3. Kinetic and dynamic elements must be used to express the real nature of time: static rhythms are not sufficient.
4. Art should stop being imitative and try instead to discover new forms.

These four axioms are not so innocent as they seem. The first one implies a decisive choice of that philosophy of life which is ambiguously called 'realism' in opposition to nominalism or materialism. If the artist makes this metaphysical choice, his activity must then, accordingly, be directed to an aesthetic revelation of the elements of reality—that is to say, to a description or concrete representation of the elements of space and time.

Moreover, it will not be a question of subjective interpretation: space and time are legal elements—they obey univerasl laws, and are misrepresented or distorted if made the expressive media of personal emotions. This point has been well brought out by Piet Mondrian, whose writings on pure plastic art are perhaps the clearest expression, by a practising artist, of its underlying principles:

'Gradually I became aware that Cubism did not accept the logical consequences of its own discoveries; it was not developing abstraction towards its ultimate goal, the expression of pure reality. I felt that this reality can only be established through *pure* plastics. In its essential expression, pure plastics is unconditioned by subjective feeling and conception. It took me a long time to discover that particularities of form and natural colour evoke subjective states of feeling, which obscure *pure reality*. The appearance of natural forms changes but reality remains constant. * To create pure reality plastically, it is necessary to reduce natural forms to the *constant elements* of form and natural colour to *primary colour*. The aim is not to create other particular forms and colours with all their limitations, but to work toward abolishing them in the interest of a larger unity.' †

The aim of constructivist artists has been to give 'a clear vision of true reality', and it might be objected that this is not essentially an aesthetic activity. Between the objectivity of science and the creativity of art there is this difference: the one aims to *inform*, the other to *please*. The pleasure afforded by the work of art need not take the channels of emotional indulgence, of sentimentality. Pleasure results from many degrees of perception, and the purest pleasure is, according to the view I am presenting here, intellectual as well as (at the same time as) sensuous. This most refined

* An idea not accepted by Gabo, who rejects entirely the idea of a constant reality. In his view reality is continuously being created anew, it has no fixed or absolute identity (a view that seems to be in accordance with the latest theories of cosmology—cf. C. F. von Weizsäcker, *The History of Nature*, and Fred Hoyle, *The Nature of the Universe*). Gabo does not feel that any one conception of reality may be thought superior to others. To his mind the conception of reality as an everchanging result of the universal, human, creative process is the essence of constructive realism. Gabo has developed his point of view in an important lecture delivered at Yale University on March 19, 1948, and published in *Three Lectures on Modern Art*, New York (Philosophical Library), 1949.

† *Plastic Art and Pure Plastic Art.* New York (Wittenborn), 1945, p. 10.

degree of pleasure is only given in response to disciplined effort. The disciplines of art are (*a*) constructive skill, (*b*) selective observation, and (*c*) unitary vision. Skill and observation are essential to any type of art, and in effective works of art do not vary much in quality (the selective observation which a Gabo practises—*cf.* his confession in the *Horizon* letter*—does not differ from the selective observation practised by a Leonardo or a Constable; Pevsner's technical skill is quite comparable to the skill of a Donatello or a Rodin). What varies enormously in works of art is the quality of intellectual vision. No amount of technical skill can compensate for the intellectual poverty of artists like Murillo and Bouguereau (a hundred other names might be substituted from the nearest museum). On the other hand, the unitary vision of a Blake or a Cézanne will go a long way to make up for defects of technique.

The particular vision of reality common to the constructivism of Pevsner and Gabo is derived, not from the superficial aspects of a mechanized civilization, nor from a reduction of visual data to their 'cubic planes' or 'plastic volumes' (all these activities being merely variations of a naturalistic art), but from an insight into the structural processes of the physical universe as revealed by modern science. The best preparation for a true appreciation of constructive art is a study of Whitehead or Schrödinger. But it must again be emphasized that though the intellectual vision of the artist is derived from modern physics, the creative construction which the artist then presents to the world is not scientific, but poetic. It is the poetry of space, the poetry of time, of universal harmony, of physical unity. Art—it is its main function—accepts this universal manifold which science investigates and reveals, but reduces it to the concreteness of a plastic symbol.

What the work of art 'expresses', in an emotional sense, depends very largely on what the spectator brings, in the way of an emotional set-up, to the work of art. Certainly the artist's business is not, and never has been, to anticipate the spectator's emotions (we can leave that to Hollywood). The artist can never control the emotional consequences of his work: he may, indeed, welcome them. But his first concern, his only concern in the act of creation, is with the structural elements of reality: and these elements,

* 'Constructive Art: an Exchange of Letters between Naum Gabo and Herbert Read.' *Horizon* (London), x. 55 (July, 1944). See pages 238 to 245.

according to the constructivist theory, are given in the physical mutations of space and time.

The acceptance of such a philosophical basis for art still leaves a considerable latitude in the manipulation of such elements. The principles common to Gabo, Pevsner, Mondrian, Nicholson, Domela and many other 'abstract' artists lead to very different results in the works of art actually produced. These differences may to some extent be explained by the nature of the materials chosen to work in—Mondrian worked in linear forms and primary colours; Pevsner works in bronze and other metals; Gabo in plastics. But such differences are superficial; more important are differences of emphasis as between the elements of space and time, or, more concretely, as between a 'static balance' and a 'dynamic equilibrium'. Mondrian has defined this difference. A static balance 'maintains the individual unity of particular forms, single or in plurality'. A dynamic equilibrium is 'the unification of forms or elements of forms through continuous opposition. The first is limitation, the second is extension. Inevitably dynamic equilibrium destroys static balance.' 'In plastic art, the static balance has to be transformed into dynamic equilibrium which the universe reveals.'

The distinction here made by Mondrian is but one example of the new laws of composition which belong to an art of concrete realism. Such a 'rationale of composition' must one day be written, but this is not the place to sketch even its outline. To a certain extent the new science of art coincides with the old science of art: abstract the subjective associations from naturalistic or figurative art and we are still left with the mutual relations of forms, which must, in any work of art whatsoever, fulfil an expressive function. It is not in formal content that non-figurative art differs from figurative art: it is in its expressive intention, *vis à vis* the personality of the artist. It is very difficult for the artist to eliminate his personality, and most people do not wish him to make the attempt. But when he does succeed in such an attempt, the result is a work of art of an altogether different order. Mondrian, again, has expressed the difference very clearly:

'Although art is fundamentally everywhere and always the same, nevertheless two main human inclinations, diametrically opposed to each other, appear in its many and varied expressions. One aims at the *direct expression of universal beauty*, the other at the *aesthetic expression of oneself*, in other words, of that which one thinks one experiences. The first aims at representing reality objectively, the second subjectively. Thus we see in every work of figurative art the desire, objectively, to represent beauty, solely through form and colour, in mutually balanced relations, and, at the same time, an attempt to express that which these forms, colours and relations arouse in us. This latter attempt must of necessity result in an individual expression which veils the pure representation of beauty. Nevertheless, both the two opposing elements (universal-individual) are indispensable if the work is to arouse emotion. Art has to find the right solution. In spite of the dual nature of the creative inclinations, figurative art has produced a harmony through a certain co-ordination between objective and subjective expression. For the spectator, however, who demands a pure representation of beauty, the individual expression is too dominant.' *

The significant claim in this statement, and in similar statements by the Constructivists, is that 'a pure representation of beauty' cannot be achieved by 'individual expression'—that is to say, by expressive means which are personal and subjective.

That the creation of a 'pure' art in this sense is possible is certain. Apart from music and architecture, where the individual element is subordinated without exciting a protest from the intelligent public, there exists a quantity of poetry, and that of the highest order, which is manifestly 'pure' in this sense. English lyrical poetry before 1600, the poetry of Dante and Hölderlin, illustrate this impersonal beauty, this pure representation of the universal element in art. What is novel in the present situation is the attempt to create such an art by plastic means. The theoretical legitimacy of such an attempt cannot be questioned: what remains, as a difficulty if not as an objection, is the problem of 'communication'.

There is no doubt that many people, not prejudiced by emotional factors, people of general aesthetic sensibility, find difficulty in discovering an aesthetic response to non-figurative art. I believe that in most cases such people cannot separate the superficial 'decorative' appeal of a non-figurative composition from its constructive significance. They are like those people (not necessarily to be despised) who only appreciate the melodic or linear element in music, and are incapable of grasping its polyphonic depth.

* *Op. cit.* p. 50.

The Art of Naum Gabo and Antoine Pevsner

I have discussed this problem of communication with reference to constructivist art in the exchange of letters with Gabo already referred to (and reprinted as an Appendix to this essay). Essentially the problem is the same whenever the public is confronted with an original or 'difficult' type of art: it is the problem which arises when the same public is confronted with the music of Stravinsky or the poetry of Eliot. A difficulty in philosophy or science—the 'difficulty' of Heidegger or Carnap—is accepted as a necessary, or at least as a natural, price to pay. Plastic art suffers from its basic illiteracy. Because it is illiterate—a visual means of communication—there is an unwarranted assumption that it should be addressed to illiterate people. There is no logical or historical justification for such an assumption. The visual language may be just as difficult to learn as any verbal language; and within this visual language there are as many degrees of difficulty as there are in literature.

Nevertheless, the inherent difficulty of a subject, of a 'vision', does not justify any imprecision of expression. But no one, I think, has ever ventured to accuse the artists now in question of any dimness or vagueness of this kind. There is no imprecision of visual language in a construction by Gabo or Pevsner; every piece has the absolute clarity of a Euclidean theorem. The development of both artists, during the past twenty-five years, is towards an increasingly exact equivalence of vision and expression. The experimental is gradually eliminated, and anything in the nature of suggestive improvisation rigorously excluded. But in each artist there is also a development towards what I can only call an increasingly 'poetic' vision. The element of deliberation which is implied by the very word 'construction' is more and more completely fused in a spontaneous moment of vision, and parallel to this development the works themselves acquire a richer degree of 'artifice', of material quality or patina. The bronze and copper constructions of Pevsner in particular often have the substantial richness of the bronzes of Ancient China.

In addition, these works of art have what is so generally lacking in modern works of art—monumentality. Some of them are actual models for monuments in public places—airports and exhibition parks—and nearly all would gain from incorporation in architectural units. There is very little architecture worthy of their collaboration, and even where these constructions might be welcome, and might function with all the majestic rightness of Michelangelo's groups in the Medici chapel, the will and the means to collaborate with such artists are lacking. But only such a collaboration would satisfy the artistic ambitions of Gabo and Pevsner, and only in such a setting would the full powers of their creative talents be engaged.

Much—perhaps most—of the art that is specifically 'modern' is in the nature of a protestation; it is not decadent art, but it is a negative reaction to the decadence of our civilization, particularly to the defunct academic traditions of that civilization. But the art of Antoine Pevsner and of Naum Gabo is positive and prophetic, and it looks beyond the immediate convulsions of our epoch to a time when a new culture based on an affirmative vision of life will need and will call into being an art commensurate with its grandeur.

13a

Appendix to the essay on

Constructivism

An Exchange of Letters between
NAUM GABO and HERBERT READ
published originally in *Horizon*, vol. X, No. 53,
(July 1944), p. 60.

Dear Herbert,

It is now more than a year and a half since *Horizon* asked me
to write an article about my own work. At that time I light-
heartedly promised to do it and only later did it dawn on me
that I had engaged myself in an adventure full of peril. When an
artist ventures to write about himself and about his work he is
heading straight into a minefield where his first mistake will be
the end of him.

Many artists have walked innocently enough into that trap
and done themselves more harm than good. Not that their works
have actually suffered, but the misunderstandings and mis-
interpretations unloosed by their words were so confusing that it
would have been better had they kept silent.

On the other hand, looking back on the destiny of many works
of art in their historical array, and having in view their relation
to their own time and people as well as to posterity, I have come
to the conclusion that a work of art, restricted to what the artist
has put in it, is only a part of itself. It only attains full stature
with what people and time make of it.

I realize that in making such a statement I may already have
struck a mine—in fact I even sense the distant reverberations of
explosions in many artistic camps, friend's and foe's.

I will therefore not walk one step further in this dangerous
field without help and guidance from someone who knows the
ground and who cares enough about my work and the idea it
stands for. After all, my art, as all visual art, is by nature mute.
Had the painter or sculptor been able to say in words what he

wanted to express with pictorial and spatial means, I do not think there would have been so many pictures and sculptures for the public to look at and for the students of art to explain.

Here is where you come in. You know more than I ever will what the public ought to know in order to judge in fairness about my work. You know both my creed and my work; could you, would you, lend me a hand and lead me through this field to safety?

Ever since I began to work on my constructions, and this is now more than a quarter of a century ago, I have been persistently asked innumerable questions, some of which are constantly recurring up till the present day.

Such as 'Why do I call my work "Constructive"? Why abstract?'

'If I refuse to look to Nature for my forms, where do I get my forms from?'

'What do my works contribute to society in general, and to our time in particular?'

I have often tried to answer these questions. So have you and others. Some people were satisfied, but in general the confusion is still there, and the questions still persistently recur.

I am afraid that my ultimate answer will always lie in the work itself, but I cannot help feeling that I have no right to neglect them entirely and in the following notes there may be some clue to an answer for these queries.

(1) My works are what people call 'Abstract'. You know how incorrect this is, still, it is true they have no visible association with the external aspects of the world. But this abstractedness is not the reason why I call my work 'Constructive'; and 'Abstract' is not the core of the Constructive Idea which I profess. This idea means more to me. It involves the whole complex of human relation to life. It is a mode of thinking, acting, perceiving and living. The Constructive philosophy recognizes only one stream in our existence—life (you may call it creation, it is the same). Any thing or action which enhances life, propels it and adds to it something in the direction of growth, expansion and development, is Constructive. The 'how' is of secondary importance.

Therefore, to be Constructive in art does not necessarily mean to be abstract at all costs: Phidias, Leonardo da Vinci, Shakespeare, Newton, Pushkin, to name a few,—all were Constructive for their time but, it would be inconsistent with the Constructive

Idea to accept their way of perception and reaction to the world as an eternal and absolute measure. There is no place in a Constructive philosophy for eternal and absolute truths. All truths and values are our own constructions, subject to the changes of time and space as well as to the deliberate choice of life in its striving towards perfection. I have often used the word 'perfection' and ever so often been mistaken for an ecclesiastic evangelist, which I am not. I never meant 'perfection' in the sense of the superlative of good. 'Perfection', in the Constructive sense, is not a state but a process; not an ultimate goal but a direction. We cannot achieve perfection by stabilizing it—we can achieve it only by being in its stream; just as we cannot catch a train by riding in it, but once in it we can increase its speed or stop it altogether; and to be in the train is what the Constructive Idea is striving for.

It may be asked: what has it all to do with art in general and with Constructive art in particular? The answer is—it has to do with art more than with all other activities of the human spirit. I believe art to be the most immediate and most effective of all means of communication between human beings. Art as a mental action is unambiguous—it does not deceive—it cannot deceive, since it is not concerned with truths. We never ask a tree whether it says the truth, being green, being fragrant. We should never search in a work of art for truth—it is verity itself.

The way in which art perceives the world is sensuous (you may call it intuitive); the way it acts in response to this perception is spontaneous, irrational and factual (you may call it creative), and this is the way of life itself. This way alone brings to us ultimate results, makes history, and moulds life in the form as we know it.

Unless and until we adopt this way of reacting to the world in all our spiritual activities (science above all included) all our achievements will rest on sand.

Unless and until we have learned to carry our morality, our science, our knowledge, our culture, with the ease we carry our heart and brain and the blood in our veins, we will have no morality, no science, no knowledge, no culture.

To this end we have to construct these activities on the foundation and in the spirit of art.

I have chosen the absoluteness and exactitude of my lines, shapes and forms in the conviction that they are the most immediate medium for my communication to others of the rhythms and the state of mind I would wish the world to be in. This not only in the material world surrounding us but also in the mental and spiritual world we carry within us.

I think that the image they invoke is the image of good—not of evil; the image of order—not of chaos; the image of life—not of death. And that is all the content of my constructions amounts to. I should think that this is equally all that the constructive idea is driving at.

(2) Again I am repeatedly and annoyingly asked—where then do I get my forms from?

The artist as a rule is particularly sensitive to such intrusion in this jealously guarded depth of his mind—but, I do not see any harm in breaking the rule. I could easily tell where I get the crude content of my forms from, provided my words be taken not metaphorically but literally.

I find them everywhere around me, where and when I want to see them. I see them, if I put my mind to it, in a torn piece of cloud carried away by the wind. I see them in the green thicket of leaves and trees. I can find them in the naked stones on hills and roads. I may discern them in a steamy trail of smoke from a passing train or on the surface of a shabby wall. I can see them often even on the blank paper of my working-table. I look and find them in the bends of waves on the sea between the open-work of foaming crests; their apparition may be sudden, it may come and vanish in a second, but when they are over they leave with me the image of eternity's duration. I can tell you more (poetic though it may sound, it is nevertheless plain reality): sometimes a falling star, cleaving the dark, traces the breath of night on my window glass, and in that instantaneous flash I might see the very line for which I searched in vain for months and months.

These are the wells from which I draw the crude content of my forms. Of course, I don't take them as they come; the image of my perception needs an order and this order is my construction. I claim the right to do it so because this is what we all do in our mental world; this is what science does, what philosophy does, what life does. We all construct the image of the world as we wish it to be, and this spiritual world of ours will always be what and how we make it. It is Mankind alone that is shaping it in certain order out of a mass of incoherent and inimical realities. This is what it means to me to be Constructive.

(3) I may be in error in presuming that these maxims are simple to explain and easy to understand. I cannot judge, but I know for certain that for me it is much more difficult to prove the social justification for my work at this time.

A world at war, it seems to me, may have the right to reject my work as irrelevant to its immediate needs. I can say but little in my defence. I can only beg to be believed that I suffer with the world in all the misfortunes which are now fallen upon us. Day and night I carry the horror and pain of the human race with me. Will I be allowed to ask the leaders of the masses engaged in a mortal struggle of sheer survival: '. . . Must I, ought I, to keep and carry this horror through my art to the people?'—the people in the burned cities and scorched villages, the people in trenches, people in the ashes of their homes, the blinded shadows of human beings from the ruins and gibbets of devastated continents. . . . What can *I* tell *them* about pain and horror that they do not know?'

The human race is ill; dangerously, mortally ill—I offer my blood and flesh, for what it is worth, to help them; my life, if it is needed. But what is the worth of a single life—we all have learned to kill with ease and the road of death is made smooth and facile. The venom of hate has become our daily bread and only nurture. Am I to be blamed when I confess that I cannot find inspiration for my art in that stage of death and desolation.

I am offering in my art what comfort I can to alleviate the pains and convulsions of our time. I try to keep our despair from assuming such proportions that nothing will remain in our devastated life to prompt us to live. I try to guard in my work the image of the morrow we left behind us in our memories and foregone aspirations and to remind us that the image of the world can be different. It may be that I don't succeed in that at all, but I would not accept blame for trying it.

Constructive art as a whole, and my work as part of it, has still a long way to go to overcome the atmosphere of controversy that surrounds it. It has been and still is deliberately kept from the masses on the grounds that the masses would not understand it, and that it is not the kind of art the masses need. It is always very difficult to argue with anybody on such obscure grounds as this; the simplest and fairest thing to do would be to allow the masses to make their own judgment about this art. I am prepared to challenge any of the representatives of public opinion and put at their disposal any work of mine they choose to be placed where it belongs—namely, where the masses come and go and live and work. I would submit to any judgment the masses would freely pronounce about it. Would any leader of the masses ever accept my challenge—I wonder!

Meantime I can do nothing but leave my work to the few and selected ones to judge and discriminate.

Yours as ever,

GABO.

Dear Gabo,

It was unnecessary to apologize for the way you explain the constructive idea in art; like all artists who feel and think deeply about their work, you have said things which no critic could say for you, and said them with an eloquence which he might well envy. Certainly I myself could not improve on your statement, either by refinement or addition. All I can do, in this brief reply to your letter, is to anticipate some of the misunderstandings to which your words might be open.

You have done two things. You have shown why your art is called and rightly called 'constructive'; and you have tackled the problem of 'communication'—the most difficult problem which the artist in a democratic society has to face.

It is unfortunate that there are many sensitive and intelligent lovers of art, with no overriding prejudice against the modern movement as such, who yet fail to respond to so-called 'abstract' art. They find themselves unable to distinguish between a formal arrangement of line and colour which they rightly regard as merely 'decorative': and a constructed object which has a formal life and independence, which exists with an organic vitality all its own.

It seems to me that we shall have to search rather deeply for the true explanation of this phenomenon. Our modern civilization has to a large extent lost the sense of form—or, to be more exact, the faculty of immediately apprehending formal values. Even in music, where this faculty is absolutely indispensable, a great many listeners get on very comfortably without it, allowing their senses to be flooded formlessly and indiscriminatively by the *flow* of sound. Here, where I personally am incompetent, it is possible to see the enormity of the failure: form, in music, is for me a unity only dimly realized, in some few preludes and fugues of Bach, for example. Knowing my limitations in this art, it is easier for me to sympathize with those lovers of art who but dimly apprehend the formal unity of one of your constructions. They see lines meeting and crossing, radiating from certain points, planes intersecting—and there they stop, perhaps secretly longing for the colour and opacity which you have denied them —for colour is something that their atrophied senses may still be able to appreciate.

Why do they stop at that point? My dear Gabo, if we could confidently answer that question we should be close to the secret of the failure of our civilization. We are up against one of the fundamental inhibitions of our society—an inhibition which affects more segments of life than this aesthetic one we are discussing. It affects, most fatally, as I think you realize, our relations with one another—the simple exchange of sympathy and affection, the *reciprocity* which is the secret of social happiness. It is as though a vizor had fallen in front of our eyes, blocking some essential channel of communication. I am speaking in metaphors, but actually I believe that we are dealing with a physiological displacement. Since the triumph of scholasticism in the Middle Ages, the educated classes in Europe have been subjected to an intellectual discipline which has over-developed certain areas of the brain at the expense of others. I can give you the scientific formula for the process: 'The specialized area represented in the forebrain or neo-pallium, and its connections with adjacent special senses, supersedes and tends in its functions even to exclude the reactions which, through the diencephalon, mediate the function expressive of man's organism as a total process.'* And this physiologist, who is also a psychologist, then points out that 'this enormous disproportion of function now directed toward the cortical or neopallial segment, due to the preponderant use of the symbol, has made far-reaching and unsuspected encroachments upon the primary feelings and sensations of man as a total organism'. And this is the point which you, as well as I, try to make. You say 'the way in which art perceives the world is sensuous . . . the way it acts in response to this perception is spontaneous, irrational and factual . . . and this is the way of life itself'. Yes, indeed; but it is not the way of life in Europe in this time of Armageddon, which is a time of prejudice,

* *The Biology of Human Conflict*, by Trigant Burrow, M.D., Ph.D. New York (Macmillan Company), 1937, p. 117.

of calculated hatred, of deliberate destruction. For even war, in our 'scientific' civilization, has lost its spontaneity.

I only introduce these larger aspects to show that the problem is not limited to the field of art: we are not opposed merely by a few stupid academicians or jealous rivals: we are fighting a mass neurosis which has its roots in the historical developments of the past five centuries. It would therefore be foolish to be very optimistic about our immediate success.

This brings me to the only other comment I wish to make. You betray a social conscience. As a Russian who has experienced in person the terrors and exaltations, the high hopes and frustrations of the greatest social revolution of modern times, you might reasonably have taken refuge in some escapist philosophy. But you still retain a faith in the masses, and you are even confident that these masses would understand and appreciate your constructive art, if allowed a free and unbiased contact with it. To a degree you are perhaps right: I have always found that simple unsophisticated people have a more natural, serious and sound reaction to abstract art than the neurotic climbers who cling desperately to some rung of the social or educational ladder. But do not ask for the 'judgment' of the masses. That is to encourage the very attitude of intellectual detachment which we are most anxious to avoid. Erect your constructions in public places by all means; but then wait and see . . . The metaphor of the catalyst has been overworked in modern criticism, but it is a very useful one. You must not expect a direct reaction from a work of art in modern society: but dropped like a foreign substance into that agitated sea, it might, without losing either its identity or its purity, effect a transformation both rich and strange.

Yours ever,

H. R.

IV

14
English Art

In any attempt to define the essential characteristics of English art (and that is to be the aim of this essay), we must begin with an explanation of what we mean by the word 'English'. Geographically we know what England is, and though there seems to be a good deal of doubt about the question, we could perhaps arrive at a satisfactory racial definition. But none of these senses would suit our purpose. Art has a way of defying boundaries, whether of land or of blood, and what we seek is actually a definition of something at once so subtle and so penetrating as the English spirit. Of certain works of art, say of the seventh and eighth centuries, we can say with confidence that they were made in England, and with the Celtic tradition to sponsor them, there is no reason to suppose that the artists were not natives of this country. But such works speak no English to us, and what we have to determine is at what period does art become specifically English, by style and not by provenance, and in what does this English style consist. We can then attempt to trace this style in its various manifestations.

Matthew Arnold, in his *Study of Celtic Literature*, ventured to affirm that the Celtic races have shown a singular inaptitude for the plastic arts. Today, with a considerably greater knowledge of the forms of their art, and of its psychological implications, no one would venture to be so dogmatic. The very contrast which Matthew Arnold draws between the German and the Celtic races, on a plus and minus scale, we would now rather regard as a direct opposition of modes of artistic experience. The basis of what Arnold regarded as the German superiority in this respect was 'their fidelity to nature'—a basis which the Celts would instinctively have rejected. So when Arnold goes on to say that this inaptitude for the plastic arts 'strikingly diminishes as soon as the German, not the Celtic element, predominates in the race,' he is merely affirming his own particular conception of art. How that conception was still further limited is shown in the restriction he has yet to make on English art. 'There is something,' he says, 'which seems to prevent our reaching real mastership in the plastic arts, as the more unmixed German races have reached it.' He asks what European jury would give our greatest geniuses, Reynolds and Turner, the rank of masters along with Raphael and Correggio, Dürer and Rubens, and concludes that they lack *architectonice*, a favourite word of his, by which he meant 'the highest power of composition, by which painting accomplishes the very uttermost which it is given to painting to accomplish'. Their success, such as it is, is of another kind; 'they succeed in magic, in beauty, in grace, in expressing almost the inexpressible; here is the charm of Reynolds' children and Turner's seas; the impulse to express the inexpressible carries Turner so far, that at last it carries him away, and even long before he is carried away, even in works that are justly extolled, one can see the stamp-mark, as the French say, of insanity. The excellence, therefore, the success, is on the side of spirit.'

Though his argument is based on a limited conception of art, and more particularly on a misconception of classical art common to the eighteenth century (whose child Arnold was), nevertheless he has arrived at a conclusion which as a generalization at first sight seems acceptable enough, and worth testing in a more detailed survey. Perhaps it does not amount to more than saying that English art has been predominantly romantic, and Matthew Arnold's further characterization of our artists, as being 'a little over-balanced by soul and feeling', and as working too directly for these, makes it quite clear that this interpretation of the matter was at the back of his mind.

That style which is the first to be distinct as a style, and to be associated with a racial blend that was henceforth to be distinctively English, was formed during the so-called Anglo-Saxon period—that is to say, during the two centuries which preceded the Conquest. About the origins of that style there are two opinions. English art historians, with a characteristic modesty, look abroad and find our inspiration in the Carolingian style. But other, chiefly German scholars, with what seems to me a finer critical insight, and a higher degree of historical probability, find the origin of this style in England itself—even assert that it was England which inspired the Carolingian schools. When it is agreed that this style has for its main characteristic a certain calligraphic or linear freedom, what seems more likely than the supposition that it was derived directly from the linear style *par excellence*, the Celtic style, which in these islands maintained its existence and its vitality long after it had disappeared from the Continent? This would seem to contradict Matthew Arnold's talk of Celtic inaptitude in the plastic arts, but I have already suggested that this was based on very incomplete knowledge.

This linear quality, 'the bounding line and its infinite inflections and movements', as Blake was to express it, is clearly discernible in all types of Anglo-Saxon art—in the Alfred Jewel no less than in the Bayeux Tapestry, but most of all in the illuminated manuscripts of the Winchester school. Of the origin or foundation of that school we know nothing, and it is merely gratuitous to assume a derivation from the school of Rheims, which it most nearly resembles. The Winchester school and the typical contemporary Byzantine style of the Ottonian school stand apart not only in stylistic extremes, but also in extremes of geographic latitude, and it would seem natural to assume that what is intermediate not only in style but in position, namely the school of Rheims, was anything but a source of origination. But the point is of little importance; what is essential to recognize is the supreme vitality of the Winchester style, the most superb style in the whole range of mediaeval illumination. The earliest Winchester manuscript (the Charter of Edgar, British Mus. Vesp. A. viii) is dated 966; the most famous is the Benedictional of St Æthelwold belonging to the Duke of Devonshire, probably completed about 980. This latter manuscript represents the style in all its richness, and at the point of its greatest vigour. Here, indeed, is magic, beauty, and grace, and a capacity to express almost the inexpressible (or as we might say, the divine); and as for *architectonice*, whatever that may prove to be when we come to analyse the claims of the classical style, we must conclude that it is something of no great importance if it is lacking here. The freshness and the freedom of these drawings, their incredible sureness, these qualities have often been noted and duly praised; but less than justice has been done to the high sense of form, the instinct for composition, displayed on every illuminated page. Two types of composition, one fixed and symmetrical, a rigid but crisp scaffolding, the other free and floating through the framework like a careless banner, play together in faultless harmony.

England, we might therefore say, in this tenth century stood for freedom and for grace; and these qualities were expressed as only they can be expressed in the plastic arts—by the infinite inflections of the line, the line which alone is capable of giving plastic expression to rhythm. Nothing proves the vitality of this style more impressively than its survival throughout the succeeding Romanesque period. Romanesque signifies static in architecture, which is physically a static art, the new style triumphs naturally. The underlying linear rhythm is reduced to a fret round the massive arches. In sculpture, as notably at Malmesbury, the linear style survives unchecked; it is perfectly represented in the twelfth century relief of the Virgin and Child in the Chapterhouse at York. We find the style effectively translated into the new art of stained glass, reinforced here by the technical necessity of the lead lines. But illumination continues to be the distinctively English art, and though the Continental schools are now in full rivalry and the Winchester school has become a little outmoded, a little mannered (but can still produce a masterpiece like the Winchester Bible), there are now a number of English schools, all amazingly competent, and all decidedly English. They are English—the Bibles and Psalters from Bury St Edmunds, St Albans, Dover, Durham and York—in precisely the same characteristics: in their forceful linear rhythm, in their comparative freedom from Byzantine solemnity.

This brings us to a second general characteristic of English art which is perhaps present from the beginning—I mean what Ruskin, in rather shocked tones, called 'our earthly instinct': 'a delight in the forms of burlesque which are connected in some degree with the foulness of evil', a quality, Ruskin held, which has precluded our art from ever being properly sublime, and is present as a blemish in Chaucer and Shakespeare, and which renders 'some of quite the greatest, wisest, and most moral of English writers now almost useless for our youth'. But though he deplored this quality, Ruskin was honest enough to admit that 'whenever Englishmen are wholly without this instinct, their genius is comparatively weak and restricted'. At first sight it seems an odd quality to find in combination with the spiritual virtues of magic, beauty, and grace which we have already admitted; but if we do no more than rely on André Gide's observation, that in all great works of art extremes meet, we must be prepared to reconcile these two apparently contradictory qualities in English art. Actually, however, the contradiction only arises in minds bound, like Ruskin's and Matthew Arnold's, to a puritanical conception of spirituality, or to an idealistic conception of sublimity. It possibly did not occur to Chaucer or to Shakespeare, or to the earlier artists we are now considering, that anything created by God could be inapposite; and the whole virtue of the monkey in the margin, and of the grotesque in general, is that it should remind us of the immeasurable distance between the human and the divine.

Whatever the motive, it is certain that already in the eleventh century English art is characterized by a detailed observation of nature, a realism, by no means inconsistent with the absolute qualities of grace and rhythm conveyed by the linear conventions. The result is, that when the great change of sentiment came over the Christian world in the twelfth century, and a new movement of thought began which was the prelude to realism in philosophy, to humanism in science, to charity, and simplicity in religion (in short, Franciscanism), and to naturalism in art, English artists were again ready to take the lead. Indeed, no abrupt transition is observable in English art. The line still dominates the composition. It is suaver, more restrained in the interests of realism, the sentiment expressed is sweeter. But it is the same sentiment, in the illuminator of the Benedictional of St Æthelwold as in Matthew Paris, and the same means are adopted to express it: the linear style. How we regard the consequences will depend on our aesthetic standards; if, with Matthew Arnold we regard 'fidelity to nature' as the only standard, then the English style, as we progress through the thirteenth and fourteenth centuries, can only seem increasingly insular. And actually that style itself could not hold out indefinitely against the forces arranged against it, chief of which was the increasingly uniform character of Christian culture in Europe. The Church was gathering its scattered sheep into a closer fold, and in that closer fold the communication of fashions became rapid and inevitable. It was not an age to encourage individuality of any kind, and the English artist was to discover that, in competition, his insular methods were ill-adapted to express the exact shades demanded by 'fidelity to nature'. The sentiments of humanism are too vague to be bounded by a line. The line could still have its way—its erratic and unnatural way—in the depiction of the folds of a garment, and it had its way with a vengeance in such an English oddity as the Perpendicular style in architecture. It survives, in its persistent manner, well into the sixteenth century; but it is gradually petering out, and with it disappears an essential quality in English art, a quality which English art, in spite of the sporadic effort of William Blake, was to be long in recovering.

Not that the process of change was without its compensations. But unfortunately they do not belong to the plastic arts—they are to be sought in our literature, an art infinitely more resilient. There our other national characteristic, our earthly instinct, found full scope, and in the poetry of Chaucer and Shakespeare the most natural aspects of humanism found perfect expression; our spiritual quality being at the same time not inadequately represented by the *Faerie Queene*. By keeping a comparative view of the various arts one can realize the inadequacy of external causes, such as the Great Plague, to explain the disappearance of any one art. It might be suggested that the plastic arts, being so manual, are more dependent on an unbroken tradition; and that a catastrophe which left perhaps no more than one artist in ten alive to carry on such a tradition is a sufficient explanation of the different destinies. But that is to take a superficial and dilettante view of the craft of literature, which is no less dependent on its man-power and its accumulated wisdom. We are left to conclude that the plastic arts all but disappeared in England between the fourteenth and the eighteenth century simply because they were superseded by a more powerful and an alien mode. The quest which began with Giotto and Masaccio simply did not, and it might be said that for some reason it *could* not, enter into the plastic consciousness of an English artist. To enquire into the cause of that inability would take us too far from our present subject, and into the doubtful fields of social psychology. Whatever the cause, we have to confess that for four centuries English art (which is different from art in England) did not exist.

If, as I believe, the source of our technical inspiration had failed in its depths, it might conceivably have happened that the other tributary to our national genius in art would have been strengthened. Our earthly instinct might have found a new mode of expression in the plastic arts comparable with the freedom it had found in poetry and drama. But here the essential distinction between the plastic and the literary arts becomes evident. Literature is a refinement, or at any rate a variety, of our normal and natural mode of communication. The plastic arts, on the other hand, have become a special or abnormal mode, and depend on the perfection of an additional and, biologically speaking, vestigial instrument. That instrument, in English art, had been the line. When the line, owing to the development of new instruments of plastic communication, no longer served its purpose, the whole equipment of the English artist was out-of-date, and he had no aptitude for the new instrument. He might, so long as he retained the line, have dispensed with medieval grace and spirituality, and then turned his earthly instinct to account. But in the circumstances he could only wait for a new plastic consciousness to evolve, and that takes centuries. Even in the native land of the alternative tactile values, a whole century elapses between Giotto and Masaccio. It would not have been too long to have waited two centuries in England. But meanwhile a very different consciousness evolved, a consciousness which not only inhibited any growth of the sensuous southern mode of spatial realization, but which threatened and finally destroyed the earthly instinct in our literature: the moral consciousness of puritanism.

I cannot speak without prejudice on this subject, so I shall not dwell upon it. To anyone who is inclined to base his whole philosophy of life on aesthetic values, what we gained in moral fibre and eventually in economic prosperity by that change of spirit which culminated in the Reformation can never compensate for what we lost in magic, beauty, and grace. From any other point of view, social, religious, economic, a contrast has been drawn which is largely sentimental in its bias. But from the point of view we are concerned with, there is no possible confusion of values, because the contrast is between the presence and the absence of an indigenous will to art. Now and then, as in the miniatures of Nicholas Hilliard, we may fancy we see a flicker of the national tradition. But actually it is not until the appearance of William Hogarth, and then only in its earthly aspect, that the English artist is once more conscious of his birthright.

iii

Though Hogarth* was openly and aggressively national in

* I have dealt with the special case of Hogarth in an essay which is printed as an appendix to *Art and Society*, London (Faber & Faber), 1945.

sentiment, the art of painting in England had for so long been dominated by foreigners that it would have needed a genius of the highest rank to restore the native tradition. With all his virtues, Hogarth was not such a genius; he was too dependent on the conventions of his age, and when he came to paint English scenes and interpret English life, the methods he employed were those of the Dutch and Venetian artists whose presence in the country he so much resented. But though he has his subtleties in the use of light and shade, and individuality in the disposition of his paint, his general attainments are not to be compared with those of a Tiepolo, a Vermeer, or even a Jan Steen. It is only in an isolated miracle like *The Shrimp Girl* that he gives us any indication of what he might have done had he thrown the foreign conventions to the wind, and so anticipated the nineteenth century revolution. Nevertheless, Hogarth's is the first great name in what is known historically as the English School, and we should be doing violence to the facts if, for the sake of our categories, we refused to find anything specifically English in his art. Baudelaire, in his notes on certain foreign caricaturists, written in 1857, deals with Hogarth and Cruikshank, and the specifically English qualities he finds in them are in effect medieval qualities. 'Je retrouve bien dans Hogarth ce je ne sais quoi de sinistre, de violent et de résolu, qui respire dans presque toutes les oeuvres du pays du spleen.' What the French, and particularly Baudelaire, imply by the Englishman's spleen has never been quite clear to me. It is perhaps explained by another sentence in Baudelaire's criticism of Hogarth: 'Le talent de Hogarth comporte en soi quelque chose de froid, d'astringent, de funèbre. Cela serre le coeur.' Speaking on the same page of another artist, Seymour Haden, whom one is rather astonished to find in such company, Baudelaire says: 'Dans Seymour, comme dans les autres Anglais, violence et amour de l'excessif; manière simple, archibrutale et directe, de poser le sujet.' Though the feeling, in Hogarth and Cruikshank, is of a narrowly defined type, we are back again at Matthew Arnold's structure of the English artists, that they are a little over-balanced by soul and feeling, and work too directly for these. But what Arnold regards as an aesthetic limitation, Baudelaire regards as a positive virtue, the expression of an inevitable sentiment. But for Baudelaire, who had escaped from the false identification of art and beauty, the grotesque was a mode of the imagination, and moreover an intelligent mode (l'intelligence du fantastique), and he is enthusiastic in his praise of Cruikshank's 'abondance inépuisable dans le grotesque'. 'Le grotesque coule incessament et inévitablement de la pointe de Cruikshank, comme les rimes riches de la plume des poëtes naturels. Le grotesque est son habitude.' And it is an English habitude, a form of burlesque connected in some degree with the foulness of evil, as Ruskin would have it; its virtue being precisely in its realism, its refusal to shut its eyes to the presence of evil in the world.

But the phrase, 'the English School', does not generally call to mind the names of Hogarth and Cruikshank. The first, and in some ways the most typical, representative of this school is Thomas Gainsborough. Here certainly there is no ambiguous quality like spleen, but nevertheless there is something so exclusively English about Gainsborough, that in spite of all he owed to his predecessors in Italy and the Netherlands, we should expect to find his English character reflected intimately in his methods of painting.

Reynolds, in his well-known tribute to Gainsborough, freely admitted him to comparison with the great Italian masters, and yet held that his distinction as the founder of an English school rested upon his originality. When artists communicate to their country a share of their reputation, he said, and so justify the appellation English, it is a portion of fame not borrowed from others, but solely acquired by their own labour and talents. But his analysis of Gainsborough's originality is a little limited; he mentions, 'as the fundamental', the love which he had to his art, and beyond that, his capacity for observation. 'He had a habit of continually remarking to those who happened to be about him whatever peculiarity of countenance, whatever accidental combination of figure, or happy effects of light and shade, occurred in prospects, in the sky, in walking the streets, or in company. If, in his walks, he found a character that he liked, and whose attendance was to be obtained, he ordered him to his house: and from the fields he brought into his painting-room, stumps of trees, weeds, and animals of various kinds; and designed them, not from memory, but immediately from the objects. He even farmed a kind of model of landscapes on his table; composed of broken stones, dried herbs, and pieces of looking-glass, which he magnified and improved into rocks, trees, and water.' There is a naïvety about such a method which we English love, and

Gainsborough was a naïve person. But we are far from an excess
on the side of spirit; there is nothing here 'a little overbalanced by
soul and feeling, working too directly for these'. And as we
have already accepted Matthew Arnold's diagnosis of the
national characteristics in our art, we can only conclude that by
Gainsborough's time a profound modification had taken place.
Reynolds's definition of his genius is of the familiar Carlylean
kind—an infinite capacity for taking pains. It belongs to that
aspect of English genius more typical of our science and philosophy—that gift for tireless detailed observation, the foundation
of our reputation as empiricists. This gift was actually fostered by
the Puritan tradition, with its general distrust of imagination and
sensuous perception; and Hogarth, for example, was decidedly a
Puritan moralist, a little overbalanced, shall we say, by virtue
and indignation. But there was nothing of the moralist in the
personal make-up of Gainsborough; his sensibility was pure of
any prejudices external to its operations; which is to say that he
was, like all great artists, predominantly a sensualist. Again, our
earthly instinct. But in this case the instinct had a preceptor in
Rubens, and a comparison of Gainsborough with Rubens might
restrain our generalizations. Perhaps the racial differences involved are small—Gainsborough being a native of the least
Celtic part of England, the part nearest to the land of Rubens.
However much he gained from Rubens, however much Rubens
is responsible for the change that came over Gainsborough in his
Bath period, the differences between the two men remain wide.
Gainsborough never sacrificed his spontaneity, his greatest gift,
and he never, like poor Romney, attempted to emulate the
grandiose conceptions of his foreign masters. He kept his feet
firmly on English soil, and did not ever paint against the grain of
his English temperament. He was much nearer than any painter
had been for three hundred years to the characteristic technique
of our early artists. His thin brush strokes, deft and dexterous,
feathery in their lightness—what do these express but a joy in
linear rhythms, a desire for clarity and concision, for the determinate and the definite?

From a wider point of view, these are the classical virtues too
—at least, the virtues of the classical technique. And the century
of Gainsborough was to see a classical revival in Europe, not the
first, and assuredly not the last. It is probable that none of the
nostalgias for the past, particularly for the antique world of

Greece and Rome, ever succeeds in re-creating the reality of their life and art. Actually there was no unity in that world, and we are left to choose between the Greece of Parmenides and the Greece of Plato, or, as Nietzsche expressed it, between the cult of Dionysos and the cult of Apollo. Renaissance classicism seems to recover some at least of the superficial aspects of ancient life and ancient art, but the classicism of Reynolds and his French predecessors in the theory of art was surely based on a complete misunderstanding of the Greek point of view. A contemporary French critic, in a brilliant study of Nietzsche, summarizes the distinction which Nietzsche laboured so passionately to make between a realistic and a romantic conception of classicism, and with some modification we shall find the distinction one that we can use to explain our dissatisfaction with eighteenth-century classicism. 'Nietzsche,' writes Monsieur Maulnier, 'applied to classical art that critical gift which, more even than his gift as a poet or as a metaphysician, was his birthright. He first brought to light the fundamental virtue of such art—the perfect union of inner richness and tragic simplicity, of lucidity and violent instincts. The classical era is thus for him the apollonian era *par excellence*, that in which the passions only acquire their moral profundity behind a rigid discipline, that of the *mask*. Classical man is masked; that is to say, Nietzsche finds in him, not only the strength of the most violent passions, but also the strength of a heroic hypocrisy, the art of self-mastery, the grand style . . . When, analysing tragic realism, he observes that tragedy is metaphor, the transmutation of life into discourse, and is in consequence as far from pretending to imitate life as the musician is from imitating cries of passion in his music, he puts his finger on what is perhaps the central truth of classical art, and of great art in general, a mode of expression different from life, more perfect than life in that it avoids all clumsiness, insignificance and incoherence. No one, perhaps, has come so near to defining the enduring value of the classical discipline, which aims at rendering the most ardent and most audible passion, not at moderating or mutilating it. . . .' * Now observe how subtly, but how vitally, this conception of classical art varies in Reynolds: 'The whole beauty and grandeur of Art consists . . . in being able to get above all singular forms, local customs, particularities, and details of every kind. All the objects which are exhibited to our view by

* *Nietzsche*, by Thierry Maulnier. Paris, 1933.

Nature, upon close examination will be found to have their blemishes and defects. The most beautiful forms have something about them like weakness, minuteness, or imperfection. But it is not every eye that perceives these blemishes. It must be an eye long used to the contemplation and comparison of these forms. The painter who aims at the greatest style . . . corrects Nature by herself, her imperfect state by her more perfect. His eye being enabled to distinguish the accidental deficiencies, excrescences, and deformities of things, from their general figures, he makes out an abstract idea of their forms more perfect than anyone original. . . . The idea of the perfect state of Nature, which the artist calls Ideal beauty, is the great leading principle by which works of genius are conducted.'

It will be observed that Reynolds has left out the passions. His mask is perfect, his discipline rigid; but it is an abstraction, an intellectual calculation of the highest common denominator to be observed in the calm features of nature. What was meant as a discipline of the emotions, Reynolds converts into a discipline of the mind. The empirical bias of the Puritan, of the de-natured Englishman, triumphs in the last sanctuary of instinct and sensibility, and a stultification sets in. Well might Blake say that Reynolds was 'hired by Satan to depress art'.

Significantly his art is the art of the portrait painter. His excursions into allegory and the heroic are not his happiest efforts. But in portraiture he could exercise his talent for observation, though he could hardly, by this means, arrive at an abstract idea of man. His gift was psychological; and beyond this, an infinite capacity for taking pains. Sometimes he so far forgets his principles as to achieve spontaneity, as in the portrait of Nelly O'Brien. Otherwise, and in general, he reflected the Englishmen about him; but this is too passive a rôle to have anything distinctively English about it. It is not the matter, but the manner, that is significant for this enquiry.

iv

The course of this argument leads inevitably to William Blake. For Blake embodied consciously and consistently the original characteristics of our art, and though the very universality of his genius involved technical limitations (for all the faculties and instincts have to be concentrated in one channel to ensure perfection of expression), he so clearly represents the national temper and with such power of imagination, that any judgment relative to these standards must give him the highest rank. The artists of the Middle Ages are anonymous; but of those who belong to subsequent ages, only Turner is of equal significance; and Turner, beside Blake, is intellectually naïve. Blake's reaction to Reynolds may be studied in his literary works. It is the reaction of a terribly sincere spirit to something he believes to be sham and sophisticated. Sure above all of the validity of his spiritual sensations, and of their superiority to all merely rational modes of apprehension, Blake set himself the task of making his vision determinate, of giving imagination an outline. His art is an attempt to combine the greatest intensity of subjective thought and feeling with the greatest clarity of objective representation. And that is precisely the character of all great art—of classical art in Nietzsche's right conception of it, of Christian art in its Byzantine and early Gothic manifestations, and of the isolated art of an individual like Blake.

Literally speaking, Blake was not completely isolated. His friend and contemporary, John Flaxman, is an artist who must be rehabilitated in the light of these considerations. His conception of classicism was superficial and rational; but it encouraged a linear technique, and the grace and delicacy of his line is in the English tradition. But it was not realized; it was not fed by a vision like Blake's. If only from his close association with Flaxman, Blake was conscious of the values of classical art, but he held that 'we do not want either Greek or Latin Models if we are but just and true to our own Imaginations, those Worlds of Eternity in which we shall live for ever in Jesus our Lord'. This is, of course, the voice of the mystic, but it is not easy to dissociate the mystic from the poet and the painter, and the genius is constant for every aspect of the man. That he did not use paint like a genius was a conscious choice rather than a personal limitation. He did not believe that the technique of oil paint was sufficiently definite for his purpose, and the failure of his experiments in tempera and other media was due to defective chemistry rather than to inefficient handling. When the chemistry is sound, as in his watercolour drawings, his illuminated printing and his 'colour-printed drawings', the hand is sure and instinctive. And unless what Matthew Arnold calls *architectonice* is to be measured by the square yard, that quality too is present in the highest degree. Indeed, so powerful is the sense of composition in many of Blake's drawings, that they seem to transcend the scale and medium of their execution, and expand in our receptive minds to the dimensions of a Michaelangelo or a Rubens. Nowhere else in the whole range of plastic art, unless in Giotto, is the capacity of the line for rendering three-dimensional form so amply demonstrated, and nowhere is solidity so compatible with movement and ethereal light.

That qualities more profound than style and technique are involved in the establishment of a tradition is shown by the fate of Blake's immediate followers—George Richmond, Edward Calvert and Samuel Palmer. Their engravings, woodcuts and watercolours have a lyrical appeal which is valid enough, but we feel that their inspiration is literary, and in the damning sense. Blake could take a poet's images and translate them into their visual equivalents, but his followers take poetic ideas and illustrate them. There is a world of difference—the difference between an equivalent and a derivative. It is a difference worth observing in certain contemporary movements.

The scope of this essay does not allow for the consideration of several artists of the eighteenth and nineteenth century who undoubtedly as individuals and as craftsmen occupy a distinguished place in the history of English art, but who are, in comparison with foreign artists, unjustly depreciated. Generally provincial in their origins, often self-taught and endowed with remarkable natural genius, they are too mute and inglorious to rise to a representative status. In a sense there is something very English about them all; their very eccentricity is English. They have English characters and they paint English scenes, but in the intimate or spiritual sense they are not English at all. Chief of these is Richard Wilson, who might as well have been a Dutchman or an Italian so far as any of our racial characteristics find expression in his style of expression. And though superficially they reflect the forms and colours of our land and people, even such painters as Stubbs, Morland and James Ward can be dismissed as insignificant for our purpose. The case of William Etty (and, a generation later, of Alfred Stevens) is almost pathological in its absolute denationalization—its utter remoteness for any consciousness of an English tradition. But with the rise of the English school of landscape painting, which begins with Girtin

and ends with Turner, we are once more face to face with a
phenomenon which is completely and peculiarly English in its
essence.

v

In its essence it would be possible to regard the English school
of watercolour painting as a return to the grace, the clarity and
the brilliance of our medieval illuminators. A pedantic designa-
tion insists on the term watercolour *drawing*, and the method is
essentially a linear one. In a casual way, Ruskin somewhere
draws a distinction between drawing with a brush and painting
with a brush—a distinction which in our own time has been
brilliantly elaborated by Heinrich Wölfflin. In Wölfflin's sense,
the English watercolourists are always linear, and never *malerisch*.
In its origins the method was used principally for topographical
sketches, and it was chosen as a medium for this purpose precisely for its precision. That this technique was raised to the
dignity of an art is due to the genius of Girtin, who in his short
lifetime left sufficient masterpieces to determine the future
course of English landscape painting. It is not often possible to
prove an influence (which does not always imply an imitation),
and in matters of technique a single revelation is sufficient to
deflect the course of an artist's development. There is, of course,
sufficient documentary evidence to show that both Constable
and Turner studied Girtin to good effect; what must remain a
matter of opinion is the extent to which the development of the
later masters would have been retarded without the example of
Girtin. Girtin, who died, we must remember, at the age of
twenty-seven, was probably the greatest genius of the three; he
impresses us by at once using his talents with intelligence. Not
only his hand, but his mind was spontaneous.

It would be pushing our categories once again to paradoxical
limits to suggest that the English qualities of our water-colourists
can be explained as a re-emergence of the basic linear signature
of our race. There is much more to it than that. There is, in
fact, a certain sublimity, product not only of line, but also of tone
and composition and of the whole romantic conception of landscape, a conception not confined to painting, even finding its
supreme expression in the poetry of Wordsworth. Laurence
Binyon, in his interesting lectures on *Landscape in English Art
and Poetry*, has suggested that this love of landscape was always

present in our national character, being part of our Celtic heritage; he quotes an early Welsh poem by the bard Taliesin, and says 'it is quite inconceivable that any poet of the classical tradition, any poet who had absorbed the Mediterranean mind, could have written thus, or indeed have written on such a subject. Taliesin identifies himself, as he sings, with the intangible, the invisible; with the wind that symbolizes the mystery of the world.' The validity of this comparison depends entirely on what Laurence Binyon means by the phrase 'identifies himself . . . with the intangible, the invisible'. In the fragment of the poem he quotes, the process is rather one of actualizing the intangible, the invisible (in this case the wind); and though I am not familiar enough with Celtic poetry to express any opinion about its general character, I feel that the typically English attitude towards nature is always more objective than Laurence Binyon implies. In my book on Wordsworth I have already pointed out how realistic, in his case, the so-called romantic attitude to nature was—how it was related to the empirical school of philosophy represented, in Wordsworth's time, by Hartley. Wordsworth's attitude towards nature is not, of course, a simple one—it is not what the psychologists would call a direct extrovert attitude. In his case it was a reaction from an opposite tendency. In his well-known note on his childhood he wrote: 'I was often unable to think of external things as having external existence, and I communed with all that I saw as something not apart from, but inherent in, my own immaterial nature.' This is certainly an identification 'with the intangible, the invisible'. But Wordsworth goes on to say: 'Many times while going to school I grasped at a wall or tree to recall myself from this abyss of idealism to the reality', and in my study of Wordsworth, I suggested that his whole poetic development, in relation to nature or the outer world, was an attempt on the poet's part to recall himself from an abyss of idealism to the reality. That is how, I think, Wordsworth came to create the actuality and vividness of his visible world. It was a process of realization, of objectification, determined by an intense psychological need. I suggest, therefore, that this Celtic strain in the English race, pressing us on, in Matthew Arnold's words, 'to the impalpable, the ideal', is at once, as he would have it, the cause of our impotence in the higher branches of the plastic arts, but also, as he did not perceive, by a process of compensation or reaction perhaps induced by other elements in our racial blend, the cause of the minute particularity of our objective vision. Constable himself described his purpose as 'a pure apprehension of natural fact'. The phrase is perhaps more significant than he intended it to be; for 'pure apprehension' implies something different from the analytical observation of the scientist, while 'natural fact' warns us against any idealistic interpretation. Unfortunately we have no record of Constable's state of mind during childhood, but can we doubt, when the products are so similar, that it was of the same cast as Wordsworth's? Constable was humbler; it was not for him to 'breathe in worlds to which the heaven of heavens is but a veil', not for him to pass Jehovah with his thunder and the choir of shouting angels, unalarmed. Compared with Wordsworth, as compared with Turner, he is without vision; but perhaps some deep common sense warned him of the instability of human visions. Certainly today, whilst we differ among ourselves irreconcilably about the genius of Turner, we accept the purer if more limited genius of Constable without reserve. We recognize that none of our artists has given fuller expression to our interests in natural phenomena, has more fully satisfied our desire to have these phenomena recorded in all their variety and aspects. But Constable does more than record; he communicates excitement by his method of recording—and does so, not merely by his deftness in seizing the actualities of light and colour and atmosphere, but by giving us a surplus which is the man himself, his sense of style and his creation of form.

vi

I have already said that there is no settled opinion about the greatness of Turner. Some people, no doubt, have been adversely affected by Ruskin's eloquence, and by the completeness of his exposition; for most critics are human enough to want to discover their own reasons for liking an artist, and it may be doubted whether Ruskin has left unexpressed a single possible reason for admiring Turner. But when we have discounted personal prejudices of this kind, we are left with obstinate questionings. A comparison with Constable should quickly reveal the differences involved. Turner studied nature as humbly and intently as Constable. He was able by his technical deftness to reproduce equally well and perhaps with more ease the specific details of natural fact. At a time when Constable was still fumbling in the wake of the Dutch landscape painters, Turner could produce such a magnificent transcript of natural fact as we find in *Calais Pier*; and no painting in the whole range of the naturalistic school is so subtly and so truly observed as his *Frosty Morning*. But Turner was not satisfied to be fed in a wise passiveness. He became inspired by what, for want of a better phrase, I am in the habit of calling a sense of glory. It is not quite fair of Ruskin to say that 'Constable perceives in a landscape that the grass is wet, the meadows flat, and the boughs shady; that is to say, about as much as, I suppose, might in general be apprehended, between them, by an intelligent fawn and a skylark. Turner perceives at a glance the whole sum of visible truth open to human intelligence.' This is at once to depress Constable's genius to a level below what is implied in his expression 'pure apprehension of natural fact', and to exalt Turner's genius to a universality which, frankly, it did not possess. Rather than possessing a universal mind, Turner was conscious of the qualities which such a mind gave to the art of painting. He knew that such a mind, however much it grounds itself on patient observation, must finally lift itself on the wings of the imagination. Turner's emulation of Claude, which has so often been treated as technical in aim, is, as I conceive it, more imaginative. It was not Claude's light, nor his limpidity, but his sublimity that Turner wished to rival. If it were a question of technical achievement, Turner must have been conscious that already in a score of paintings, pictures like his *Windsor*, *The Sun rising through Vapour*, and *Abingdon*, he was master of more effects than Claude, in his sedateness, had ever attempted. And as Turner so triumphantly demonstrated, there was no question of his hero's superior sense of form. But in painting a subject like *Dido building Carthage*, Turner was trying to demonstrate that with all his talents he too was capable of this further grace, this apex of sublimity, which justified the Grand Style. If Turner had been satisfied with this achievement we should have the measure of his limitations. He would have fallen into the same error as Reynolds, and all his observation would have been dammed up against a static idealism. But largely through the medium of watercolour, Turner was gradually discovering what might be called the autonomy of colour. He was discovering that colours could be organized into a harmony independent of nature. So long as he confined himself to watercolours, the experiment could pass with its significance unobserved—however remote from nature, they could be regarded as studies that would be absorbed and corrected in some finished oil-painting. But with *Ulysses deriding Polyphemus* (1829) Turner boldly transferred his experiments to canvas, and the first stage in the revolution which was to lead to the modern position was completed (the second and final stage had to wait for Cézanne). Ruskin might ingeniously maintain that Turner's colours were after all natural colours, once you had abstracted the shadows from objects; but except in the sense that all colour is given in nature, his argument is a vain paralogism. From that moment, until he reaches the logical conclusion of his method in paintings like the *Interior at Petworth*, Turner is on a path which leads him to what Matthew Arnold regarded as the verges of insanity, but which we, with surely a broader vision, regard as an alternative mode of expression to any conceived by Matthew Arnold. If we ask what, in the process and from Matthew Arnold's point of view, has been sacrificed, we are led back to the ambiguous phrase 'fidelity to nature'. Arnold would no doubt have murmured about his *architectonice*, but if by this he meant the formal organization of the picture, we must claim that even in his freest harmonies, the order is adequate for the material. What has been lost is definition, and this is sacrificed for the sake of intensity. It is interesting to speculate on Blake's possible reaction to Turner's later work. It is natural to assume that he would have condemned it outright, as he condemned Rembrandt. But it is just possible that he would have hesitated, recognizing that Turner, in destroying chiaroscuro, was on the side of the angels —without knowing it.

vii

By the strangest of destinies, all that was gained by Constable and Turner—all that was recovered of the native virtues of our art—was to be lost to France. The effect of Constable on Delacroix is one of the most dramatic events in the history of art, just as the letter written by a group of French Impressionists acknowledging their debt to Turner is one of the most moving.* I have no ready explanation for the seeming perversity of our national

* Quoted by Clive Bell, *Landmarks in Nineteenth Century Painting* (1927), p. 136.

trend. It is hardly that the men were lacking. Stevens at least had all the necessary natural ability; so, I am inclined to think, had some of the Pre-Raphaelites, Millais and Madox Brown. But for some reason they shut their minds against the modern consciousness revealed in the work of Constable and Turner, and escaped into odd sanctuaries of pedantry and snobbery. It is a phenomenon not confined to painting; in poetry the early Wordsworth is followed by the late Wordsworth, Keats by Tennyson, whilst, by contrast, in the freer atmosphere of France a Baudelaire emerges. It is, in fact, to something stultifying in the atmosphere of England that we must look for an explanation. Personally, I cannot find it in anything else but that final triumph of the puritan spirit—our industrial prosperity. The true explanation of the Pre-Raphaelite movement is the Great Exhibition. Looking, as we may still do, through the pages of the sumptuously illustrated catalogue of the masterpieces of art and craftsmanship then displayed, we are revolted by the ugliness and vulgarity of every single object; but we cannot deny them, in the mass, an astonishing vitality. They are the expression of the taste of the age, and they are appalling or shaming; but granted the economic and moral ideals of the age, they are inevitable. Before such inevitability, the sensitive soul could only retreat.

NOTE

'The Modern Epoch in Art' was written as an introduction to *The History of Modern Painting*, Geneva (Skira), 1949. 'Surrealism and the Romantic Principle' was a contribution to a volume on *Surrealism*, London (Faber & Faber), 1936. 'Realism and Abstraction in Modern Art', originally delivered as a lecture at two or three centres in the United States, was first printed in *Eidos*, vol. I, June, 1950. 'Human Art and Inhuman Nature' is a composite essay, with material from a broadcast and from an article published in *World Review*. 'The Situation of Art in Europe at the end of the Second World War' was delivered as a lecture in the United States and Germany, and printed in the *Hudson Review* (New York), vol. I, No. 1, Spring, 1948. 'The Fate of Modern Painting' was originally given as a lecture to a conference organized by UNESCO in Paris and later appeared in *Horizon*.

'Gauguin' is the text of a volume in the Faber Gallery; so is the essay on Klee. 'Picasso' was a contribution to *Great Contemporaries*, London (Cassell), 1934. The essays on Henry Moore and Ben Nicholson were written as introductions to volumes on their work published by Lund Humphries & Co. (London), 1944 and 1948. The essay on Paul Nash is a composition from three sources: the Penguin Modern Painters volume (1944), the Lund Humphries publication on this artist (1948), and from an introduction to his autobiography, *Outline*, London (Faber & Faber), 1949.

The essay on 'English Art' was originally contributed to *The Burlington Magazine*, vol. lxiii (December, 1933).

Index

Abingdon (Turner), 266
Abstraction in art, 37–38, 48, 50–51, 76, 86–7, 88 *ff.*, 173, 179, 216 *ff.*, 227
  realism contrasted with, 88–104
  See also Art, abstract
Abstraktion und Einfühlung (Worringer), 100, 216, 217
Aesthetik (Hegel), 116, 117, 118
Alastor (Shelley), 48
Alice in Wonderland (Carroll), 124
Angst, 49, 95, 101, 102, 219
Apollinaire, 167, 226
  on the function of artists, 224–25
Archipenko, 41, 201
Architectonice, 250, 251, 261–2, 267
Architecture, 66, 252
Arnold, Matthew, 267
  on English art, 250
  on German and Celtic races and art, 249–50
Arp, Hans, 55, 202, 223
Art, 31–2, 40, 68, 73, 74, 96, 141, 156, 157, 224, 230, 232, 233–4, 235
  abstract, 50, 76, 128, 159, 223
  changes in the history of, 19–20
  classical, 259
  common man, the, and, 63
  'communication' and, 235–6, 243
  communism and, 96
  Constable on, 28, 79
  current ideas of a period and, 19
  education and, 66
  English, 80 *ff.*, 106, 175 *ff.*, 187–8, 194, 249 *ff.*
  evolution of, 19, 26
  function of, 53, 150, 212
  geometrical and vital, 217–18
  Hegel and, 116
  idea and image in, 230
  imitative, 85, 86
  kinds of, 217–19
  'life of forms' of, 208 *ff.*
  modern, 17 *ff.*, 42–3, 76, 88 *ff.*, 173, 237

Nash, Paul, on, 180–81
  new and old science of, 234
  organic and constructive principles in, 201–2
  origins of modern, 17 *ff.*
  ornamental, 91
  Pater and, 156
  photography and, 18–19, 59
  physical laws and, 200–1
  plastic, 232 *ff.*
  poetic, 85–6
  polarity in, 22
  primitive, 91
  'pure' and purity in, 49, 235
  revolutionary, 45 *ff.*
  Ruskin and, 87, 252, 263, 265
  schools of Rheims and Winchester, 251, 252
  scope of, 64, 207
  synthesis and, 45 *ff.*
  theories about, 156–7 *et passim*
  three types and ends of, 84–5
  two stages in works of, 31
  vital, 202, 209, 217
  vitality and, 20, 87, 207
Art of Spiritual Harmony (Kandinsky), 169, 216
Artists, 18, 26 *ff.*, 42, 103, 110, 171, 210
  function of, 224–5
  intention of, 90
  temperament and, 83–5
Artists on Art (1945), 168
Art schools, 66–67
Art services, 61–62
Aurier, Albert, 149
Automatism, 41, 53, 110, 137

Barlach, 196
Battle of Britain, The (Nash), 183
Baudelaire, on Hogarth and Cruikshank, 256–7
Beauty, 34, 198, 200, 234, 235
  three types of, 117
Beckmann, Max, 37, 56
Bell, Clive, 176

Index

Belle Angèle, La (Gauguin), 150

Berçot, 56

Bernard, Emile, 17, 31
  Gauguin and, 148, 149, 150
  'synthètisme' of, 25, 29

Binyon, Laurence, on English landscape in art, 263–64

Blake, William, 7, 125, 137, 138, 175, 251, 260–62, 267

Blaue Reiter, group, 101, 167, 169

Boccioni, 38, 167

Bonington, 79, 80

Boogie-Woogie (Mondrian), 26

Bosch, Jerome, 56

Boucher, 29

Bradley, A. C., on poets, 121

Brancusi, 201
  Henry Moore on, 201

Braque, 37, 40, 45, 48, 49, 100, 223, 226, 227

Breton, André, 41, 52–3, 54, 106, 110, 134
  surrealism and, 52–53

Brown, Madox, 267

Browne, Sir Thomas, 192

Butler (Reg), 57

Byron, 80, 121, 122, 123

Cahiers d'Art, 159, 172

Calvert, Edward, 262

Calais Gate, 81

Calais Pier (Turner), 265

Calder, Alexander, 196

Carrà, 44

Carroll, Lewis, 124

Cézanne, 17, 20, 21, 24, 29 ff., 38, 39, 75, 127, 154, 179, 200, 226–7
  'Baigneuses' series of, 127
  Gauguin and, 33
  Letters quoted, 28, 29–30
  'modulation' of, 29–30
  nature and, 29–30, 31
  style of, 37, 155–56

Chagall, 37, 56

Change, art and, 57, 87

Chardin, 184

Chelsea, 194

Chilterns Under Snow (Nash), 179

Chirico, 38, 41, 44, 45, 48, 190

Cirque, Le (Seurat), 127

Classicism, 79, 107–9

Claude, 32
  Turner and, 266

Coleridge, on Sir Thomas Browne, 192

Collage, the, 128

Colour, 29, 38, 75, 152, 266
  scientific theory of, 18
  Gauguin and, 151

Colquhoun, Robert, 56, 57

Commencement du Monde, Le (Brancusi), 197

Constable, 17, 28, 29, 75, 78–9, 80, 81, 82, 86, 126, 263, 265, 266, 267
  on art, 28, 79
  Ruskin on, 79, 266
  Turner and, 265–66

Constructivism, 17, 38, 44, 51–52, 93, 94–5, 202, 217, 226 ff.
  Manifesto of 1920, 231

Contes Barbares (Gauguin), 150

Corot, 80, 184

Courbet, 17, 20, 27, 28, 35, 74, 80, 185

Creation, artistic, 22, 55, 98–9, 103, 104

Critique of Judgment (Kant), 90

Cruikshank, Baudelaire on, 256–7

Cubism, 17, 32–33, 38, 39, 44, 48, 49–50, 76, 89, 92, 169, 216, 217, 226, 232
  analytical, 49–50, 76, 92
  non-figurative, 50
  synthetic, 49, 76, 92

Culture, 91, 118

Dada group, the, 41, 44

Dahlias (Nash), 179

Dali, Salvador, 41, 126, 128, 137

David, Gérard, 17

Dead Spring (Nash), 180

Decadence in art, 27, 91

Degas, 28, 74, 86
  Gauguin and, 148

Delacroix, 17, 35, 74, 80, 267

Delaunay, 37

Demoiselles d'Avignon (Picasso), 100, 155

Denis, Maurice, 148

Derain, André, 48

De Smet, 56

Dialectical materialism, 17, 19

Dialeticism and, dialectics, 108, 109, 115–16, 137

Dido Building Carthage (Turner), 266

Discourses (Reynolds), 75–76

Index

Disquieting Muses, The (Chirico), 86
Dix, Otto, 56, 85
Domela, 234
Dreams, 129 *ff.*, 182
 formation of, 129 *ff.*
Dubuffet, 56
Duchamp, Marcel, 37, 41
Duchamp-Villon, 201
Dvořák, Max, on naturalism, 17

Education, 66, 69
Edward Munch (Hodin), 36
Egyptian Art (Worringer), 219
El Greco, 86, 153
Emotion, 25, 34
 art and, 24–25, 56
Erni, Hans, 103
Ernst, Max, 41, 54, 128
Etty, William, 262
Evolution, 13
 creative, 68, 99
 human, 13, 22
Europe, contemporary art in, 44 *ff.*
Exhibitions, 139
 Carfax, 176
 First Impressionist, 147
 International Surrealist, 105
 Paris (1947), 52
 Paul Nash's, 176, 178
 Post-Impressionist, 175–76
 Post-revolutionary Russian art, 228
 Surrealist, 181
Existentialism, 21, 45, 46, 95, 102,
 219, 220
Expressionism, 34, 36–37, 44, 48–49,
 55–6, 81, 83, 169

Falling Stars, The (Paul Nash), 176
Fauvism, 17, 40, 44
Fear, 102, 103
 See also Angst
Feeling, 79
Fiction, art and, 124
Flaxman, John, 261
Form, 54–5
 in art, 29, 33, 51
 pure, 226 *ff.*
Focillon, Henri, 'life of forms' and,
 55, 208, 209, 221–22
Formalism, 91
Freedom, 99
 in art, 76–77, 102

Freud, dream formation of, 129 *ff.*
 hypothesis of the unconscious and,
 40
Frosty Morning, A (Turner), 81, 266
*Further Letters of Vincent Van Gogh to
 his Brother*, 35
Futurism, 38, 41, 44

Gabo, Naum, 37, 44, 51–2, 93–4,
 202, 217, 227, 228, 230, 231,
 233, 234, 236, 237
 on his philosophy, 93–5
 letters between Herbert Read and,
 233, 236, 238–45
 reality and, 94, 232
Gainsborough, Thomas, 125, 257–8
 Reynolds and, 257–8
Gauguin, Paul, 17, 20, 25, 29, 33–34,
 36, 38, 145 *ff.*
 egoism of, 136
 his family and, 146–47
 his letters, 145, 146, 147, 151–2
 on composition, 33–34
 paintings of, 150
 technique of, 133
Gauguin, le peintre et son oeuvre (Malin-
 gue), 25
Gestalt, the, 31, 32, 121
Géricault, 74
Ghiberti, 196
 'Commentaries' of, 196
Giacometti, 202
Girl in the Tree (Klee), 166
Girtin, 262, 263
Gleizes, 37, 38
Graves, Robert, 64
 on his writing, 58
Grierson, Sir Herbert, 107, 109, 165
Gris, Juan, 37, 76, 92, 93, 97, 98,
 222, 223
 cubism and, 92
 on his art, 92
Grohmann, Will, on Klee's art, 168
Gropius, Walter, 171
Grosz, George, 56
Grunewald, Mathias, 56

Haden, Seymour, 256
Hals, Franz, 84
Hamlet (Shakespeare), 120
Hampstead Heath (Constable), 81
Harmony, 76, 77, 151
 surrealism and, 41

Index

Hausenstein, Wilhelm, on Klee, 169
Haywain, The (Constable), 74
Hegel, 29, 40, 112
  philosophy of art of, 91, 114, 115, 116–17
Heidegger, 29, 95, 97, 102, 219
Hepworth, Barbara, 98, 202, 223
  on her art, 98–9
Hilliard, Nicholas, 255
Hogarth, William, 59, 78, 79, 80, 255–6, 258
  Baudelaire on, 257
Holden, Dr Charles, 210
Holmes, Sir Charles, 151
  on Gauguin's works, 151
Horizon, 233, 238–45
Housman, A. E., poetic inspiration and, 129
Hulme, T. E., on kinds of art, 217–19
Human consciousness, 22
Human mind, the, 23, 24
Humanism, 27, 36
Husserl, 29, 102
Huysmans, 139, 148

Icons, Byzantine, 85
Ideas, 117
  art and, 26 *ff*., 51
Ideal, the, 117
Idealism, 83, 117, 231
Images and imagism, 22, 23, 24, 29, 43, 53–4, 73, 88, 93, 94, 95, 134, 135, 165, 203
  cubism and, 92
  dream, 129 *ff*.
  metaphors distinguished from, 134–5, 165
  poetic, 135–6
  reality and, 95–6
  symbols and, 19, 22, 23, 24, 29
Imagination, the, 77 *ff*., 126, 148, 184
  Ruskin's ideas about, 77 *ff*., 81, 82
Impressionism, 29, 33, 74–5, 86, 148
Improvisations (Kandinsky), 216–17
Industrial revolution, the, 26, 27
Inspiration of the Poet (Poussin), 86
Instincts, 114, 124,
  repression of, 123–4
Interior at Petworth (Turner), 81, 82, 267
Interpretation, 21
  illustration and, 19
Intimate Journals (Gauguin), 33

Isomorphism, 85, 94, 168n
Israels, 35

Jacob wrestling with the Angel (Gauguin), 149
James, William, 89
Jerusalem (Blake), 137, 138
Jung, Carl G., psychology of, 54, 83–4, 163, 190

Kairuan oder eine Geschichte vom Maler Klee (Hausenstein), 169
Kandinsley, Wassily, 37, 51, 101, 167, 169, 173, 216–17
Keats, John, on poetry, 161
Kierkegaard, 40, 96
Klee, Johann Wilhelm, 165
Klee, Paul, 37, 41, 42, 45, 46, 48, 101, 164 *ff*., 184
  Diary, 167
  Grohmann on, 168
  influences of, 167
  last work, 172
  lecture on composition of, 171
  on his work, 167–68, 169–70, 172
  personality of, 166–7
  post at the Bauhaus, 171–72
Koffka, K., on art, 31–32
Kokoschka, Oskar, 37, 56, 81

Lam, Wilfredo, 54
Landscape, 32, 81
  English, 263–4
Landscape in English Art and Poetry (Binyon), 263–64
Laurens, Henri, 55, 201
Lawrence, D. H., 40
Lear, Edward, 124, 175
Léger, Fernand, 45, 48, 57
Leonardo da Vinci, 80, 195
Lewis, Wyndham, 37, 44, 126
Life of Forms in Art, The
  See Vie des Formes
Life-process, the, 97, 105, 116
Lipchitz, 55, 201
Lipps, 100
Literature:
  ballads, 119
  English, 254
  romantic principle and, 119–24

MacBryde, Robert, 56, 57
Macke, August, 169, 173

Index

Madonna and Child (Moore), 55, 97, 211, 212
Maillol, Aristide, 199, 200
Malevich, Kasimir, 37, 44, 167, 228
Man, docility of, 114
Manet, 17, 28, 35, 74
Manuscripts, 252
  tenth-century English, 251
Marc, Franz, 101, 167, 169, 173
Marcel, Gabriel, 102
Marinetti, 44, 167
Marriage à la Mode (Hogarth), 78
Marriage of Heaven and Hell, The (Blake), 138
Martin, John, 126
Marxism and Marx 27, 115, 116–17
  art and, 86–7, 228 *ff.*
Masson, 41
Mathematicians, and mathematics, art and, 86–7, 92
Matisse, Henri, 20, 38, 40, 41, 45, 48
  on art, 40
Matta, 54
Menin Road, The (Nash), 185, 190–1
Michelangelo, 84, 118–19
Millais, 267
Millet, 28, 35
Minotauromachia (Picasso), 125
Miro, Joan, 41, 54, 223
Modern Painters (Ruskin), 77, 81, 82
Moderne Kunst, Ueber die (Klee), 171
Mondrian, Piet, 26, 37, 38, 44, 51, 93, 223–4, 234
  on art, 26, 234–35
  on pure plastic art, 232
Monet, Claude, 28, 74, 127
Moore, George, 175
  on Sickert, 174–75
Moore, Henry, 55, 97–8, 103, 195 *ff.*
  Brancusi on, 201
  drawings of, 210, 213, 214
  evolution and aims of, 208 *ff.*
  human form, the, and, 204 *ff.*
  materials and forms and, 206
  mine drawings of, 214
  on his *Madonna and Child*, 211–12
  on his work, 205, 207, 211–12, 213
  on vitality, 207
  post-war sculpture of, 214–15
  'shelter drawings' of, 214
  spiritual essence and appearances and, 203

Morality, poets and, 122–23
  surrealists and, 139–41
Morris, William, 20
Munch, Edvard, 17, 36, 55–6
My Father Paul Gauguin (Pola Gauguin), 145
Myths, 54

Nash, Paul, 174 *ff.*
  activities of, 178
  autobiography of, 189, 192–4
  book illustration of, 178
  letter of, 191
  Read, Herbert, and, 177, 183–4
  Unit One and, 180–1
  Urn Burial and 180, 192
  work of, 176 *ff.*, 185 *ff.*
Nature, 73
  art and, 21, 38, 73 *ff.*, 86, 158, 198, 199, 208
  Paul Nash and, 177
Naturalism, 198, 226
  Dvořák on the origins of, 17
Neo-plasticism, 38, 44, 223, 224
New English Art Club, the, 176
New Introductory Lectures (Freud), 130, 131
Nicholson, Ben, 37, 50–51, 98, 216 *ff.*, 234
  on abstract art, 223
  symbols and, 220, 221
  work of, 220 *ff.*
Nicholson, Sir William, 223
Nicolson, Benedict, on the Post-Impressionist Exhibition, 175n
Nierendorf, Karl, on Klee, 165–66, 167, 170
Nietzsche, 101, 102, 259
Nietzsche (Maulnier), 259
Nirvana (Gauguin), 150
Northwind (Moore), 210
Notes on Poems and Reviews (Swinburne), 123

Old Guitarist (Picasso), 154
Olympia (Manet), 74
Ontology of the Vital (Woltereck), 102–3
Originality, 19 *ff.*, 22
Outline (P. Nash), 189, 192–4

Painter's Object, The (Moore), 212, 213

Index

Painting and painters, 58 *ff.*, 195
  'cabinet,' 65–66
  composition in, 32
  easel, 66, 67
  glass-, 65
  English, 124-27, 263
  metaphysical, 165, 169, 190
  portrait, 80
  research and, 158–9
  State, the, and, 64
  water-colour, 263
Palmer, Samuel, 126, 262
Paolozzi, 57
Parade, La (Seurat), 127
Pater, Walter, theory of art of, 156
Patronage of art, 58 *ff.*, 18, 26 *ff.*,
  58 *ff.*, 64, 65–6
Paul Cézanne (Mack), 28, 29–30
Paul Klee: Leben, Werk, Geist (Kahn),167
Paul Klee: Paintings (Ed. Nierendorf), 165–6, 170
Perception, 23, 31–32, 86
Permeke, 56
Personality, 89
  art and, 75, 89, 110, 129
Pevsner, Antoine, 44, 51–52, 202,
  228, 229, 230, 231, 233, 234,
  236, 237
Philosophy, 21–2, 46–7, 95, 100 *ff.*,
  111 *ff.*, 203, 219, 231
  Hegel and art and, 91, 114, 115,
  116–17
  metaphysical, the, 230 *ff.*
  modern, 227
  relativism in, 21
  revolutionary, 46–7
Photography and photographic methods, and art, 18–19, 59
Picabia, Francis, 41
Picasso, Pablo, 37, 39, 40, 45, 46 *ff.*,
  50, 55, 57, 76, 82, 100, 103, 126,
  128, 153 *ff.*, 167, 219, 223, 226,
  227
  diversity of, 161
  influences in his work, 163–4
  interview with Westheim, 158–9
  later pictures of, 160
  'Negro period', 155
  on cubism, 39
  on truth and art, 42, 158–9
  on his visions, 159
  papiers collés of, 157
  perversity of, 161–2
  work of, 154 *ff.*

Picasso (Barr), 39
Pissarro Camille, 20, 28, 29, 74,
  147–8, 150
  Letters to his Son Lucien (ed. J.
  Rewald), 148, 149
  on Gauguin's art, 149
Plastic Art and Pure Plastic Art
  (Mondrian), 232, 234–5
Plato, on the poet, 111–12
Poems, 1938–1945 (Robert Graves),
  58
Poetic inspiration, 129, 130, 132 *ff.*
Poetry, 104, 184
  Keats on, 161
  metaphysics and, 121, 165
  'pure', 235
  Vico on, 135
Poets, 23, 58–9
  morality and, 122–3
  Plato on, 111–12
  symbolism and, 23
Pointillism, 18, 74
Pond (Nash), 179
Portrait of Kahnweiler (Picasso), 92,
  100–1
Post-impressionism, 44, 176
Pottery, Chinese and Greek con-
  trasted, 89–90
Poussin, 21, 38, 85
Pre-Raphaelites, the, 126, 268
Priestley, J. B., on Surrealists, 139,
  140
'Problems in the Psychology of Art'
  (Koffka), 31–32
Pryde, James, 223
Psycho-analysis, 54, 136
Psychology, 110
  art and, 68, 75, 110
  Freudian, 52–3
  Jung and, 54, 83–4, 163, 190
Psychology and Alchemy (Jung), 163
Publicity, artists and, 18

Rain, Steam and Speed (Turner), 78, 81
Realism, 37, 48, 88 *ff.*, 226 *ff.*
  abstraction and, 88–104
Reality, 21–2, 26, 94, 95–6, 231,
  232 *ff.*
  art and, 29, 37–38, 102, 224
  changing concept of, 21
  Gabo and, 94, 232
  interpretation and, 21, 231
  philosophy of, 29
  subjectivity and, 21, 56

276

Index

Religion, art and, 211, 212
  medieval, 125
Renoir, 28
Resonance, 102, 103, 151
  modes of, 97
Reverdy, Pierre, on images, 134, 135
Reynolds, Sir Joshua, 38, 79–80, 261
  on art, 75–6, 259–60
Richmond, George, 262
Rilke, Rainer Maria, 170
Rodin, Auguste, 28, 197, 198–199,
  200, 201
Rodschenko, 229
Romanticism, 80, 101, 107, 111
  classicism and, 107 ff.
  romantic principle, 119–24
  Surrealism and, 105–41
Rothenstein, William, 176
Rouault, Georges, 37, 48, 56
Rousseau (Douanier), 125
Ruskin, art and, 87, 252, 263, 265
  imagination and, 77 ff., 81, 82
  on Constable, 79, 266
  Turner and, 79, 81 ff., 126, 266,
    267
Rubens, 258
Russia, 43, 44, 96
  art and, 228–9

St Pancras Lilies (Nash), 179
Sartre, Jean-Paul, 95
  philosophy of, 46, 47
Schelling, on artistic creation, 104
Schlemmer, 202
Schuffenecker, Emile, 146, 151
Schwitters, 20
Science, art and, 38, 42, 75, 232, 233
Sculpture, 59, 195 ff.
  animal style in, 204
  base in, 196–7
  Greek, 203–4
  human form, the, in, 204–7
  modern, 198 ff.
  'truth to material', 199
Sensations, 22, 31, 86, 150–1, 191
Sensibility, 18, 19, 20, 21, 111, 157,
  223
Sentimentality, art and, 154–5
Seurat, 28, 74, 75, 125, 200
Severini, 44
Shakespeare, 119–20
Shelley, Percy Bysshe, 121, 122, 138
  metaphysics and, 138

Shrimp Girl, The (Hogarth), 256
Shy, Timothy, on the common man
  and art, 63
Sickert, Walter, 174
  George Moore, on, 174–5
Signac, Paul, 74
Slave Ship, The (Turner), 82
Society and the social context, 19, 20,
  21, 108
  art and, 17–18, 20, 26 ff., 42–3, 58,
    109, 130, 215, 228
  synthesis and, 108
Speculations (Hulme), 217–19
Speculations on Metaphysics (Shelley),
  138
Spiritual in Art, On the (Kandinsky),
  101
State, the, art and artists and, 59 ff.
  principles and aspects involved,
    60 ff.
Stepanova, 229
Stevens, Alfred, 262, 268
Still-life (Nash), 179
Stravinsky, 45, 46
Study of Celtic Literature (Arnold), 249
Style in art, 37, 83, 89, 209, 210
Subjectivism, 40
Sun Rising through Vapour, The
  (Turner), 266
Sunflower and Sun (Nash), 189, 190
Supernaturalism, art and, 125
Superrealism, 48, 52–3, 106
Suprematism, 44, 51, 228 ff.
Surrealism, 17, 40–41, 44, 52–54,
  105 ff., 181
  Breton and, 52–3
  first Manifesto of, 40, 52
  morality and, 139–41
  Priestley and, 139, 140
  Romantic principle and, 105–41
Swan Song (Nash), 179, 180
Swinburne, Algernon Charles, 121,
  122–3
  on art and morality, 123
Symbolism: its Meaning and Effect
  (Whitehead), 23–24
Symbols and symbolism, 22, 23–26,
  36, 37, 43, 47, 53, 85, 149, 150,
  166–7
  images and, 19
Symbolists, the, 227
Synthesis, and art, 34, 47–8, 108,
  109, 116, 209
'Synthétisme', 25, 29, 148–9

Index

Tailleux, Francis, 56
Taliesin, 264
Tanguy, Yves, 54
Tatlin, Vladimir, 37, 44, 167, 202, 228, 229
Temperament, art and, 83–4, 85, 89
Texture in art, 89
Thackeray,
  Turner's *The Slave Ship* and, 82
Toulouse-Lautrec, 154
Truth, 47
  art and, 42, 79, 158–9
Tradition and art, 20–21, 34–5, 80, 83, 227
Turner, 32, 78, 79, 81 *ff.*, 126, 190, 250, 261, 263, 265–7
  Constable and, 265–6
  Ruskin and, 79, 81 *ff.*, 266, 267
  work of, 265–7
Type-psychology, 83–84

Unconscious, the, 40, 54
  art and, 53, 54–5, 109, 160–1, 182
  images and, 135, 136, 160, 162, 163
  Picasso and, 160, 162, 163
Unit One, 180–1, 182, 187–8
Unit One: The Modern Movement in English Architecture, Painting and Sculpture (ed. H. Read), 182, 187–8
United States, the, 50
Urn Burial (Sir Thomas Browne), 182, 191–92

Values, 90–1
  aesthetic, 118, 128, 157
  formal, 13, 90, 222
  malerisch or painterly, 128
Van den Berghe, Fritz, 56
Van Doesburg, 44

Van Gogh, Vincent, 17, 28, 34–37, 55, 101
  Letters of, 24, 35, 101
  on his painting, 35
Vchutemas, the, 229
Vico, theory of poetry of, 135
Vie des Formes (Focillon), 55, 208–9, 221–2
Virgin and Child with the Burgomaster Meyer and his family (Holbein), 26
Vision at Evening (Nash), 190
Visual Arts, The (Report of Dartington Hall Trustees), 59–60
Vorticism, 44
Vrubel, 227

War, 112–13
  paintings of, 163, 177–8, 183
Westheim, Paul, interview with Picasso, 158–9
What Happens in Hamlet (J. Dover Wilson), 120
Whistler, 28, 77
Whitehead, on the artistic perception, 23–24
  on symbolism and art, 24–25, 26
Wilde, Oscar, on art, 73, 74
Wilson, Professor Dover, 120
  and the problem of *Hamlet*, 120
Wilson, Richard, 262
Windsor (Turner), 266
Wölfflin, Henrich, 263
Woltereck, 97, 102–3
Woman with a Guitar (Picasso), 92
Wonder, 141
Wood, Christopher, 223
Wordsworth, 81, 263, 264, 268
  on external things and reality, 264
Worringer, Wilhelm, *Abstraction and Empathy*, 100, 216, 217–18
  on abstract art, 216 *ff.*

Yellow Christ (Gauguin), 26, 149

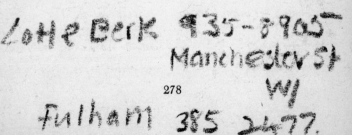